Color Confidence

The Digital Photographer's Guide
to Color Management

Color Confidence

The Digital Photographer's Guide to Color Management

Tim Grey

SYBEX®   San Francisco • London

Associate Publisher: Dan Brodnitz
Acquisitions Editor: Bonnie Bills
Developmental Editor: Pete Gaughan
Production Editor: Leslie E.H. Light
Technical Editor: Jon Canfield
Copyeditor: Kathy Grider-Carlyle
Compositor: Franz Baumhackl
Graphic Illustrator: Tom Webster, Lineworks, Inc.
Proofreader: Nancy Riddiough
Indexer: Lynnzee Elze
Cover Designer: Richard Miller, Calyx Design
Cover Photographers: Tree Frog: Linda Peterson;
                    Tree in Silhouette: John Shaw;
                    Puppy: Corbis

Library of Congress Card Number: 2003115582

ISBN: 0-7821-4316-4

Manufactured in the United States of America

10 9 8 7 6 5 4 3 2 1

To Lisa—

my wife and best friend.

I'm the lucky one.

Acknowledgments

First and foremost, I want to thank my incredible wife Lisa. She has inspired me to pursue my goals, provided encouragement, made me laugh, been incredibly patient when I had to work crazy hours to meet a deadline, understood my insanity at taking on far too many projects at once, and through it all has been my best friend. No matter what she says, *I'm* the lucky one.

My daughter Miranda is my best reader, and she is an incredible young lady. I'm more proud of her than she can ever realize. Her frequent queries about my writing progress kept me motivated, and I hope she enjoys reading dad's books, even if they don't compete with *Harry Potter*. She inspires me to write the best I can, because I know she'll be able to read even the biggest words and tell me if they're wrong!

My daughter Riley Savannah was supposed to arrive about the time this book hit the shelves, but she decided to make an early (by almost three months!) entrance. Thoughts of her kept me motivated to write late into the night.

Without my lifelong friend Bruce Heller, this book probably would have never been written. He provided an ear for listening, encouragement to follow my dreams, and assurance that I really could succeed. He has inspired me to become a better person and a better writer.

George Lepp showed me that beautiful photography really can be in color, not just black-and-white. Without that, I may not have become obsessed with color and color management, and I might not have written this book. I appreciate his support and encouragement.

Peter Burian is an excellent author that I am proud to call a friend. He shared the knowledge of his own experience, encouragement for me to pursue this project, frequent advice, the latest information on products and trends, and a dialogue for sorting out thoughts and ideas. I consider myself lucky to count him as a friend and associate.

Jeff Greene is an incredible assistant for my courses at the Lepp Institute of Digital Imaging, an excellent photographer always available in a pinch when I need a specific image, and most importantly a valued friend.

Many teachers have helped guide me down the path to where I am and where I am going. My fifth-grade teacher, Margaret Shea, was an incredible influence on me in many ways that I didn't even realize until years later. My high school photography teacher, Margaret Bower, helped nurture my passion and tolerated (even encouraged) my many hours in the wet darkroom. My high school journalism teacher, Cyril Baird, provided me with my first for-hire writing assignment. He helped me become a better writer, and he showed me there was a chance I might actually be able to make a little money with my writing!

I appreciate those who have published my writing and always been supportive and helpful, including Rob Sheppard, Chris Robinson, Ibarionex Perello, Wes Pitts, Jim Erhardt, and Angela Arndt.

Jack Davis convinced me that this book really did deserve to be published, and he provided creative inspiration and ever-entertaining Monty Python quotes.

Bob "Bug Bob" Allen helped ensure that I included accurate information for Macintosh users. I appreciate his generous help, his support, and his friendship.

Some of my readers and students have been particularly supportive and helpful, including John Huss, John Norton, Ben Pridemore, Cam Garner, and Ellen Anon. Thank you.

I appreciate all the photographers who allowed me to use their beautiful images in this book, including George Lepp, John Shaw, Dewitt Jones, Art Morris, Jack Davis, Peter Burian, Jeff Greene, Ira Meyer, Alice Cahill, Jon Canfield, Linda Peterson, and Chris Robinson.

I couldn't have written this book without the support of many individuals at various companies who have provided equipment for testing, information for learning, and other resources that have proven invaluable. I'd like to thank Dave Metz at Canon USA; Michael Rubin and Chuck De Luca at Nikon; Kim Evans at Lexar Media; Dan Steinhardt and John Jatinen at Epson; Brian Levey, Peter Bradshaw, and Matthew Chilton at Color Vision; Arlene Karsh for Gretag Macbeth; Lorenzo Gasperini at Mamiya America for Monaco Systems; and Jenny Cooley for Hewlett-Packard.

I also want to thank the team at Sybex who helped guide me through the process of making this book become something of which I am proud. Bonnie Bills believed in me and the concept for this book from day one. Her support and guidance have been greatly appreciated. I'd also like to thank developmental editor Pete Gaughan, production editor Leslie Light, compositor Franz Baumhackl, technical editor Jon Canfield, copyeditor Kathy Grider-Carlyle, and proofreader Nancy Riddiough. Thanks also to Tom Webster at Lineworks, Inc. for the wonderful illustrations. Each of these people has helped me along the journey of producing this book, and I appreciate them all.

Dear Reader,

Thank you for choosing *Color Confidence*. This book is part of a new wave of Sybex graphics books, all written by outstanding authors—artists and teachers who really know their stuff and have a clear vision of the audience they're writing for. It's also part of our growing library of truly unique digital imaging books.

Founded in 1976, Sybex is the oldest independent computer book publisher. More than twenty-five years later, we're committed to producing a full line of consistently exceptional graphics books. With each title, we're working hard to set a new standard for the industry. From the paper we print on, to the writers and photographers we work with, our goal is to bring you the best graphics books available.

I hope you see all that reflected in these pages. I'd be very interested to hear your comments and get your feedback on how we're doing. To let us know what you think about this or any other Sybex book, please visit us at www.sybex.com. Once there, go to the product page, click on Submit a Review, and fill out the questionnaire. Your input is greatly appreciated.

Please also visit www.sybex.com to learn more about the rest of our graphics line. Best regards,

DAN BRODNITZ
Associate Publisher
Sybex Inc.

Katrin Eismann

Foreword

Take a dollar bill out of your wallet, tear it up into tiny little pieces, and throw the pieces away. Now take another dollar bill out and tear it up into tiny little pieces, and throw the pieces away. Keep at it until you either run out of dollar bills or become so frustrated that you wonder why in the world I have you doing this.

Every time you take an 8-by-10-inch sheet of inkjet paper out of its package and make a print you're taking out a dollar bill in the hope that the print will look good. What happens if you don't like the print? You tear it up, throw it away, and go back to Photoshop to tweak the color or print driver controls and hit the Print button again—with the hope that the next print will look better. If it doesn't, you start the entire process over again. How many dollars and how much time have you wasted in the elusive hope of creating the color print that is in your mind's eye? I won't tell you how many times I've gone through this scenario and how many prints I have that are simply not right.

If you think that making a print that looks like the image on your monitor isn't too much to ask for—if the overwhelming and often conflicting information about working with color makes you yearn for the classic black-and-white darkroom—then you are in luck. Tim Grey's book on color management, *Color Confidence*, is long over-due. This has nothing to do with Tim's enviable work ethic or his talent for expressing the complex in a straightforward manner. It is overdue because every single digital photographer I know needed this book yesterday. All we want to do is take good pictures, enhance them in Photoshop, and make color prints that convey the sense of the scene we photographed. This book will help you do exactly that while avoiding the frustration, wasted time, and disappointment that making color prints has too often entailed in the past.

Tim's book is not about complex color science or rarefied opinions on color aesthetics. Rather, it is your stepping stone to making the prints that express your vision. And isn't that what photography and digital imaging are really about? I've often joked with my classes that I need a "Make It Good" keyboard button—well, I think I've found it in Tim Grey's *Color Confidence*. Enjoy the journey: you have found an experienced and articulate guide who will lead you where you want to go before you tear up another dollar bill in wasted time, effort, and materials.

KATRIN EISMANN
www.photoshopdiva.com
Artist, educator, and author
Photoshop Restoration & Retouching
Real World Digital Photography

Contents

"My emphasis is on putting color management  to work for you, not the other way around."

Introduction

Color management has a reputation for being an incredibly complicated subject. Certainly the science of color is very complicated. In fact, there is still much we don't fully understand about the human visual system and color theory. But you might not consider a book that provides a detailed look at our present understanding of color theory to be good reading.

Fortunately, this is not that book. Instead, this book is a practical guide to getting the best results possible in your digital darkroom by implementing a color-managed workflow.

Throughout *Color Confidence*, I cover the individual subjects that together form a complete color management system for the photographer, and I show you exactly what steps are required to achieve the best results. I don't just teach you the theory and leave you alone to work out the real issues. My goal in writing this book is to provide practical information that you can actually use in producing images with the most accurate color possible. Although I provide you with an understanding of how things work and why, the emphasis is on putting color management to work for you, not the other way around.

My assumption is that photographers who are serious about color management are also using the industry-leading Adobe Photoshop software to optimize their images. Although a color-managed workflow can be implemented with many other software tools, I focus on Photoshop in this book.

Who Should Use This Book

If you've ever been frustrated by a print that doesn't match what you see on your monitor (and I don't know a single photographer working with a digital darkroom who hasn't faced this challenge), then this book is for you. Whether you're taking pictures with film or a digital camera, if you are optimizing your images and producing your own prints using a computer, this book will help you get the very best results.

What's Inside

This book covers all of the topics related to color management through the full work-flow in your digital darkroom. This book is designed to be read from start to finish; however, if you've already started implementing some aspects of a color-managed workflow, you may be able to skip ahead to the specific topics you need to address. Here's a quick guide to what each chapter covers.

Chapter 1: Foundations provides a foundation in color theory that will help you better understand color, how it is produced, and how color management works.

Chapter 2: Photoshop Setup helps you configure Photoshop properly, and shows you what the various dialog boxes and warning messages mean.

Chapter 3: Display guides you through the process of selecting an appropriate monitor, as well as the process of calibrating and profiling that monitor.

Chapter 4: Scanning shows you the features to look for in a film scanner and demonstrates how to produce the best scans possible, including the use of custom scanner profiles.

Chapter 5: Digital Capture details the various options available for producing the most accurate color in your digital captures.

Chapter 6: Optimization offers techniques for getting the best color in your images using Photoshop, so that you can produce exactly the colors you are trying to achieve in your images.

Chapter 7: Output demonstrates the methods available to produce prints that match your monitor, the "Holy Grail" of color management.

Chapter 8: Workflow puts all the color management pieces together, providing a summary of the basic process involved in putting color management to work for you.

How to Contact the Author

Sybex strives to keep you supplied with the latest tools and information you need for your work. Please check their website at www.sybex.com for additional content and updates that supplement this book. Enter the book's ISBN—4316—in the Search box (or type **color confidence**), and click Go to get to the book's update page.

If you'd like to provide feedback about this book, or input on the types of books you'd like to see from me in the future, you can contact me via e-mail at tim@timgrey.com. More information about my writing and appearances can be found on the Web at www.timgrey.com. That is also where you'll find the book's companion website.

About the Author

A lifetime of working with computers and a love of photography combine as the perfect passion for Tim Grey. He loves learning as much as he possibly can about digital imaging, and he loves sharing that information even more. He does so through his writing and speaking appearances. His articles have been published in *Outdoor Photographer*, *PC Photo*, and *Digital Photo Pro* magazines, among others. He is also co-author of *Real World Digital Photography, 2nd Edition*. He teaches courses at the Lepp Institute of Digital Imaging (www.leppinstitute.com), and he lectures and makes public appearances at other venues.

Tim also publishes a regular "Digital Darkroom Questions" e-mail list where he answers questions related to digital imaging for photographers. To add your e-mail address to the list, visit www.timgrey.com.

Foundations

Although this is a very practical book, you must have some understanding of the foundations of light and color, as they relate to photography, in order to use its practical information effectively. This chapter provides a basic look at color and color management. It won't make you a color expert, but it will help you understand how color works and how a color management system can help you.

1

The Nature of Light

Although the science of color is incredibly complicated, the subject of color management doesn't need to include a steep learning curve. The first topic on that learning path is how light carries and contains color (Figure 1.1).

Figure 1.1
Dewitt Jones has made a career of transforming the light reflected off a scene into dramatic images that truly captivate the viewer. By understanding how light works, you are better equipped to produce the very best results possible. In this image Dewitt has started with a digital infrared photographic image, and then hand-tinted the color in Photoshop to produce the final image. (Photograph by Dewitt Jones, www.dewittjones.com.)

Note: Tempted though you may be to skip ahead in this book and get your hands dirty (figuratively speaking), I encourage you to read this chapter first. It will give you a stronger foundation to build on as you implement color management in your own workflow. Learning the concepts presented in this chapter will make the rest of the topics in this book much easier to understand.

Light is a fascinating thing. The light from the sun travels over 93 million miles—in about eight minutes—through the void of space to meet the earth. It provides the heat that makes life possible and also allows us to see and helps make life more enjoyable. Light allows us to enjoy the golden rays of a sunrise, the cool blue of deep shade, the vibrant green of a lush hillside, the dramatic yellows, oranges, and reds of a sunset (see Figure 1.2), and the pink haze of twilight. Even after the sun has disappeared below the horizon, its light can be reflected from the moon to illuminate our world in magical ways. Our fascination with color begins at an early age, and for photographers it certainly continues to be a fascination. Although photographers who focus on black-and-white photography may not place as much emphasis on color, they are very much in tune with the subtleties of light in general.

Figure 1.2 Light provides the source of color that we enjoy capturing in photographs. (Photograph by Ira Meyer, www.irameyer.com.)

Light is energy. Energy travels as waves, with a wavelength that defines the energy level of a particular source. These various ranges of wavelengths are categorized in sections, from gamma rays and x-rays, through ultraviolet, to the visible spectrum, and infrared, and on to microwaves, radar waves, and radio waves. Color is observable if it falls within the "visible spectrum," which is a range of wavelengths from approximately 380 to 780 nanometers (see Figure 1.3). One nanometer is one billionth of a meter, so we're talking about pretty small waves of energy.

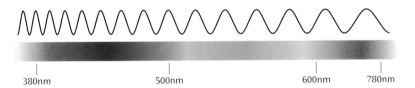

380nm   500nm   600nm   780nm

Figure 1.3 The visible spectrum includes light that ranges from wavelengths of about 380 nanometers to 780 nanometers.

In a sense, you could say that color doesn't exist. Light energy does not actually have color as a tangible property. Rather, various wavelengths of energy cause our optical system to perceive particular colors. For example, red is around 650 nanometers, green is around 525 nanometers, and blue is around 450 nanometers. When energy at these wavelengths reaches our eye, it causes us to perceive red, green, or blue. Although color can be defined based on specific wavelengths of light, it isn't a physical attribute of light by itself, but rather the way we perceive the energy at particular wavelengths. The very real property we perceive as color is created in our minds as a response to the specific wavelengths of light observed.

Quite literally, all the colors of the rainbow—red, orange, yellow, green, blue, indigo, violet—are found on the visible spectrum, with red at the longer wavelength end (around 650 nanometers) and violet at the shorter wavelength end (around 380 nanometers). This range of colors represents the full spectrum of visible light.

Note: You may have learned the name "Roy G. Biv" in science class while you were growing up. This serves as an acronym (Red, Orange, Yellow, Green, Blue, Indigo, Violet) for the colors found in the rainbow, extending from the longest wavelengths (red) to the shortest (violet).

Our eyes contain photoreceptors that enable us to convert light into signals in the brain, providing the experience of vision. The photoreceptors are of two types: rods and cones. The rods number around 120 million, and are very sensitive to light but aren't able to perceive color. There are around 6 to 7 million cones, and they provide color sensitivity. The human visual system allows us to perceive a huge range of colors, and all at the same time. When we look at a landscape before us, as shown in Figure 1.4, we are seeing many colors at once, and we are able to perceive all of them concurrently.

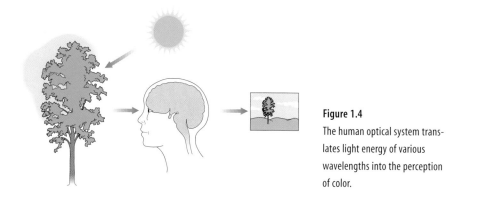

Figure 1.4
The human optical system translates light energy of various wavelengths into the perception of color.

In the real world, of course, color is a bit more complicated than I've made it sound so far. The colors we see are created by the reflection of light observed by our eyes. Although objects do not actually possess color from a technical standpoint, they have properties that cause them to absorb and reflect particular wavelengths of light. If an object absorbed all light, it would be perceived as completely black. Of course, the only object that can achieve this is a black hole. All other objects reflect some degree of light, but perhaps not enough for us to distinguish it. If an object reflected all light, it would be perceived as being pure white. Again, real world objects aren't going to have this purity, but the basic concept holds true. Most objects, of course, absorb and reflect various wavelengths of light in various combinations.

While we can define a specific color based on a wavelength of light, a single observed color is actually composed of light at a variety of wavelengths, which means that a single color is built from many other colors. The amount of light at different wavelengths used to form a specific color can be described using *spectral curves* like the one in Figure 1.5. These are charts that illustrate the amount of light energy at various wavelengths is contained within a specific color being measured.

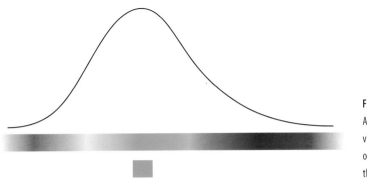

Light and color are intertwined, and they represent the foundation of photography and the genesis of color management. While color management is a science unto itself, involving an effort to control color in one form or another, understanding the underlying light and color you are trying to tame with a color management system is helpful for photographers at all levels.

Light in Photography

Photography has everything to do with light. In fact, you could say that photography is nothing more than controlling—to the extent possible—and recording light. When you capture a photographic image, whether on film or with a digital camera, you are storing the visible effect of light so it can be presented again for the enjoyment of others, as depicted in Figure 1.6. Film and digital image files effectively store light so it can be reproduced to provide a similar sensation to observing the light reflected off the scene in the first place.

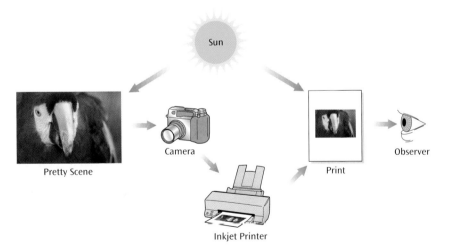

Figure 1.6 Light from an illumination source is reflected from objects and then recorded by the camera. The image can then be printed to simulate what was originally observed, again depending on reflected light to be seen.

Light is the key ingredient that makes photography possible. Light is emitted from the sun or artificial light sources, bombarding the objects in the world around us. When light energy comes in contact with an object, it passes through, is absorbed by, or is reflected by the object (in various degrees and combinations depending on characteristics of the object such as translucency). The reflected light moves outward from the object, so it can continue on in all directions. This light can then be observed by your eyes and recorded by your camera. The scene you are able to see is, in fact, created in your mind, as a response to the light energy stimulating your optic nerves.

The light reflected from a scene does much more than allow you to see what is there. Light isn't just a source of illumination. In a sense, light *is* the scene before you, because that light is what your brain is able to process as the image you perceive.

Each object has its own reflective properties, causing light of certain wavelengths to be absorbed while the rest is reflected. Capturing an image is a matter of recording that reflected light as it streams through your lens. Optimizing that image in the digital darkroom involves making judgments about the light emitted from your monitor to produce the perfect image. The final print closes the circle, reflecting light off the paper to re-create the image you envisioned at capture.

The Nature of Color

We become familiar with color at a very early age, and naming colors is one of the first skills many children learn after they are able to talk. We live with color and experience it constantly. Despite our familiarity with color, many are not familiar with the terminology used to describe color. Understanding these terms so that you have a better understanding of color, and are better able to deal with variations in color once you establish your color-managed workflow, is important. The following terms describe the various attributes of color:

Hue is what we usually refer to as "color." Of course, color consists of properties other than hue, but the hue is what we consider the color to be. The names we use to describe colors, such as "red" or "blue," represent the hue of that particular color. If you prefer a more technical definition of hue, it is the dominant wavelength of light in a particular color. For example, red consists of mostly red light, but unless it is absolutely pure it also contains some component of light at other wavelengths.

Saturation refers to the purity of the color, and it is what we would normally consider the vibrancy of a particular color. High saturation represents a very vibrant color, while low saturation would represent less vibrant colors, or a shade of gray. Saturation can also be referred to as chroma.

Brightness, also referred to as luminance, is a measure of the amount of light emitted or reflected from a subject. When referring to a color, it refers to the brightness or lightness of the color.

Together, these three primary components allow you to precisely describe a color in general terms. They form the basis of the HSB (hue, saturation, brightness) system for defining specific colors. Even with other color models (which will be discussed later in this chapter), these terms are used to describe the attributes of color.

Perceived Color

So far the presentation of color makes it sound rather absolute. An object absorbs and reflects light energy of different wavelengths in a particular combination, and the combination of reflected wavelengths determines what color is seen. Of course, it isn't quite that simple.

Color, as we perceive it, is the product of three individual factors working together:

The light source, also referred to as the illuminant. When talking about basic color theory, we usually assume a light source that is pure white, meaning that it contains all wavelengths of the visible spectrum. As a photographer, you already know that the sources of light available to you for your photography are anything but white. The actual color of the light illuminating your subject has a significant effect on the final color appearance of that object. The standard illuminant for color management is 5000 degrees Kelvin, often referred to as D50.

The object, which reflects the light from the light source. Each object has its own properties that affect the wavelengths of light that get reflected or absorbed, and to what degree. These properties affect the appearance of the light reflected off the object and, therefore, the color that is observed for an object under particular lighting conditions.

The observer of the reflected light. The ultimate observer is, of course, a human observer. But when it comes to the effect on a photographic image, there are other observers to consider. For example, the camera is an observer of reflected light, and it reacts differently than the human optic system does. Furthermore, filters and other devices can be used to modify how the light reflected from an object is observed. Other observers include the devices used for calibrating and profiling various devices, which will be discussed in later chapters.

Each of these three factors plays its own role in the creation of the perceived color (see Figure 1.7), and so changes to any of them affects the final perceived color.

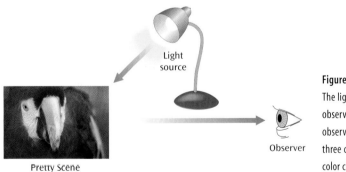

Pretty Scene

Light source

Observer

Figure 1.7
The light source, object, and observer each influence the observed color. If any of the three changes, the perceived color changes.

The Color Wheel

A color wheel (such as the one in Figure 1.8) is a very effective tool for understanding the relationships between colors. Earlier in this chapter, I referred to the full visible spectrum, which includes all the colors of the rainbow. The color wheel arranges the range of colors in the visible spectrum into a circle. Instead of a linear representation based on wavelength of light, hue is defined based on the position on the wheel, measured in degrees around the circle.

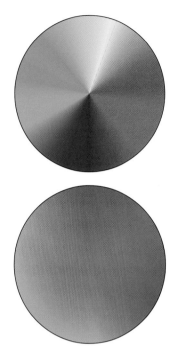

Figure 1.8
The color wheel provides a way to visualize the color spectrum in a way that illustrates the relationships between different colors. This basic color wheel shows only actual hues at pure saturation.

Figure 1.9
This color wheel shows both hue and saturation in one display.

Saturation is often shown on a color wheel with highly saturated colors at the edge and unsaturated colors in the middle (see Figure 1.9). This allows more information about specific colors to be represented on a single graphic.

A color wheel generally doesn't show lightness (brightness) information, simply because it would require a three-dimensional construct to show all three values of hue, saturation, and brightness. With software that uses some form of color wheel to select a color, hue and saturation can often be viewed at one time, with a separate control for brightness (see Photoshop's version of this in Figure 1.10). With some programs, you can change the representation of the color wheel being displayed so you can view any two properties of color at once, with a separate control for the third.

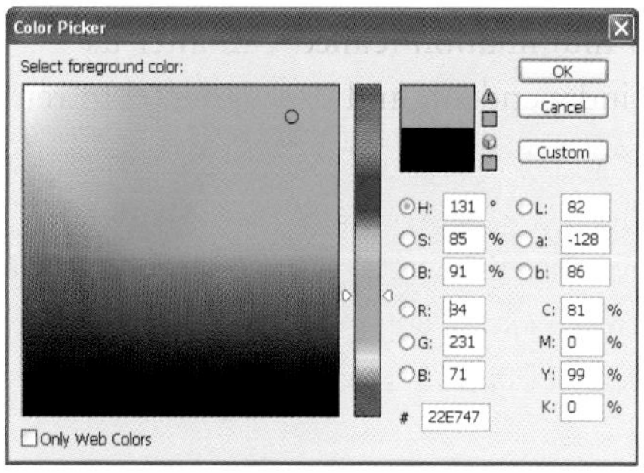

Figure 1.10
The Photoshop Color Picker provides a visualization of the relationships of the three color attributes of hue, saturation, and brightness. The selected attribute is shown on the smaller bar, while the other two attributes are displayed on the larger box along the horizontal and vertical axes.

Colors on opposite sides of the wheel are opposite—or complementary—to each other. Adjusting color balance shifts the colors in your image from one side of the wheel to the other on a specific axis. For example, as you're adjusting the color balance for the green/magenta axis, you are shifting the pixel values in your image between more magenta on one side of the color wheel and more green on the other side of the color wheel. I'll talk more about color balance adjustments in Chapter 6, "Optimization."

Understanding the relationships of adjacent colors on the color wheel is also important. On each side of a color on the color wheel are the colors that produce that color. For example, cyan is found between blue and green on the color wheel, and cyan is composed of blue and green. Understanding the intricacies of these color relationships can be incredibly helpful as you are adjusting your images, and also as you are evaluating your color management workflow to confirm accurate results.

Color Models

Color in the real world is all about wavelengths and intensity of light. When we work with digital images, we need a way to translate those values so color can be accurately described. Color models provide an organizational system for color in digital imaging. These color models can either be device-independent or device-dependent.

A device-independent color model does not depend on any device to describe color. LAB and CIE XYZ are examples of device-independent color models. They are modeled on the way the human visual system translates color, but they can be challenging to work in for many photographers who do not have experience working within this color model. The benefit of a device-independent color model is that it can precisely describe a color without referencing a specific device.

Device-dependent color models, on the other hand, revolve around providing instructions to devices in an effort to match a device-independent color value. The fact that we work with color using device-dependent color models does a lot to explain why profiles are critical to get predictable results in the digital darkroom. Because these color models don't describe a true color, but rather provide color values to a device that is expected to produce the intended color from those values, a method to translate color between devices is required.

The following color models are those used most often in photo-editing applications or with color management tools in general:

The CIE XYZ color model is a device-independent color model developed in 1931 by the International Commission on Illumination (called CIE after its French name). This color model is device-independent, and it is designed to represent color based on the way it is actually perceived under very specific viewing conditions (defined as the "CIE 1931 Standard Observer"), so that it describes actual color as it is perceived by an individual with normal color vision. Each of the values it defines (termed X, Y, and Z) represent imaginary primary values based on a mathematical model rather than real color values.

Note: Although not used as a color model for any photo-editing software, CIE XYZ is the basis of most device-independent color models in use today.

The LAB color model (CIE LAB) is the most commonly used variant of the device-independent color models that have been developed by CIE. The LAB color model consists of three channels to describe a color. The Lightness channel, as the name implies, defines luminosity. The "A" channel describes color on an axis between blue and yellow, and the "B" channel describes color on an axis between red and green. For those already familiar with the other color models, this may seem like an odd arrangement. However, it is based on the way the human vision system perceives color, and it provides an effective way to describe color in a device-independent way. The LAB color model provides the reference color space for most color management systems.

The RGB color model is device-dependent, and it is used when describing color as emitted light, such as that on a monitor. Colors are described by specifying a value for red, green, and blue. In other words, RGB values specify how much light of each of the three constituent colors should be blended to produce the intended result. Mixing all three colors at their maximum value will (in theory at least) produce pure white, and omitting all three colors completely will (again, in theory) produce pure black. Most images you will work on will be edited using an RGB color model, as that is the way monitors, digital projectors, and inkjet printers deal with color.

The CMYK color model is the other commonly used device-dependent color model. It describes colors based on the subtractive primaries of cyan, magenta, and yellow. The obvious example of this is for inks, which absorb and reflect light to produce the colors we see. When none of the colors are included, the result is white (in theory; the color of the paper to which the ink is printed is a significant source of variation here). When all of the colors are mixed at their full values, the result is black (in theory). In reality, because the inks used are not perfectly pure, mixing all the cyan, magenta, and yellow inks won't produce black (it usually creates a muddy brown), so black ink (the Key color, providing the "K" in CMYK) is added to the mix. Although most images are adjusted using an RGB color model, you may have occasion to use the CMYK color model, as I'll discuss in later chapters.

Primary Colors

Within any particular color model, specific attributes are used to describe a color. These attributes are referred to as "primaries," and the values of the primaries describe a specific color. In the case of CIE XYZ or LAB, these primaries are not based on how we actually create color, but rather are based on how we perceive color. For this reason, they tend to be a bit complicated, and not an easy way to adjust color in your photographic images.

Therefore, most digital photo editing is performed using the RGB or CMYK color models. Each of these color models uses specific colors for their primaries, thereby making use of "primary colors." Understanding the concept of primary colors is important both for adjusting your images and for understanding color management.

An understanding of primary colors will help you understand what changes are required to produce the result you are trying to achieve in your images when you are adjusting them.

Each color that we produce on a monitor or printer is composed of some combination of primary colors. For emitted light, the three primary colors are red, green, and blue. They are called *additive primary colors* (see Figure 1.11) because you create white by adding all three colors together, and each of the individual components is adding color to the mix. The absence of all three primary colors represents black because it represents a complete absence of light. The presence of all three primary colors at their maximum value represents white, as shown in Figure 1.12.

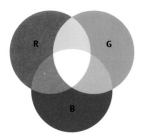

Figure 1.11

The additive primary colors of red, green, and blue can be blended to produce all possible colors with light. Combining all three at maximum value produces white.

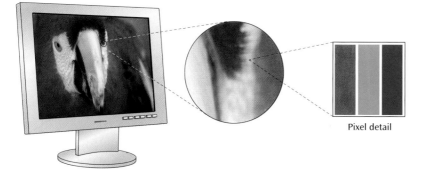

Pixel detail

Figure 1.12 The display on a monitor is composed of the three additive primary colors of red, green, and blue. Each pixel is formed by these three colors, with the intensity of each modified to produce the appropriate color.

For reflected light—such as with the inks used in a print—the three primary colors are cyan, magenta, and yellow. These colors are called the *subtractive primaries* (see Figure 1.13) because each of the primary colors is absorbing light (subtracting light) so that only light of certain wavelengths is reflected back. The absence of all three primary colors represents white because no light is being absorbed—although in fact, "white" would be the color of the paper because the CMYK color model is used primarily for printed output. The CMYK color model represents the colors of inks (cyan, magenta, yellow, and black) used to produce printed output for virtually all printers. The presence of all colors represents black (at least in theory) because all light is being absorbed.

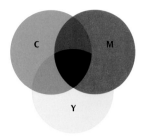

Figure 1.13
The subtractive primary colors of cyan, magenta, and yellow can be blended to produce all possible colors with reflected light. Combining all three at maximum value produces (in theory) black.

The additive and subtractive primary color groups are related to each other in terms of the relationships between colors, as diagrammed in Figure 1.14. Each primary in one group has an opposite color in the other group. These relationships are important to understand when working with your own images in the digital darkroom and making prints of those images.

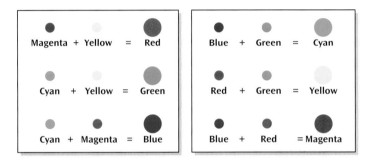

Figure 1.14 The additive and subtractive primary colors are opposites of each other. Each additive primary color can be formed by combining the two subtractive primary colors that are not its opposite, and each subtractive primary color can be formed by combining the two additive primary colors that are not its opposite.

In the color wheel, the opposite color for a given primary is exactly opposite it. For example, red is a primary color for the RGB color model. On a monitor, red is produced by emitting red light at maximum intensity with no green or blue light included. The opposite of red is cyan, which is a primary color in the CMYK color model. Cyan absorbs red light, reflecting back green and blue. Red and cyan are opposites.

You can also refer to the color balance control in most color management software, which usually provides sliders that allow you to shift the balance between each of the primaries. An easy way to remember the colors that are opposite each other in the RGB and CMYK color models is to think of them in order. The first colors in each (red and cyan) are opposite each other, as are the second (green and magenta) and third (blue and yellow). Understanding how these colors interact makes color adjustments much easier, and it will help you better understand what is going on behind the scenes in your color-managed workflow.

Metamerism

If you ever need to impress someone at a cocktail party, try to work the term "metamerism" into the conversation. Microsoft Bookshelf defines metamerism as "The condition of having the body divided into metameres, exhibited in most animals only in the early embryonic stages of development." If you're having a difficult time understanding what that has to do with color management, you're not alone. When it comes to color management, metamerism seems to be a word that is rarely understood, and usually scorned.

Metamerism, despite its bad reputation among those who have actually heard of it, is actually a very good thing. Metamerism is a phenomenon where two colors match under one lighting condition, but don't match under different lighting (see Figure 1.15). That may sound like a bad thing, and in many cases it is, but it is also the underpinning of a very good thing.

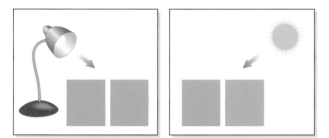

Figure 1.15
Metamerism is a phenomenon where two colors match under one lighting condition, but don't match under different lighting.

Each color has specific spectral properties. In fact, every object that reflects light has specific spectral properties. These properties are the properties of the reflected light, and they are generally defined as how much light is emitted or reflected at each specific wavelength. Because of metamerism, objects with very different spectral responses can actually appear as the same color to the human eye. This is very significant.

Metamerism makes it possible to create the same color using a variety of inksets, for example. Without metamerism, we would have to use exactly the same pigments to produce a particular color. It would also require that to produce a specific color, you would need an ink of that specific color. That would not be very practical. You can imagine how many different inks we would need in our inkjet printers if every color we wanted to produce needed an individual ink. With metamerism, we can produce a variety of colors that will produce a specific color experience despite the spectral properties of the colors used to produce the colors.

Metamerism has a pitfall, of course, or it wouldn't have such a bad reputation. For one thing, it is possible to produce two colors that look like a perfect match under one lighting condition, but don't appear to match in a different lighting condition. This could be a huge problem if you are trying to match two different printed items with the same colors. They could appear to match until you deliver them to the client.

For photographic images, it can also be a problem, though usually not in the color matching sense. Instead, it can create a problem where the relationship between colors appears different under certain lighting conditions. Colors that have an appropriate relationship under certain lighting may not match under other lighting. In this type of situation, different lighting would effectively cause different changes in different areas of the print, which could obviously be a problem. However, it is not a common problem.

There are several situations where metamerism has gained a bad reputation it doesn't deserve. One of the most common relates to observing a printed image under differing light sources. This goes back to the discussion of perceived color earlier in this

13

■

THE NATURE OF COLOR

chapter. If you change the illumination source, you change the perception of the print. A print that looks perfect in the lighting of your digital darkroom may not look very good under incandescent lighting, for example. This is not metamerism. This is a change in the illumination that causes a change in the appearance of the image because a different light source means different color will be reflected, which in turn means that different colors will be observed. You can't expect a print to look exactly the same under all lighting conditions, any more than you would expect a mountain range to look the same at sunrise as it does at high noon.

Another issue that has given metamerism a bad name should be referred to as *bronzing*. This is a situation where certain inks have different reflective properties, causing them to appear slightly different under certain lighting It is most common with black ink, particularly with pigment-based inks. For example, photographers using the Epson Stylus Photo 2000P printer frequently complain about bronzing.

For most photographers, understanding metamerism is purely academic. It is a major issue underlying the science of color management and worth understanding so that you will have a greater appreciation of what is involved with producing prints with matching colors. You can't do anything to change the fact that metamerism exists, so it is better to understand it, appreciate the benefits it provides, and accept the potential pitfalls it can produce.

Color Profiles

Profiles are a major component of any color management system. They are what actually makes it possible to produce prints that match what you see on your monitor or produce scans that accurately reflect what is contained in the piece of film you are scanning.

A profile is a data file that describes the color behavior of a specific device. The color values stored in an image can be thought of as instructions for the device that will display or reproduce those colors. In order to maintain accurate colors, those values must be related to a device-independent color model. The profile contains a table that lists the specific device-dependent color values and their equivalent values using the device-independent LAB color model.

Most image files that photographers work with are in either the RGB or CMYK color model, where values are assigned to the additive or subtractive primary colors, defining the color of each pixel. The color values provide instructions for how much of each primary color should be used to produce the intended color. The results are dependent upon the specific primary colors used. For example, each printer uses specific inks, and so "cyan" for one printer is different from "cyan" on a different printer, because the cyan ink for each has a slightly different color value. Even the paper used to print can result in different values, because of the way the inks are absorbed by the paper. Therefore, the color values used in the RGB or CMYK color models don't have any meaning by themselves. They only have a specific color meaning when a device is used to produce output based on the color numbers.

A profile translates these values stored in a digital image to a device-independent color model—usually LAB—so that they have a specific color meaning. In this way, profiles allow consistent colors to be produced by a wide range of devices, because each device can have a specific profile that allows it to translate the colors in your image file.

This translation is key to producing accurate results, and so it is important that the ability to interpret those color values is maintained for each image file. They can, therefore, be "tagged" with a profile, which means that a profile is attached to the file so an application used to read the image file can know exactly what color is represented by each of the color values stored within the image file. In effect, the translation of the color values is contained within the image file itself, so that the meaning of each color value can be accurately determined.

The profiles used by most applications and operating systems now comply with the standards developed by the International Color Consortium (ICC) and are commonly referred to as "ICC Profiles." The ICC was founded by Adobe, Agfa, Apple, Kodak, and Sun Microsystems to create industry-wide standards for color management. The profile specifications that the ICC created have become the standard used by most operating systems and photo-editing software.

Profiles can be created for input devices such as a digital camera or film scanner, or output devices such as monitors, digital projectors, or printers. Ideally, a profile will be specific to a particular device—not just any scanner of a specific model, but the exact scanner sitting on your desk. This would be a custom profile, and it represents the ideal. However, because manufacturing tolerances are generally very fine, profiles can be made for a specific model of a device with good results. These profiles are referred to as generic or "canned" profiles. For example, each model of inkjet printer includes canned profiles for different types of papers that can be used with that printer.

Profiles can also be used for a more arbitrary purpose when used as a working space. Such a profile does not relate to a specific device, but rather provides a range of colors—a *gamut*—that are available for your images (see Figure 1.16). The available color values are mapped to specific values, typically using the LAB color model, so that each value represents a device-independent color value.

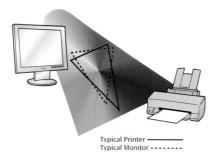

Typical Printer ————
Typical Monitor ········

Figure 1.16

Each device has an individual color gamut that defines the range of colors it is able to produce.

Note: In later chapters I'll show you how to build and use custom profiles and how to utilize generic or canned profiles when you aren't able to obtain custom profiles.

Regardless of their specific implementation, whether to describe the color behavior of a specific device or to define a working space for photo editing, profiles provide a way to relate the color values stored in an image file or interpreted by an input or output device to actual colors based on the way the human visual system perceives color. Profiles, therefore, perform what is arguably the most important task within a color management system.

For color displayed on a monitor, profiles allow a conversion of color values from those stored in your image file to the LAB color model before they are then converted to appropriate RGB values that will cause the monitor to display the same color accurately. For prints, the color values in an image file are similarly translated to LAB before being converted to values that the printer understands to produce the specific colors in the image. Similarly, when a digital camera or film scanner reads color values, a profile can help map the values that are "seen" into correct values in the LAB color model, so that they can then be interpreted for accurate display on any output device.

Any of these translations of color values from one profile to another require conversions that are calculated by a color management engine in the software performing the operations. Because each device has a specific color gamut, which is the range of colors it is able to capture or produce, not all of the colors in the source profile will be available in the destination profile. A method of conversion of image data from one profile to another must include a strategy for dealing with both colors that are within the destination profile's color gamut, and those that are not. That method is implemented by one of four rendering intents.

Rendering Intents

In a color-managed workflow, images will need to be converted from one profile to another for various reasons. During such a conversion, colors in the source profile may not be available in the destination profile. Colors that exist in both profiles can be converted quite easily. The out-of-gamut colors need to be dealt with more carefully. The *rendering intent* determines how the color conversion is performed.

In later chapters, we'll look at the different situations where conversions will be performed and how to choose the right rendering intent, but for now we want to gain an understanding of how the rendering intents behave. Four rendering intents are available: saturation, relative colorimetric, absolute colorimetric, and perceptual. They are demonstrated in Figure 1.17.

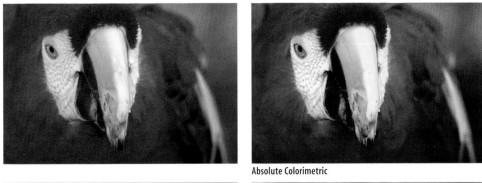

Absolute Colorimetric

Perceptual

Relative Colorimetric

Saturation

Figure 1.17

Each rendering intent will have a slightly different effect on an image. These pictures show the result of converting the same image to the same profile using each of the four rendering intents. As you can see, saturation causes a shift in color values while maintaining saturation, while the other three produce good (though slightly different) renderings of the image.

Saturation

With the saturation rendering intent, as the name implies, the most important property of each color is the saturation. This is the purity of a color, and it is what we think of as having vibrant colors.

The saturation rendering intent does not change colors that are within the gamut of the destination profile. For out-of-gamut colors, the color is changed to maintain the saturation of the color without regard for the hue. In other words, a highly saturated green that doesn't exist in the destination profile could be converted to a highly saturated red hue if that is the closest match in terms of saturation. This could be an obvious problem for photographic images. Although the results will not be as garish as changing a color from green to red, the important point is that the actual color appearance can potentially change quite dramatically, causing problems for photographic images.

Because of the way the saturation profile works, it is not recommended for use with photographic images. It is designed for situations that require saturated colors where you don't care about the hue, such as when using charts in a PowerPoint presentation.

Absolute Colorimetric

The absolute colorimetric rendering intent maintains the appearance of colors that are within the gamut of the destination space, but changes the values of colors that are out of gamut to the closest reproducible hue. Saturation and lightness may be sacrificed in order to obtain the closest matching hue. Absolute colorimetric includes white in the conversion, so that the "color" of white in the source profile is reproduced in the destination profile. That means that white in your image may not match paper white, which can cause the image to look like it has a color cast. This is because the human visual system is incredibly capable of adapting to different light sources, always translating white to appear white. With absolute colorimetric, the eye may adapt to paper white, resulting in a color cast if the white of the image doesn't match paper white. Black is not adjusted with the Absolute Colorimetric rendering intent.

This issue may cause you to avoid using absolute colorimetric as a rendering intent, and in general I would say that is a good decision. However, there are some situations that make it useful. For example, if you are using your printer as a proofing device of a different output method, the absolute colorimetric rendering intent can allow you to proof what white will look like in the final print, producing a more accurate proof.

Relative Colorimetric

Relative colorimetric is virtually identical to absolute colorimetric, in that it keeps colors that are within the gamut of the destination space unchanged, but it changes the value of colors that are outside that gamut to the closest matching hue. The difference with relative colorimetric is that it maps white in the source profile to white in the destination profile, so you can achieve an accurate white that is as pure as possible based on the destination profile.

Perceptual

The perceptual rendering intent attempts to retain the perception of colors within the image by maintaining the relationships between those colors. When there are colors outside the gamut of the destination profile, the colors are effectively compressed to fit within that profile. All colors are shifted so that the relationships between colors are maintained, even if the actual colors shift slightly. This can cause a loss of saturation for many colors, which can be a problem for some images. It may be necessary when there are significant colors outside the gamut of the destination profile.

The perceptual rendering intent is best suited for photographic images that contain a significant number of colors that are outside the gamut of the destination profile, because the relationships between all colors in the image will be maintained, producing the best visual result. We'll talk more about how to determine if there are significant colors that are outside the destination color gamut in later chapters.

The Right Rendering Intent

There is no single best rendering intent. As a general rule for photographic images, I would only use the relative colorimetric or perceptual rendering intents. I tend to favor the perceptual intent for many images printed to inkjet printers, but for color space or profile-to-profile conversions, I generally prefer relative colorimetric. There is no right answer for every situation. I'll discuss the selection of rendering intents in more detail in later chapters, but understand that you may want to use a different rendering intent for different images even with the same output process.

Introducing Color Management

Photographers who do their own color image editing in the digital darkroom tend to have a love/hate relationship with color. They use color as their way to express creativity, and they love what they are able to express through color. They capture light on film or with digital sensors, but they do so much more than capture the light. They control that light through various lenses, filters, editing techniques, and printing methods. Nothing provides more satisfaction for the photographer than to use all the tools at their disposal to blend the palette of colors into a beautiful image.

And yet, as much as photographers love color, it seems nothing can frustrate them as easily as when colors don't match, or the color they expected isn't produced. Making the final print match what they envisioned when they clicked the shutter can present a tremendous challenge, particularly when you consider how many steps the image must pass through from capture to final print.

Color management provides the tools to ensure that the photographer is able to produce a print in the digital darkroom with predictable color. The tools to do so are available; however, learning what they are and how to properly use them seems to be one of the most misunderstood issues in digital imaging.

The complexity of color management is partly due to the number of components involved in working with digital images. Capture devices, such as digital cameras and film scanners, read the color in the original image. A monitor displays the color that is stored within the digital image file and provides the photographer with a visual representation on which to base adjustments to the image. Software settings determine the available colors in the image file. Finally, a printer attempts to reproduce the colors stored in the image file. Each of these components must be controlled to ensure proper color throughout the workflow.

As mentioned earlier in this chapter, color management revolves around profiles, and those profiles provide a common translation for color throughout the color-managed workflow (see Figure 1.18). You can build a custom profile for your digital camera or film scanner so that the colors recorded are as true to the scene that was photographed as possible. A custom profile also ensures that the color information in the image file is presented accurately by the monitor, because the values are translated to those that will produce accurate color on the monitor. This ensures that when you adjust the image, you are doing so based on an accurate view of the image and, therefore, the adjustments will truly produce the results you intend. Finally, when it comes time to print the image, a profile translates the numbers in the image file to the appropriate color information for the printer, resulting in a print that accurately reflects the color information in the image file.

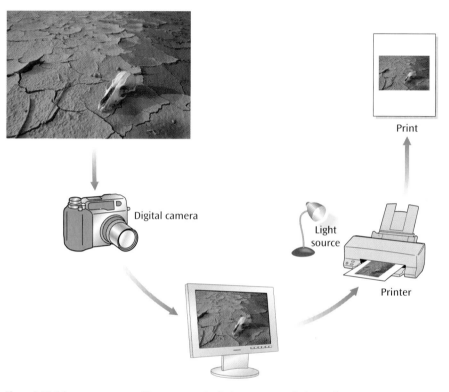

Figure 1.18 Color management provides a way to maintain the appearance of colors as the image moves through each device in the color-managed workflow.

In later chapters, I'll address each of the components of the digital darkroom in turn, providing solutions to achieve accurate and consistent color through the full process of optimizing your digital images.

Limitations of Color Management

I hate to burst your bubble, but color management isn't perfect. If you were hoping to buy this book and suddenly be able to produce a print that is indistinguishable from the display on your monitor, I'm going to have to bring you back down to earth.

Understanding the limitations of color management is just as important as understanding how color management works and what is involved in implementing a good color-managed workflow. We still don't have a complete understanding of all aspects of human vision, and new technology related to color is continually being developed. We have come a long way in understanding color and implementing color management solutions, but it isn't a perfect science.

Although you can achieve excellent results with a color management system, having realistic expectations is important. For example, the holy grail of color management for photographers is a print that matches the monitor. You need to understand that a print will never look exactly like the image on the monitor (see Figure 1.19). For one thing, both use very different mediums to present an image. A monitor emits light to present an image, while a print depends upon reflected light. Although the colors themselves can be very accurate, the experience of viewing each image is very different. The monitor is able to produce an image that is very luminous, by virtue of the fact that the image is actually composed of emitted light. Prints, on the other hand, will never be quite as luminous because they depend upon reflected light.

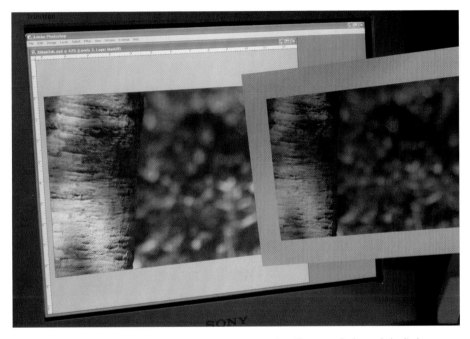

Figure 1.19 No matter how good your color management system, a print will never perfectly match the display on your monitor due to the differences in how the image is produced.

As I'll discuss in later chapters, evaluating your prints requires a certain amount of interpretation. If you understand the different properties of the different devices used in a color-managed workflow, you'll better understand the limitations of color management.

Of course, that doesn't mean you can't expect excellent results with a proper color-managed workflow. Quite the contrary, you can achieve incredibly accurate prints that exactly reflect what you intended the image to look like. Although it is important to understand that there are limitations in color management, you can get excellent results with an appropriate workflow.

One point I would emphasize is that while you may not get prints that exactly match what you see on the monitor in all respects, you can achieve predictable results. If you accept the inherent limitations involved, you can learn to interpret the results you achieve, learn to get the most accurate results, and ensure that you can get consistent, accurate, and predictable output for your images.

Photoshop Setup

Before you implement a color management system to get your digital camera, film scanner, monitor, and printer capturing or producing accurate color, you'll want to make sure Photoshop is properly configured.

Once you understand how Photoshop works and how to best configure it to meet your specific needs, you'll have much greater success producing excellent results with your color-managed workflow.

Chapter Contents
Color Settings
Warnings
Assigning and Converting Profiles

Color Settings

The Color Settings dialog box (see Figure 2.1) is "command central" for color management in Photoshop. It allows you to establish settings for how your images will be dealt with in a color-managed workflow. Having the right settings in this dialog is important for getting the best results with your images (Figure 2.2).

Figure 2.1

The Color Settings dialog box is "command central" for your color management settings in Photoshop.

Figure 2.2

As editor of *Digital Photo Pro* magazine, Chris Robinson knows the importance of proper Photoshop color settings. The right settings lay the foundation for proper optimization and accurate output. (Photograph by Chris Robinson.)

Keep in mind that there aren't any absolutes that define the best color settings. The optimal settings will depend in part on the type of output for which you are preparing images. Some of the settings also depend on personal preference. In this section, I'll explain what each of the settings is for and how to choose the best setting for your specific needs. I'll also offer recommended settings for some of the options based on typical workflows. The best settings may vary from one project to another, making it all the more important that you understand what each setting affects. This also means it is important to remember to check your color settings before you embark on a new project that will use different output methods than you are accustomed to, or than your current settings are geared toward.

The Color Settings dialog box is accessed by choosing Edit > Color Settings from the menu (Photoshop > Color Settings for Macintosh OS X). You can also use the shortcut key Shift+Ctrl+K (Shift+Command+K on Macintosh).

Saving and Loading Color Settings

If you will be working with images destined for a variety of different output methods, you'll likely need custom Color Settings for each of those situations. In that case, saving the settings that apply to each type of work you will be doing is very helpful, so that you can easily load the appropriate settings whenever you begin working with a new set of images. Even if you only need to have a single set of Color Settings, saving them just in case the settings get changed accidentally can be very helpful, and I strongly recommend doing so.

Settings Dropdown

The Settings dropdown menu at the top of the Color Settings dialog box (see Figure 2.3) allows you to choose from a list of stored settings with values set for all options. Selecting one of these options will simply change the values in the Color Settings dialog box. based on the settings saved for that preset. Note that you can only select color settings that have been saved to the default location. If you save to a special location, you'll need to use the Load option to load your specific settings.

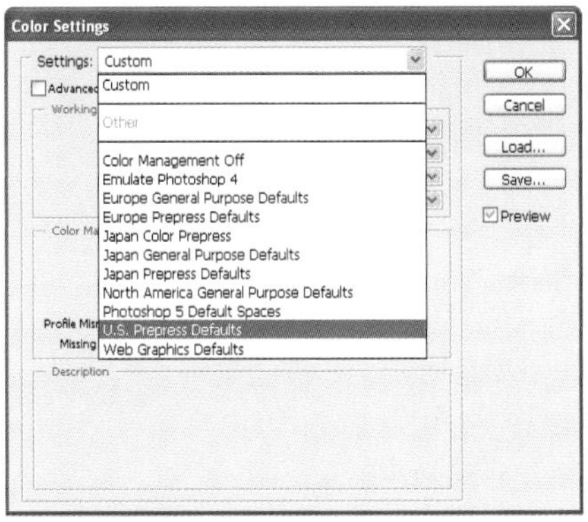

Figure 2.3
The Settings dropdown on the Color Settings dialog box allows you to quickly select from saved settings.

Save Settings

Saving a set of Color Settings is a simple matter of configuring all the settings the way you want them and then clicking the Save button. You will be prompted to provide a name for the settings, as well as a location to save the file that will store those settings.

I strongly recommend that you give the settings a name that will be meaningful for you based on the type of output you will be producing with those settings. For example, you might save settings called "Standard Inkjet Printing" for images you'll print yourself on an inkjet printer. If you are working on a particular project providing CMYK images for use in a catalog called "Wonderful Widgets," you might save settings as "Catalog CMYK - Wonderful Widgets." The name you use to save the settings should give you a clear indication of exactly what type of output you'll be producing with particular images, so that you can select the right settings based on the type of job on which you're working.

You will also be prompted for a location to save the settings file. If you save the settings in the default location that Photoshop uses to store color settings files, you will be able to select your settings from the Settings dropdown list. Otherwise, you'll have to use the Load option to recall those settings.

Location for Saving Color Settings

Many photographers prefer to save their custom settings to a separate folder they create for this purpose. This can help keep the files more organized, make them easier to share with others, and ensure that they will remain safe even if Photoshop and all related files are removed from your system.

The advantage is having all of your settings saved in a single location that you manage yourself, so you'll know exactly where all of the files are.

The disadvantage is that settings saved outside the default location will not display on the Settings dropdown, and their Description information will not be visible, until after you have specifically loaded a setting.

I recommend saving the settings in the default location unless you have a compelling reason to keep them somewhere else.

After you have selected a location and provided a filename for the settings, you will be prompted to provide a description for the settings (see Figure 2.4). This is an excellent way to provide a detailed explanation of how the settings should be used. When you choose a setting at the top of the Color Settings dialog box, its description is displayed at the bottom.

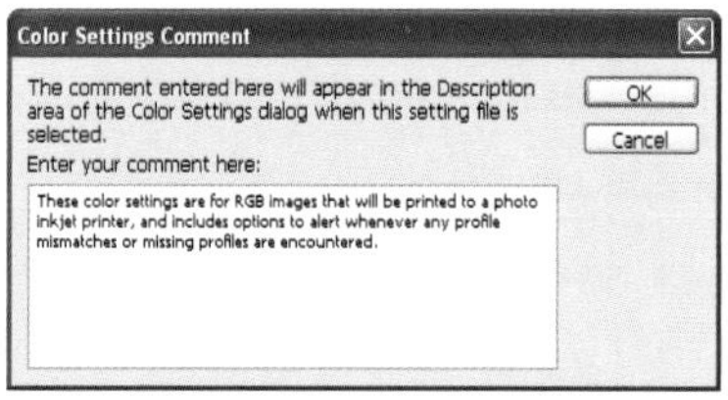

Figure 2.4

When you save color settings so they can quickly be selected in the future, you can also assign a description that will help you remember exactly for what the settings are optimized.

Load Settings

If you have saved settings to a location other than the default used by Photoshop, they will not be available from the Settings dropdown at the top of the Color Settings dialog box. In that case, you will need to click the Load button and navigate to the location where you save the settings. You can then select the settings by filename. With the settings loaded, the name of the saved settings will show up on the Settings dropdown, even though it will not remain there permanently. If you included a description when you saved the settings, you can read the description by holding your mouse pointer over the Settings dropdown. This is a good way to confirm the settings you've loaded are the correct ones for the images on which you plan to work.

Advanced Mode

By default, the Advanced Mode checkbox at the top of the Color Settings dialog box is not checked. For most users, the options available by checking Advanced Mode don't need to be adjusted.

When the Advanced Mode checkbox is checked (see Figure 2.5), it causes two changes in the Color Settings dialog box. First, it will expand the list of profiles for each of the Working Spaces to include all profiles installed on your system, rather than just those defined as working space profiles. Second, it will expand the Color Settings dialog box to include Conversion Options and Advanced Controls sections, which will be explained later in this chapter.

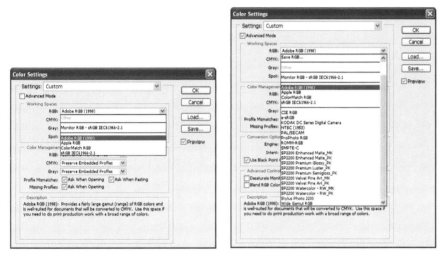

Figure 2.5 When you check the Advanced Mode checkbox, the Color Settings dialog box expands to include additional options, and the Working Space dropdown lists include all profiles installed on your system, rather than only those designated as working spaces.

Figure 2.6 shows the Color Settings dialog with the options that I recommend already selected. The following sections detail each of these choices and how you should make them.

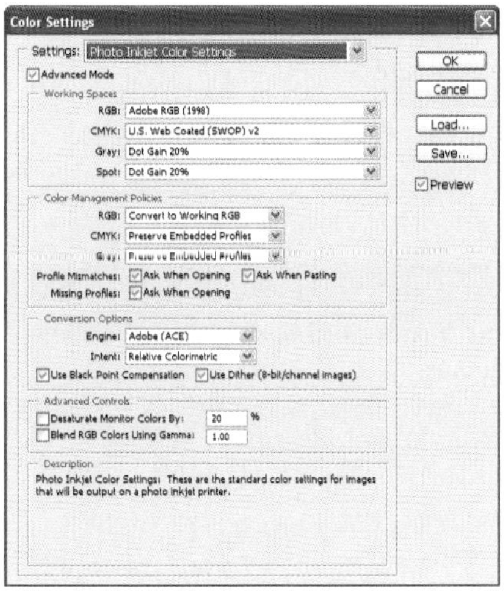

Figure 2.6
These are the standard Color Settings I recommend for most photographers.

Working Spaces

A *working space* defines the range of colors available to you as you edit your images. You can think of this as being similar to a painter's palette. If a color isn't on the palette, you can't include it in the painting. With digital images the same situation applies, although there are a very large number of colors available. At first glance you may think that you want to have as large a working space as possible, so that a huge range of colors is available. However, bigger isn't always better. In the case of a working space, bigger means covering a broader range of colors, but it doesn't mean you actually have more colors available.

A digital image can store a finite number of possible colors. With 8-bit-per-channel (24-bit) images, that number is over 16.7 million colors (16,777,216 to be exact). That's a pretty big number, but it is a limitation. In reality, you aren't going to be able to reproduce all of those colors because a printer can only produce a certain range. Also, as you edit the image, you're going to lose even more color possibilities. Even though a large number of colors still comprise your image, the bottom line is that the number of colors available is finite.

A working space effectively defines the outer limits of colors available from the visible spectrum. This range of colors is the effective color gamut of the working space. Keep in mind that the color gamut of the monitor or printer used to reproduce the image may not be as wide as the working space. That means you can have colors in your image that can't be reproduced on certain (or any) devices.

A very wide-gamut color space extends to highly saturated colors that may not be reproducible, depending on the output method. In other words, it has a wider range of possible colors, but those colors might not do you any good.

Bigger is not necessarily better when it comes to working spaces. While a wide-gamut color space extends to a broader range of possible colors, the total number of colors available for a given image does not change. If the same number of possible colors is spread across a broader range of the color spectrum, the space between each color is much larger (see Figure 2.7). The result is a greater risk of losing smooth gradations of color in your image. The best solution is a working space that most accurately represents the color range you are likely to actually use in your images for the various output methods you will utilize. There are situations where a wide-gamut color space may be desirable. For example, when working with images from Ektachrome films that you intend to optimize and put back onto film with a film recorder, the Ektaspace color space would be a good choice (though it isn't provided with Photoshop, so you'll need to obtain it elsewhere). For most photographers, there are few—if any—situations where a wide-gamut color space would be necessary.

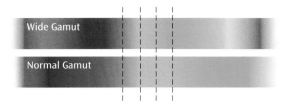

Figure 2.7

A wide-gamut color space provides a broader range of colors, but that means the distance between the finite number of possible color values is bigger, increasing the risk of banding or posterization.

Setting a working space does not mean that every image will be limited to the range of colors for that working space. The working space settings simply provide default color spaces for each of the color modes. You still have the option to leave an image in the color space it has been saved with, or convert it to a completely different working space. The space you set as the working space will also be used as the default color space for any new documents you create.

RGB Working Space

For most photographers working in the digital darkroom, the only color space that is important is RGB. As will be discussed later in this book (see Chapter 7, "Output"), even though photo inkjet printers use CMYK inks, they should be considered RGB devices and the images should be kept in the RGB color space during editing and printing. Because most photographers intend to print their images, I recommend using the Adobe RGB (1998) working space rather than the default of sRGB.

The Wrong Working Space

Knowing which working space should *not* be used is perhaps as important as knowing how to select an appropriate working space. Besides choosing from a variety of profiles designed as working spaces, some experts recommend setting your working space to the profile for your printer or monitor.

The problem with this approach is that it limits the range of colors available to those that can be produced with a single device. Your printer can produce many colors that are not included in a monitor profile. If you use a printer profile, there will be colors that other printers could produce that won't be available to you

This is why it is best to use a working space that offers a good balance between colors that can be produced on your monitor and colors that can be printed with a wide variety of printers.

sRGB   For images destined for display on a monitor, such as for e-mail, web, or digital projection, the sRGB color space is an excellent choice. This color space is designed to match the typical monitor display. Although every monitor is indeed different, this space does a good job of including the colors that will be available with most monitors, even if they aren't calibrated. If you are working with images primarily for this type of usage, then the sRGB color space is probably your best option.

The sRGB color space has a reputation as being "useless" for images that will be printed. This is an undeserved reputation, and excellent prints can be produced with images in this space. However, sRGB is not the best option for images that will be printed, because it doesn't include as many printable colors as the Adobe RGB (1998) color space. If you will use your images for more than one purpose, you should probably consider Adobe RGB (1998), converting images destined for display on a monitor to sRGB during final preparation. This topic will be covered in more detail in Chapter 7.

Adobe RGB (1998)   The Adobe RGB (1998) color space is widely regarded as the best choice for images that will be printed on photo inkjet printers. It very closely matches the available color gamut of photo inkjet printers, so that very few colors are clipped. At the same time, the color space is not significantly larger than the color gamut of most photo inkjet printers, so that smooth gradations aren't lost due to a color space that is larger than necessary. For images that will be repurposed to a variety of output methods, and in particular for images that will be printed using photo inkjet printers, I consider this the best choice and, therefore, recommend setting it as the default RGB working space in the Color Settings dialog.

ColorMatch RGB   The ColorMatch RGB color space fits somewhere between sRGB and Adobe RGB (1998) in terms of color gamut. It offers a wider gamut than sRGB, but not as wide as Adobe RGB (1998). It is a very good choice for images that will be repurposed for a variety of output methods, but not as good a choice as Adobe RGB (1998).

CMYK Working Space

For most photographers, working with CMYK images isn't an issue. Even when it is, it generally won't be frequent enough and for the same output device that a common CMYK working space can be established. In general, keeping your images in RGB mode for as long as possible is preferred, because a conversion to CMYK involves a conversion to a color space specific to particular output conditions. Once you have converted an image to CMYK, you will have sacrificed some degree of color and tonal range in the image, in most situations. This is part of the reason that I recommend that you keep your archival master image files in the RGB color mode and only convert a copy of the master image to CMYK for specific output needs.

If you are required to convert to CMYK for a particular output process, that conversion should be one of your last steps in preparing the file. In those situations, you should use a custom CMYK profile for the specific output device to be used. Otherwise, I would leave the CMYK conversion to the printing lab.

If you work with a large number of RGB images that you must convert to CMYK, or you actually have to process CMYK images, all for the same output conditions, then it is a good idea to set the profile for the specific output conditions as your working space, so that when you open CMYK images or change images from RGB mode to CMYK, the appropriate profile will be applied.

Because the CMYK profile used for images that must be converted to or edited in CMYK mode is device specific, you probably can't really settle on a standard CMYK working space, but instead will need to adjust the CMYK working space on a per-job basis when you have the need to produce CMYK files. If you have no idea what sort of CMYK profile or output process might be used in the future, I recommend setting the CMYK working space to U.S. Web Coated (SWOP) v2. Just remember that this is a generic working space that won't necessarily provide you with an accurate picture of what your images will look like in print. It is a reasonably good generic working space, in that most output in the U.S. is conducted on web offset presses. However, to get the most accurate results, you'll need a custom CMYK profile from your printer.

Gray Working Space

The Gray Working Space sets the default color space for grayscale (black and white) images. Because grayscale images by definition don't have any color information, this isn't a matter of matching color so much as it is a matter of matching tonal values. For grayscale images that will be used primarily on a monitor or digital projector, I recommend using the Gray Gamma working space that coincides with the gamma you have targeted your monitor to during calibration (see Chapter 3, "Display," for more details on monitor calibration). In general, that means Gray Gamma 2.2 (or Gray Gamma 1.8 if you calibrate to that target gamma, in which case you'll want to read my recommendations in Chapter 3 very carefully).

For grayscale images destined for print, the primary issue that will affect the appearance of tonal values in the final display will be *dot gain*. This is the spreading of ink on paper, which causes tones to look darker because there is more blending of the individual dots used to produce the various tonal values. For images destined for print, I would use a Dot Gain setting that matches the approximate dot gain of the output method you will be using—most often Dot Gain 20%.

Keep in mind that in most situations it is better to keep your grayscale images in the RGB color mode, making the Gray Working Space setting relatively unused.

Spot Working Space

If photographers are unlikely to work with CMYK images for editing, they are highly unlikely to use spot color, which produces images with a single ink color. This obviously doesn't result in good tonal range in the final result, although spot color can be added to CMYK images to extend tonal range. Spot color would be more of an issue for a graphic design firm, or other companies producing printed pieces that include images, rather than photographers producing prints of their own images. In the rare situation where you do need to use spot color for an image (such as a low-budget newsletter), the important factor is dot gain. If you need to use spot color, get the specific dot gain specifications for the particular printer. As a general starting point, I recommend setting the Working Space for spot color to Dot Gain 20%.

Color Management Policies

The Color Management Policies section of the Color Settings dialog box allows you to instruct Photoshop how to deal with particular situations related to profiles embedded (or not embedded) in existing images. The options you set will define the default action Photoshop will take when an embedded profile in an image doesn't match the working space you have defined, or when there isn't a profile embedded at all. Individual options are available to set the policy for RGB, CMYK, and grayscale color models.

The options for Color Management Policies are Off, Preserve Embedded Profiles, and Convert To Working. It is important to understand that the setting you use here is the default option, and there are ways to override the default value as explained in the following text.

Off

This setting, as you might expect, simply turns off color management. Since you're reading this book, you probably want to take full advantage of the benefits of color management, and so this option is not one you would choose. It most certainly isn't an option I recommend. With this setting, the color numbers in the image are preserved, but the meaning of those numbers will be interpreted based on the current working space. If the embedded profile in an image matches the working space, then the colors will appear correctly. If the image is not tagged with a profile, or if it is tagged with a profile other than the current working space, the color numbers will still be interpreted with the working space and, therefore, probably will not be displayed accurately. I can't think of a single good reason to use this setting when working with photographic images, so I avoid it.

Preserve Embedded Profiles

This option will preserve the embedded profile in an image if it is tagged with a profile. This allows you to see what the image looks like with the embedded profile without converting to the working space. Although such a conversion is intended to maintain the appearance of colors in the image, a significant difference in the color gamut of the source versus destination profiles can still result in a loss of information. This setting is most useful if you frequently open images that have already been tagged with a profile other than your normal working space. For example, if you have images scanned by a lab that assigns a custom profile to the images, you would want to see what the image looks like before the conversion to your working space. For most photographers, this type of situation doesn't come up very often, so it usually isn't the best choice. Particularly for photographers using a digital camera, I prefer to convert the image to the working space rather than keep it in the color space defined by the camera. However, if you work with a large number of images that have a custom profile assigned to them, such as drum scans provided by many labs, this may be a good choice.

Although the Preserve Embedded Profiles option isn't the best option for most photographers, it is the right option if you use custom profiles. I'll address custom profiles for film scanners in Chapter 4, "Scanning," and custom profiles for digital cameras in Chapter 5, "Digital Capture." When using a custom profile for film scans or digital captures, you don't want to convert the image to the working space before assigning the custom profile, and so the Preserve Embedded Profiles option makes the most sense.

As I'll discuss in Chapter 7, there are situations where different profiles are used for particular images. For example, images that will be presented on the Web, via e-mail, or with a digital projector will likely benefit from being converted to the sRGB color space; you would not want to convert to your working space of Adobe RGB (1998), for example, only to convert them again to sRGB after adjusting them. For those images, you want to preserve the embedded profile rather than converting to your working space. If this is a significant portion of the images you work with, you may want to select Preserve Embedded Profiles as your default Color Management Policy. However, for most photographers this won't represent the majority of images.

For images that do not have an embedded profile, when you have this option selected the image will be interpreted based on the current working space, and when you save the image it will still not have a profile embedded.

Convert to Working

The working space you select as your default should be chosen because it represents the best balance between the color gamut of your monitor and that of the intended output method you will use to reproduce your images, both now and in the future. Therefore, it makes sense to convert your images to that working space unless you have a very good reason for doing otherwise (such as when you are using custom profiles, as mentioned in the previous section).

Besides the fact that your selected working space is well-suited for the output methods you will use for your images, it also provides the benefit of consistency for your images. While this isn't a significant benefit, it does mean that all of your images will have the same color palette available to them, which provides some consistency for them.

If your scanner software provides the option to tag the scanned images with your working space as a profile, I recommend taking advantage of that option. Otherwise, convert those images as well. I'll discuss this and other issues related to film scans in Chapter 4.

Likewise, if your digital camera offers the option to tag your images with your preferred working space at the time of capture, I recommend using this option, in which case you won't need to convert your images to the working space after the fact. If this option isn't available with your digital camera, then convert the images to your working space when you open them. I'll discuss issues related to digital captures in Chapter 5.

If you open an image that is already tagged with your working space as the profile, then no conversion is necessary, and you won't receive a warning message when you open the image.

Profile Mismatches

The Profile Mismatches checkboxes allow you to specify whether the option you set under the Color Management Policies should be performed automatically to your image or whether you want to be asked if a different action should be taken instead. With the Ask When Opening checkbox checked, the Color Management Policy you selected will be the default action, but you will be asked for confirmation with the opportunity to change the action to be taken if you open an image tagged with a profile that differs from your current working space. If the box is not checked, the Color Management Policy selected will determine the action taken, and it will be done without offering you the option to change the action to be taken.

The Ask When Pasting option has the same behavior, except that it affects the copying of pixels from one document to another. If this checkbox is checked and you copy and paste pixels from a source document with a different profile than your destination document, you will be asked what action should be taken. The Color Management Policy will determine which action is the default. If the box is not checked, then the Color Management Policy selected will determine the action taken, and it will be done without offering you the option to change the action to be taken.

If you always use the same Color Management Policy for every image in every situation, then it is convenient to leave these checkboxes unchecked, so that you don't need to be bothered with an extra dialog box asking you a question that you answer the same way every time. However, if you turn off the checkboxes, you'll never receive a warning, which means that when you do have an exception you may not remember to change your color settings first, causing the image to be handled inappropriately. For example, if you have images you have optimized for the Web and converted to the sRGB color space, you won't want to convert them to a working space of Adobe RGB (1998) when you open them.

My preference is to keep the boxes checked at all times. It means I am asked what action I want to perform for every single image, but I prefer this for two reasons. First, I always know what is being done to my images. Second, I always have the option of changing the default behavior, so when I'm working with an image that is an exception to my normal workflow, I will get a reminder to change the setting as needed.

Missing Profiles

The Missing Profiles option provides the same Ask When Opening checkbox available for Profile Mismatches. The only difference is that this option deals with images that are untagged, meaning that no profile is assigned to them. I always leave this option turned on, so that if I open an image that doesn't have an embedded profile, I'll want to select a specific profile to assign to the image to provide the most accurate interpretation of the colors in the image.

Default Doesn't Mean Always

It is important to remember that the right setting is defined by your specific needs for the image, the source of those images, and the specific method to be used to produce the final output. While I've offered recommendations based on what settings will work best for most photographers in most situations, that doesn't mean the settings presented will always be the best choices for all of your images. By understanding what each setting means, and what determines the optimal choice for each setting, you'll be able to make an informed decision about what settings to use under particular situations.

This also reinforces the reasons I recommend keeping the Profile Mismatch checkbox and the Missing Profile checkbox selected so you will be notified when such a situation exists and can determine the best course of action for the particular image with which you are working.

Conversion Options

This section is available only if you have checked the Advanced Mode box at the top of the Color Settings dialog box.

Engine

This setting controls the Color Matching Method (CMM) that is used to convert colors from one profile to another. I recommend leaving this option set to the default value of Adobe (ACE) unless you have a good reason to use a different engine. The other available options are ColorSync for Macintosh users and Microsoft ICM for Windows users. Both of these provide an excellent alternative. However, because I trust Adobe Photoshop for photo editing, I feel perfectly comfortable trusting Adobe's engine for color management. The consensus among experts seems to be that the Adobe engine is more accurate than the alternatives. It also provides a cross-platform solution, because the other options are not cross-platform.

Intent

This option allows you to specify the default rendering intent used for conversions from one profile to another. The behavior of the available rendering intents is explained in Chapter 1, "Foundations." My recommendation is to set the Relative Colorimetric rendering intent as the default, and use it unless you have an image with a significant number of colors that fall outside the gamut of your target space. (In that case, the Perceptual rendering intent is the better option.)

Use Black Point Compensation

I feel the Use Black Point Compensation option should always be turned on. It affects the process of converting images from one profile to another and, as the name implies, has an effect on the black point in your image. With this option on, the black in your image will be mapped to the black point of your output device (typically a printer). That means that the full tonal range of the printer will be used, from the darkest black it can produce to the brightest white (defined by the color of the paper).

With this option turned off, the black point in your image would not be set to black in the output profile. Either the blacks will be lighter than black, producing a muddy image, or they will be darker than black, causing clipping in the shadow areas.

Use Dither

The Use Dither option (only available for 8-bit per channel images) provides a method of simulating colors that are not available in the destination profile during conversion. It will cause available colors in the destination profile to be blended to simulate colors that aren't available. This helps to enable colors that might otherwise be impossible to reproduce, but more importantly helps to avoid banding and posterization in the image. For images that will be printed, this is almost always a benefit.

For images that are going to be saved with compression, as would be the case when saving an image in JPEG format, the noise can result in a larger file size. If you are particularly concerned about file size with your JPEG files for web display, for example, you might turn this option off while working on those images. In all other situations, I recommend leaving it turned on.

Advanced Controls

The Advanced Controls section of the Color Settings dialog box offers a couple of options that most photographers will simply want to leave disabled.

Desaturate Monitor Colors

Many photographers initially assume the option to desaturate the colors on their monitor might be a good thing based on their understanding of the capabilities of printers and monitors. Because they know a printer can't produce the vividly saturated colors they can view on their monitor, they figure that desaturating the monitor will help produce a better match between monitor and printer. That isn't what this option is designed for, and it will likely cause more problems than it solves if you attempt to use it for that purpose. I recommend always leaving this feature turned off.

The only time it may be helpful to turn on the Desaturate Monitor Colors option would be if you are working in a color space with a very wide color gamut. In those situations, the color space will contain colors that are beyond the color gamut of the monitor. In other words, the monitor can't even display some of the colors available in the color space. Desaturating all the colors in your image allows you to bring the colors in your image within the gamut of your monitor (see Figure 2.8). That means the colors you see will not be an accurate representation of the images in your image, because the overall gamut is compressed to fit within the gamut of your monitor (if an adequate setting is used). Considerable interpretation is required to make adjustments to the image, because the entire image will be desaturated and not an accurate representation of the actual colors.

Figure 2.8
Desaturating the colors on your monitor will ensure that you are able to see a representation of all of the colors in a wide-gamut color space. However, desaturating them causes all colors to be displayed with reduced saturation (right) so that it is more difficult to accurately adjust the colors in your image.

Fortunately, most photographers don't need to work in a wide-gamut color space. The most common output processes offer a color gamut that is narrower than that of a monitor, or with very few colors out of gamut, so you don't need to worry about being unable to see colors accurately. The bottom line is that unless you are very experienced in this area, this option should be turned off.

Blend RGB Colors Using Gamma

Although photographers use light in some way at every stage of the process of producing their images, they tend to think about the dyes or pigments that produce the final result on paper when they think about the final product. For that reason, when editing an image they tend to think of colors blending with each other as if they were ink on paper. By default, Photoshop blends colors with a result that matches what you would expect when mixing inks.

The Blend RGB Colors Using Gamma option allows you to change this behavior so that colors blend as if they were light rather than ink (see Figure 2.9). For example, if you have a red background, and you paint blue over the top of it with a soft-edged brush, the edge of the stroke would be a relatively dark blue with the option turned off, and a light pink color with the option turned on.

Figure 2.9
With the Blend RGB Colors Using Gamma option turned off, colors painted over other colors blend the way you would expect inks to blend on paper (left). With the option turned on, colors blend as you would expect colored light to blend (right).

Based on the way most photographers tend to think about the blending of colors in their images, I recommend leaving this option turned off. Because most photographers don't spend a significant amount of time painting color onto their images, this option isn't of key concern anyway.

Warnings

Once you have configured Photoshop for the proper color settings, you also need to set up and understand the various warning messages that will be displayed as you open and work with your images.

Gamut Warning Preferences

To produce the best prints, it is important that all of the colors present in your image can be reproduced with the particular output method you'll be using. The Gamut Warning option in Photoshop allows you to determine which colors in the image can't be printed, based on whether the colors are available in a particular profile.

The Gamut Warning options are actually the only settings in the Preferences dialog box in Photoshop that directly relate to color management. All other settings in Preferences are largely a matter of your personal preference, and don't affect your color-managed workflow.

You can access the Gamut Warning preferences by selecting Edit > Preferences > Transparency & Gamut (Photoshop > Preferences > Transparency & Gamut on Macintosh OS X) from the menu. In the Gamut Warning section (see Figure 2.10), you can select the color and opacity of the gamut warning display on your images. To change the color, click the box labeled Color. This will bring up the Color Picker, where you can select the color to be used. My recommendation is to use a highly saturated color that is not likely to appear in your images. Keep in mind that you can always return to the Preferences dialog box to change the setting if the color you normally use actually exists in an image with which you are working. I usually use a highly saturated magenta color, but any color that will visibly stand out with most of your images is a good choice.

You can also adjust the opacity of the color by changing the value on the Opacity slider. This allows you to use a partially transparent color for the gamut warning, so you can still see the details of your image under the warning color. My preference is to keep the Opacity at 100 percent, so that the gamut warning color stands out more.

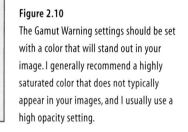

Figure 2.10

The Gamut Warning settings should be set with a color that will stand out in your image. I generally recommend a highly saturated color that does not typically appear in your images, and I usually use a high opacity setting.

I'll discuss how to use the Gamut Warning option, and how to adjust your images to ensure all colors are within gamut, in Chapter 7.

Embedded Profile Mismatch

As mentioned earlier, the Color Management Policies options available to you in the Color Settings dialog box simply determine the default behavior. If you work with images from a single source, such as a digital camera, you may want to have the same action take place with every image you open. For example, a digital camera typically captures an image in the sRGB color space by default. If your working space is set to Adobe RGB (1998), Photoshop will recognize that the profile does not match your working space.

The Color Management Policies will determine what Photoshop does by default with your image. If you always want the same action performed, you can simply clear the check from the Profile Mismatches option for both Ask When Opening and Ask When Pasting. If these checkboxes are not checked, then the Color Management Policies option you select will be performed on every image without giving you the option to intervene. This may be fine if you want all of your images to be handled the same way. However, the problem with turning off these warnings is that you won't be warned about possible exceptions with certain images that you might want to handle with a different policy.

If you work with images from a variety of different sources, or if you want to be sure that you don't forget to change the default behavior in certain situations, then it is a good idea to check the boxes under Profile Mismatches. If the Ask When Opening box is checked, Photoshop will alert you if the profile in the image does not match the working space when you open an image (see Figure 2.11). It will then give you three options, which are the same as the options available for Color Management Policies:

Figure 2.11
The Embedded Profile Mismatch dialog box allows you to determine what action should be taken when you open an image with an embedded profile that does not match your current working space.

"**Use the embedded profile (instead of the working space)**" is the same as Preserve Embedded Profiles. This will cause your image to be converted to the working space, preserving the appearance of the colors in your image to the extent possible. If you save the image, it will still be tagged with the original profile embedded in the image when you opened it.

"**Convert document's colors to the working space**" is the same as Convert To Working. This will cause the image to be converted to your working space. If you save the image, the current working space that the image was converted to will be embedded as the profile for the image.

"**Discard the embedded profile (don't color manage)**" is the same as Off. This will cause the profile to be ignored, and the color values in the image will be interpreted based on the current working space. This does not produce an accurate display of the image and, therefore, I don't recommend using this option. If you save an image after opening it with this setting, it will not have a profile embedded.

The default option in the Profile Mismatch dialog box will be the option you selected under the Color Management Policies in the Color Settings dialog box. However, you then have the option to change the default behavior before proceeding. If you generally convert to the working space, but you have now received an image that is tagged with a custom profile, this gives you the option to change the default behavior on a per image basis. It also gives you a better understanding of what is being done to your images.

For more detail on how these options work, turn back to the earlier section "Color Management Policies."

Paste Profile Mismatch

Opening an image isn't the only time that a profile mismatch can occur. If you copy-and-paste or drag-and-drop pixels from one image to another with different profiles, you must deal with the profile mismatch. If you have checked the Ask When Pasting box for Profile Mismatches in Color Settings, then you will be prompted with the Paste Profile Mismatch dialog box (see Figure 2.12) when you copy pixels from one image to another with profiles that don't match. If the box is not checked, then the action selected under Color Management Policies in Color Settings will be performed automatically.

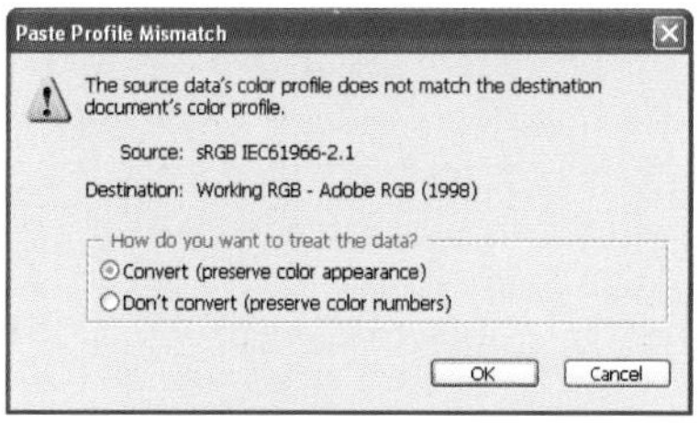

Figure 2.12

The Past Profile Mismatch dialog box allows you to determine what action should be taken when you paste pixels into an image where the source image has a different profile than the destination image. I always recommend using the Convert option.

Two options are available to you in the Paste Profile Mismatch dialog box. The option to "Convert (preserve color appearance)" is the one you'll most often want to select. This will change the color numbers in the image using a profile-to-profile conversion so that the visual appearance of the colors is unchanged, although out-of-gamut colors will need to be changed to the nearest match defined by the rendering intent set in Color Settings.

The option to "Don't convert (preserve color numbers)" will cause the color numbers for the source pixels to be retained and then interpreted based on the profile of the destination image. For photographic images, this isn't generally an option you would want to choose, because it will actually change the appearance of the colors in the image you are copying.

Note: If you copy pixels between two images with different color modes (such as pasting from an RGB document to a CMYK document), the only option is to preserve color appearance, so you won't see the Paste Profile Mismatch dialog.

Missing Profile

The Missing Profile dialog box (see Figure 2.13) is very similar to the Embedded Profile Mismatch dialog box, except that it appears when the image you have opened does not contain a profile. It will be displayed only if you have checked the box for "Ask When Opening" associated with the Missing Profile option in Color Settings.

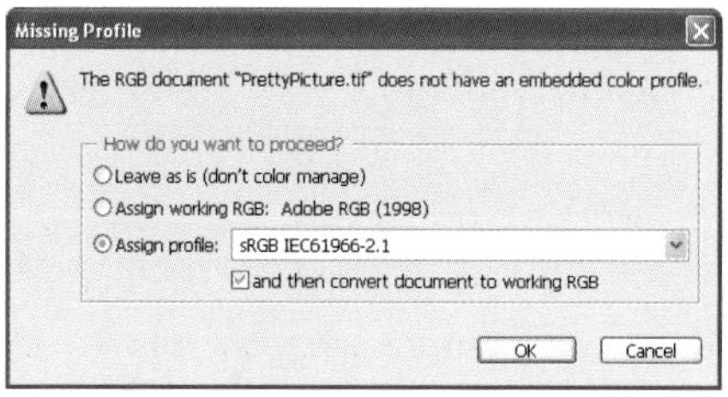

Figure 2.13

The Missing Profile dialog box allows you to determine what action should be taken when you open an image that does not have an embedded profile.

As with the Embedded Profile Mismatch dialog box, you have three options from which to choose. The default action will be based on the option selected in Color Settings.

The option to Leave As It Is (Don't Color Manage) is similar to the Discard The Embedded Profile option in the Embedded Profile Mismatch dialog box. If you select this option, the image will be interpreted based on the currently selected Working Space set in Color Settings. When you save the image, no profile will be embedded. This is generally not a good choice, as it doesn't include an indication of how the colors in the image should be interpreted.

The Assign Working RGB option (assuming an RGB image) provides an indication of what the current Working RGB color space is based on the setting in Color Settings. Because the image does not contain an embedded profile, there is no basis for interpreting the colors in the image. If you select this option, the color numbers in the image will be interpreted based on the Working Space defined in Color Settings. When you save the image, the Working Space that was used to interpret the image when it was opened will be embedded in the image, so it will now be tagged with a profile.

The Assign Profile option allows you to assign a profile to the image to determine how the color numbers should be interpreted. This option is most frequently used to assign a custom profile to a film scan or digital capture. By assigning a custom profile to those images, the color numbers are interpreted based on the profile, which should result in more accurate colors in the image. These custom profiles will be discussed in later chapters. If you do select this option, a checkbox will also be enabled that allows you to convert to the Working Space defined in Color Settings after the profile has been assigned, and I recommend checking this box unless you have a reason not to convert your image to the working RGB color space.

This is the best option in most situations, unless you know under what profile the color values in the image were originally defined. By choosing Assign Profile, you can scroll through all of the profiles available on your computer to find the one that offers the most accurate interpretation of the colors in the image. For example, if you open an image taken with a digital camera with no profile embedded, you can find the best profile to assign that will provide the most accurate colors in the image.

Embedded Profile Mismatch Alert

If you have not checked the boxes to Ask When Opening for profile mismatches, Photoshop will offer an alert to let you know what is happening with your image. This alert (see Figure 2.14) is simply warning you that the profile embedded in the image you have opened does not match the working profile. It also lets you know what action will be taken, which will be based on the settings you have set in the Color Settings dialog box. Since you set appropriate settings in Color Settings to determine what action should be taken in the event of a profile mismatch, this dialog box is not generally useful. You can click the checkbox for Don't Show Again so that this dialog box will not be shown in the future.

Figure 2.14

If you do not enable the options to be notified of embedded profile mismatches in the Color Settings dialog, you will still receive an alert letting you know what action will be taken unless you disable it.

Note that if you disable this alert message, but later decide you'd like to receive the alert, the only way to bring it back is to enable all alerts by clicking the Reset All Warning Dialogs button in the Preferences dialog box (Edit > Preferences > General).

Assigning and Converting Profiles

Besides the options available in Color Settings and with the Embedded Profile Mismatch and Missing Profile dialog boxes, you can also deal with profiles "manually," assigning them to an image or converting an image from one profile to another.

Assign Profile

The Assign Profile command (Image > Mode > Assign Profile; see Figure 2.15) allows you to assign a profile to an image. When you do so, the color numbers in the image are not changed. Rather, they are interpreted based on the profile you assign. Normally, you want to preserve the color appearance in an image, so at first glance the option to assign a profile to an image may not sound like something you would want to do.

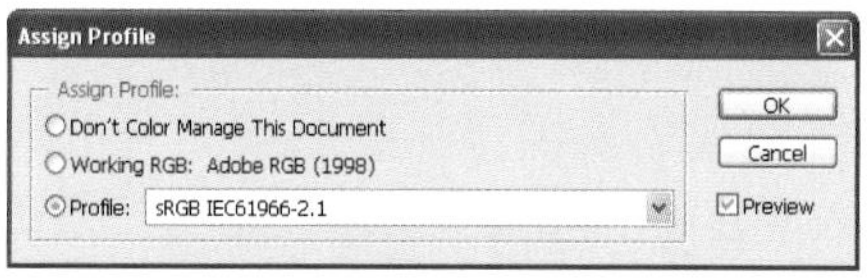

Figure 2.15

The Assign Profile dialog box allows you to specify which profile will be used to interpret the color numbers in your image. That profile will then be embedded in the image file when you save it.

However, there are situations where this would be used. The two most common are for assigning a custom profile to a film scan or digital capture. Most scanning software and digital cameras don't allow you to use a custom profile at the time of scan or capture. If you are going to use a custom profile, you'll generally have to assign it after the fact in Photoshop. The Assign Profile command allows you to do this. This will be covered in more detail in later chapters.

Convert to Profile

The Convert To Profile command (Image > Mode > Convert To Profile; see Figure 2.16) allows you to convert an image to a different profile. There are a variety of situations where you may want to convert an image to a different profile, such as when preparing it for a different output method. Each profile causes the color numbers in the image to be interpreted in a unique way. Converting from one profile to another involves changing the color numbers in the image so that the colors appear the same after being converted. The results are generally quite accurate, with no visible difference between the image before and after conversion. However, if there are significant out-of-gamut colors, the conversion will need to adjust those values based on the rendering intent selected. Specific use of the Convert To Profile dialog box will be covered in later chapters.

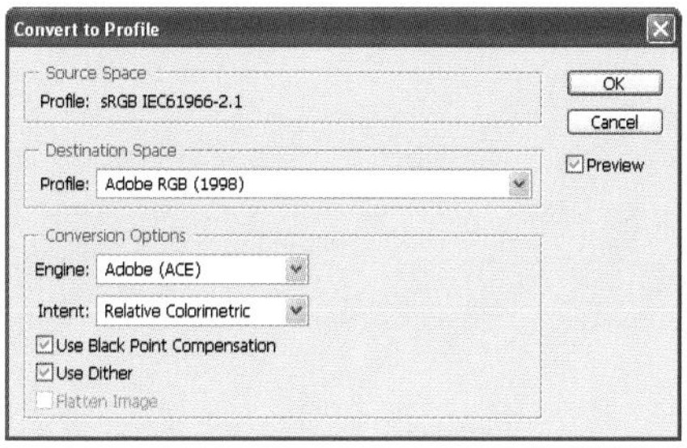

Figure 2.16
The Convert To Profile dialog box allows you to convert an image from one profile to another, specifying the profile, rendering intent, and other options for the conversion.

Display

The monitor is your window to the pixels in your image. Having an accurate display on your monitor is a critical factor in an effective color-managed workflow. If the display on your monitor does not reflect an accurate display of the pixel values in your digital image files, then the adjustments you make are based on inaccurate information. Furthermore, if your monitor is not adjusted to the established standards for color management, the rest of the workflow will be unreliable. For that reason, an accurate monitor display is perhaps the most important aspect of color management.

3

Chapter Contents

Choosing a Monitor

All too often it seems that the monitor gets taken for granted, despite the fact that photographers working in the digital darkroom spend an inordinate number of hours in front of it. The monitor is one of the most critical components of color management (see Figure 3.1). The printer tends to get all the attention, but the monitor is where all the action really happens.

Figure 3.1
Professional nature photographer George Lepp has a well-earned reputation for capturing unique images such as this digital infrared photograph, and optimizing them to produce exceptional prints. He depends upon his calibrated monitor to give him an accurate display of the image throughout this process. (Photograph by George D. Lepp, www.leppphoto.com.)

Keep in mind that color management doesn't truly revolve around getting the printed image to match the display on the monitor. Obviously, that is what you're trying to achieve, but the way it is accomplished is by having a monitor display and printed page that both match the color information in the image file.

The display on the monitor is what you use as the basis of the adjustments you make to the image. If the display on the monitor isn't accurate, the adjustments to the image won't produce the results you think you're getting. The first step in getting the print to match the monitor is to ensure the monitor is presenting an accurate view of the image data.

Having a monitor that is able to display the full range of tones and colors in your images accurately is important. Before you jump to monitor calibration, you'll want to be sure the monitor you are using (or are planning to buy) will meet your needs.

CRT or LCD?

Selecting an appropriate monitor for your digital darkroom is an important first step to a color-managed workflow. The first decision when buying a new monitor is whether you'll go with a "standard" CRT (cathode ray tube) monitor, or a "flat screen" LCD (liquid crystal display) monitor (see Figure 3.2).

Figure 3.2 When you buy a new monitor for your digital darkroom, the first decision you need to make is whether to buy an LCD monitor (left) or CRT monitor (right).

Comparing CRT and LCD monitors is like the proverbial apples to oranges comparison. Both types of monitors do the same basic job, but they have different advantages and disadvantages. When deciding which type of display to get, you need to consider the basic specifications and relative merits of each, and then determine which is right for you.

The actual process for most photographers these days tends to be trying to justify the purchase of a space-saving and "cool" LCD display.

> **Note:** Try not to focus on how cool it would be to have a skinny LCD monitor on your desk. Instead, consider the various compromises involved when choosing between a CRT or LCD monitor.

Let's take a look at the basic specifications to see what the advantages and disadvantages are for each monitor type:

Brightness is the measure of the luminosity of a display, describing the brightest white the monitor can display. LCD monitors are generally about twice as bright as CRT displays. However, because your monitor should be calibrated to a fixed luminosity value, which a CRT monitor in good condition should be able to achieve, monitor brightness isn't a significant issue for photographers.

Contrast ratio is a measure of the range from the brightest white to the darkest black that a monitor is able to display. Although LCD monitors have higher brightness than CRT monitors, they generally have a lower contrast ratio. Most current LCD displays have about a 400:1 contrast ratio, with the current high end at about 500:1. CRT displays generally have contrast ratios ranging from around 350:1 to a top value of about 700:1. This means that in general CRT displays can display a much wider range of tonal values. In particular, the lack of adequate contrast ratio in LCD displays will result in a loss of visible detail in the dark shadow areas of your images.

Viewing angle defines an arc along which you can still see an accurate display on a monitor. If you've worked on a laptop other than the latest high-end models, you've no doubt experienced the issue of limited viewing angle firsthand. With a limited viewing angle, the apparent brightness of the display will vary as you get farther away from viewing directly in front of the monitor. When you are attempting to adjust brightness and contrast in your images, this can obviously be a serious limitation. Color shifts can also occur with changes in viewing angle, causing additional problems.

Note: A wide viewing angle is probably the most important factor for the photographer to consider when selecting an LCD monitor, and this is an area that has seen a great deal of improvement with recent LCD monitors.

Color fidelity is both the accuracy of the colors displayed on the monitor and the ability of the monitor to display a wide range of colors. LCD monitors continue to improve, but they still don't match the color fidelity of CRT monitors. CRT monitors are simply able to produce more saturated colors with a wider color gamut. The result is that gradations of color tend to not be as smooth on LCD displays, and vibrant colors can't be reproduced as well. This is certainly a concern for photographers working with their images in the digital darkroom.

Refresh rate measures how fast the display on your monitor is updated with new information. Even when nothing is changing on the display, the monitor is actually refreshing it many times per second. This term is often used interchangeably to describe two different issues with CRT and LCD monitors. For CRT monitors, a high refresh rate is necessary to avoid flicker. If the rate is too low, the display will appear to flicker, which can be very distracting. Most CRT monitors are now able to refresh at rates of 85 Hz and above, ensuring a flicker-free display. LCD monitors do not have flicker, but they do suffer from problems caused by their relatively high pixel response time. This is the rate at which pixels can be updated on an LCD monitor, and it typically runs between 20 and 50 milliseconds. That may seem like a fast update; however, when things are moving quickly on the display, it is often not fast enough. This is not generally a major concern for editing still images, because there is no need to update quickly. You might notice that your mouse will fade from view if you move it quickly, or that full-motion video will be a bit choppy, but it isn't a cause for significant concern for still photographers.

Resolution options allow you to adjust the total number of pixels that can be displayed on the monitor at once. CRT and LCD monitors use slightly different methods for creating the pixels you see. A CRT monitor can easily adapt to different resolution settings because of the flexibility of the phosphors used to create the display. LCD monitors, on the other hand, use fixed dots to produce the display. For best results, LCD monitors should only be operated at their "native" resolution defined by the actual number of pixels in the display. At any other resolution setting, the monitor must scale the display, which can result in a relatively coarse look.

Focus determines how crisp the display will appear. The sharpness of an LCD display is generally very good because the individual pixels have crisp edges, compared to the "glowing" edges of the pixels on a CRT monitor. Of course, crisp focus can be a problem sometimes, such as when text starts to look coarse. For photographic images, the crisp focus is generally a good thing on an LCD monitor.

Power consumption relates to the operating cost of the monitor in terms of electricity used, and it is also related to the heat given off by the monitor. There is no question that an LCD monitor will consume less power than a CRT monitor. The problem is that it will take a very, very long time to save enough on your electric bill to make up for the increased cost of an LCD monitor. Most LCD monitors operate at about 25 to 40 watts, while CRT displays operate at about 60 to 160 watts.

Size and weight are both factors you'll want to consider, especially if you're working at a relatively small desk. I imagine I don't really need to explain this one. A major part of the appeal of LCD monitors is their smaller size and weight compared to the relative bulkiness of CRT monitors.

Glare on the surface of your monitor can be very annoying when you are trying to work on your images. If your working environment lives up to the "dark" in digital darkroom, glare shouldn't be too much of a problem with any monitor. Unfortunately, practical considerations often prevent working in a darkened environment. Ambient light can cause distracting glare, or even simply a reduction of the visible tonal range or a color shift. Minimizing the lighting in your working environment can help prevent glare. The front of CRT monitors is glass, which makes them more prone to glare even when an antiglare coating is present. LCD displays have a surface that has more of a matte finish, and it is naturally less subject to glare, even compared to a CRT monitor with antiglare coating.

Uniform brightness (or uniformity) from edge to edge can be an important factor in getting the most accurate display of your image possible. LCD monitors are often brighter at the edges than at the center. Conversely, CRT monitors are generally brighter at the center than at the edges. Most of the higher-end LCD and CRT monitors are relatively uniform across the full display.

Geometry refers to a variety of distortion effects in the image displayed by the monitor. Because of the grid pattern of pixels used to produce the display on an

LCD, the geometry (shape) is always perfect. On a CRT monitor the geometry can be inaccurate, resulting in minor problems. This is most often seen as a pincushion effect, where the straight lines forming the rectangular display are actually curved. Another problem is a trapezoid or parallelogram shape to the display rather than a perfect rectangle. These geometry errors can be corrected using the available menu options on most CRT monitors, and even if you can't correct them, it won't affect your ability to perform tonal and color adjustments to your images.

Viewable area is the diagonal measure of the area of the monitor that actually displays pixels. The advertised size of a CRT monitor generally includes a disclaimer providing the "viewable" size. Part of the tube area is unused and partially hidden behind the monitor casing. That means that when a CRT monitor is listed as being 17", for example, it will generally have a viewable area of about 16" diagonal. LCD monitors are measured by their true diagonal size, so that no translation is required. This doesn't really represent an advantage for the LCD displays, but the accuracy of information provided is certainly appealing when you are in the market for a new monitor.

Price is a factor that can't be ignored by most of us when outfitting our digital darkroom. It should come as no surprise that an LCD monitor will cost you more than a comparable CRT monitor. Comparing monitors of the same size, LCD monitors are generally around four to five times more expensive than CRT monitors, as of this writing. As greater market penetration is achieved and manufacturing efficiencies reduce costs, the price gap will narrow and LCD monitors will become more affordable.

The Bottom Line

The simple fact is that CRT monitors still have an advantage over LCD monitors in terms of general specifications. The very best monitors are still CRT monitors. However, some excellent LCD monitors are also available. You just need to be a bit more careful to ensure that a particular LCD monitor will provide you with the quality you are seeking.

Regardless of whether you purchase a CRT or LCD monitor, be sure you're getting the best display that fits your budget. Later in this chapter, I'll discuss specifications to look for in both CRT and LCD monitors, so you can make an informed decision.

You can certainly find an LCD monitor that will provide an excellent display for optimizing your images, but be prepared to pay considerably more than you would for an equivalent CRT monitor.

Color Management Issues

You may have noticed that my discussion of the features related to choosing between a CRT or LCD monitor don't seem to relate to color management. In fact, the factors that affect display quality also relate to which monitor is best from the perspective of color management. All monitors have limitations, but LCD monitors are a bit more limited when it comes to an accurate display of your images.

Viewing angle is definitely a concern for LCD monitors, because it can directly impact the accuracy of the display. As the technology continues to improve, the viewing angle of LCD monitors is becoming less of an issue. Finding an LCD monitor that doesn't offer a viewing angle of at least 120° is unusual, which is more than adequate for working on your images. We are almost to the point that with higher-end LCD monitors you don't even need to check the viewing angle (but I still would just to be safe).

Color fidelity is obviously an important consideration when it comes to color management. If the monitor can't display a full range of colors, you'll have a difficult time achieving accurate results. Fortunately, most LCD monitors offer excellent color fidelity, very nearly matching the capabilities of CRT monitors.

Contrast ratio remains as the biggest factor affecting LCD monitors. A relatively low contrast ratio will cause a loss of detail in shadow. This isn't going to affect the accuracy of colors, but it will affect the accuracy of the overall image. Detail that exists in the darker areas of your image won't show on the monitor if the contrast ratio isn't high enough, causing variations between what you see on the monitor and what you achieve in the final print.

For the best results in a color-managed workflow, you'll want to use the best monitor possible for working on your images. In the next sections, I'll review the specifications for both CRT and LCD monitors so you'll know what to look for when buying a new monitor.

> **N o t e :** If the following sections convince you that it is time to replace your current monitor, don't be too quick to discard the old monitor when you buy a new one. That old monitor can be used as a second monitor in a multiple-monitors setup, which I'll address later in this chapter.

Choosing a CRT Monitor

If you want to choose a CRT monitor until LCD monitors achieve better quality at a lower price, make sure you select a CRT that will meet your needs. Although CRT monitors in general have some advantages over LCD monitors for photographers working in the digital darkroom, that doesn't mean you can ignore the features of the CRT you buy.

Fortunately, CRT monitors aren't exactly new technology, so there are a wide variety of excellent displays at reasonable prices. In fact, a relatively high percentage of the monitors out there are more than adequate for use in the digital darkroom. You will want to consider some key features when considering a new CRT monitor (see Figure 3.3).

Size

With CRT displays, you don't have to worry too much about having a monitor that is too big. Of course, available desk space may contradict this statement, but image quality generally won't suffer too much when you use a larger CRT display. LCD monitors aren't quite as flexible, as will be explained in a later section.

Bigger is usually better when it comes to CRT monitors. Of course, if space is tight and you'll be sitting close to the display, you might want to cut back a little on the size.

In general, I consider a 17" monitor to be the minimum for digital imaging use. This is a workable size, but it will tend to feel a bit cramped in Photoshop. A 19" display is an excellent compromise between size and price, and it is a great starting point. If you have the desk space and budget, a 21" monitor will give you much more room to spread out.

Keep in mind that solutions are also available for using two (or more) monitors. This can be an excellent route for the digital darkroom. In Photoshop, you can put all your palettes on a second monitor, with your large primary monitor reserved for the image at full screen.

Dot Pitch

The dot pitch is a measure of the distance between pixels of the same color (remember that each pixel is composed of three subpixels of red, green, and blue). The dot pitch is measured in millimeters, and a lower number indicates a crisper display. In general, you'll want to look for a CRT monitor with a dot pitch below about 0.25mm.

Resolution Support

CRT monitors are more flexible when it comes to displaying at different resolutions, and they don't require that an "optimal" resolution setting be used for the best image quality as are required with LCD monitors (which will be discussed later).

Because of the flexibility of CRT monitors, you don't need to concern yourself with a specific resolution setting for these displays. Also, most CRT monitors currently on the market support very high resolutions. In fact, many of them support resolutions that are so high, most users won't want to use them because they can be hard on the eyes due to the smaller size of objects on the screen.

The optimal resolution setting will vary based on the monitor size. For monitors up to about 17", the maximum resolution most users will want to use is 1024×768. For larger displays up to about 20", a resolution of 1280×1024 is generally preferred. For displays larger than 20", a resolution of 1600×1200 is about the maximum I usually prefer to work at (see Figure 3.4).

Figure 3.4 You'll want to make sure the monitor you purchase offers the resolution you plan to use. A higher resolution allows more information to be displayed at once. The screenshot on the left represents a monitor resolution of 1024×768, while the screenshot on the right represents a monitor resolution of 2048×1536.

Refresh Rate

Flicker in a display can be incredibly annoying. Fortunately, most current CRT displays have an adequate refresh rate to avoid flicker in most, if not all, supported resolutions. Look for a monitor that supports a refresh rate above 85 Hz for the resolution you plan to use for the display.

Flatness

Not to be confused with LCD displays, many CRT monitors are promoted as being "flat-screen." This term refers to the lack of curvature in the glass at the front of the monitor. Most monitors use a tube with a curved front surface, which can add to the distortion in the image being displayed. A flat-screen CRT monitor produces a more geometrically accurate display, which is much more pleasing to the eye. It is also less prone to glare from light sources other than those directly in front of the monitor.

Color Controls

To get the best results when calibrating your CRT display, the monitor should provide the ability to adjust the color. This ability is generally offered as a gain control for each of the three (red, green, and blue) electron guns that are used to produce the image you see (see Figure 3.5).

Figure 3.5
Ideally, you want to be able to adjust the color balance of your monitor with RGB controls.

These adjustments allow you to fine-tune the monitor display before creating a monitor profile, so that the monitor is as accurate as possible and, therefore, requires only minor adjustments through the profile. This isn't a critical option, but it's a valuable one. Fortunately, many current monitors offer this capability, so finding a model that includes color controls and meets your other requirements shouldn't be difficult.

Choosing an LCD Monitor

While LCD monitors have some disadvantages, such as reduced color saturation and a loss of detail in shadow areas, a good LCD display can be used very effectively in the digital darkroom. Buying an LCD monitor requires that you understand the features that are important, and that you know what to look for (see Figure 3.6).

Figure 3.6
An LCD monitor does offer advantages in terms of size and weight, but it also represents a compromise compared to the best CRT monitors.

Brightness

LCD monitors actually tend to be much brighter than you need them to be, requiring some adjustment in the calibration process. Brightness is generally measured in candelas per square meter (cd/m^2), and most LCD monitors range in brightness from about 170 to 300 cd/m². In general, you'll want to get a display that has a brightness of about 250 cd/m² or higher.

Resolution

In general, you will probably want a monitor that supports as high a resolution as possible so you can see more of your image at once on the display. However, it is important to match maximum resolution to an appropriate monitor size for LCD monitors. The display on an LCD monitor will look best at the native resolution for that display. If you get an LCD monitor with a very high native resolution and then set it for a lower resolution, the display won't be of optimal quality.

I usually recommend a native resolution of 1024×768 for monitors up to about 17". For displays over 17", a resolution of 1280×1024 or more is generally best. For displays above 20", a resolution of 1600×1200 may be best, provided you don't have a difficult time reading small text. Of course, you can also increase the magnification of text to help overcome this problem.

Note: If you are concerned about geometric distortion, keep in mind that the 1280×1024 resolution setting varies from the normal aspect ratio. Because of this, shapes will be slightly distorted. This isn't a real concern for photographers editing images for tone and color, but it can be a distraction if you are editing images that include geometric shapes. This certainly isn't a major issue, but something that is good to be aware of, particularly if you are working with images where the correct aspect ratio can be important, such as in architectural photography.

Contrast Ratio

The contrast ratio defines the range of tones from pure black to pure white that can be displayed. The higher the contrast ratio, the more tones the monitor can display, and the smoother the gradations in tone and color. With a low contrast ratio, detail in the shadows will tend to block up so that you can't see all the detail that is actually present in the image file. A contrast ration of 350:1 would be considered a minimum. Most current LCD displays have a contrast ratio of 400:1. The highest is about 500:1, at this writing. This will continue to improve as LCD technology advances. In the meantime, look for the highest contrast ratio possible.

Pixel Pitch

With CRT monitors, dot pitch is an important measure of overall image quality and crispness. With LCD displays, this is generally referred to as *pixel pitch*. It is important, though in a slightly less direct way.

The most important factors that affect the clarity and smoothness of an LCD display are the native resolution relative to the display size. Pixel pitch is a way to express this, but simply comparing pixel pitch isn't the most accurate way to determine the overall quality of the display. Still, it is an issue to consider, and you'll want to look for an LCD monitor with a pixel pitch of under about 0.28 mm.

Pixel Response Time

Pixel response time relates to the speed at which the monitor display can be updated. This isn't a major issue for still images that are displayed on an LCD monitor. However, just because you aren't editing full-motion video doesn't mean you don't have to be concerned with pixel response time. For example, if you move your mouse pointer quickly across the screen, the pixel response time will determine whether the mouse will remain clearly visible as you move it.

The faster the pixel response time, the more quickly the display can be updated. That means your mouse is less likely to disappear as you move it across the display, and full-motion video will remain fluid rather than choppy.

Many manufacturers neglect to include pixel response time in their specifications. When you are able to obtain the specification, look for pixel response time of 30 ms (milliseconds) or lower.

Display Size

Bigger isn't necessarily better when purchasing an LCD display. While it gives you a larger display area, a bigger monitor display can actually reduce image quality. Running at the same resolution, a smaller monitor will use smaller pixels, which results in a smoother display of higher quality. If you run the same resolution on a larger monitor, the larger pixels will result in a display that is coarser and more pixilated. Keep in mind that any given LCD display will have an optimal resolution setting for that display, which is the setting that will afford the best quality.

Viewing Angle

Viewing angle is one of the most important factors to consider when purchasing an LCD monitor. Fortunately, most recent LCD monitors have greatly improved in this regard. With a low viewing angle, the relative brightness and color of the display will vary considerably with slight changes in your position relative to the display (see Figure 3.7).

Figure 3.7 LCD monitors continue to improve, so that the viewing angle isn't a significant issue. With some LCD displays, the display will look considerably darker and may exhibit a color shift if you don't view the image from directly in front of the monitor.

When buying an LCD monitor, look for a display with a viewing angle of 120°, and ideally above 160°.

Note: Because the LCD displays used on laptop computers tend to be of lower quality than the best LCD monitors, it is generally best to avoid doing any critical imaging work on your laptop display.

Special Concerns

There are some special issues to be concerned about with LCD monitors. In general, they tend to be at higher risk of damage. The surface can be scratched if sharp objects contact it or damaged if it is touched too hard. You should avoid touching the surface of an LCD monitor. If young children will have access to your computer, an LCD monitor may not be the best choice.

Another issue with LCD displays is that the manufacturing process can't always ensure that all pixels will function properly. Some pixels may be "dead" (always black) or "hot" (always white) when you buy the monitor, and the display will be considered defective (and therefore due for replacement under warranty) only if a set number of pixels are out when the monitor is new.

Choosing a Display Adapter

The display adapter (also referred to as a video card) is an important component that produces the display signal and sends it to your monitor. Fortunately, from a color management and image quality standpoint, most photographers don't have to give much thought to their display adapter.

Note: Very rarely you may find that a particular display adapter does not work properly with a monitor profiling utility. This is not common, and it is usually caused by an inability to update the video LUT (look-up table) that provides "translation" values for the signal to be sent to the monitor. Most recent display adapters will not have this problem, and it isn't an issue with most operating systems. Color Vision does offer a utility called OptiCheck on their website (www.colorvision.com) that allows you to confirm compatibility with their monitor profiling software, which in most cases would indicate compatibility with any monitor profiling tools.

When display adapters are reviewed, a great deal of emphasis is put on the amount of memory included on the card (video RAM) and how fast they perform. For photographers editing still images in the digital darkroom, this really isn't a serious concern. If you will also use your computer for playing games or editing full-motion video, then a high-performance card with plenty of video RAM may be in order. Otherwise, there simply isn't a need for this high-end performance.

If you are using an LCD display, you'll also want to consider the issue of analog versus digital for your display adapter. LCD monitors use a digital signal, while CRT monitors use analog signals. Many LCD monitors include an option to connect to the display adapter with an analog connection. However, it is best to keep the signal digital from the computer to the monitor, without any analog conversions, to avoid a loss of quality or accuracy in the display. Therefore, if you will be using an LCD monitor, you'll want to use a display adapter that offers a digital output.

For Windows-based computers, the digital output will be through a DVI (Digital Visual Interface) connection on the display adapter. For Apple LCD displays, a proprietary ADC (Apple Display Connector) connection is used. If your display adapter only offers a DVI output (as would be the case on a Windows-based computer), you can purchase an adapter to go from the DVI output to the ADC input on the Apple monitor.

Multiple Monitors

The fact that you're reading a book on color management tells me that you're pretty serious about your digital imaging. I would therefore assume you spend a fair amount of time working on your images, which means you would greatly benefit from using multiple monitors.

With a multiple-monitors setup, you can have two (or more) monitors connected to your computer, providing a much larger working space. You can move your mouse off the edge of one monitor and onto the other monitor. This allows for a much more efficient working environment in Photoshop or other applications. For example, you can put all of your palettes onto your second monitor, so that nothing but the image itself is displayed on the primary monitor.

While you can install multiple display adapters in your computer to provide support for multiple monitors, I strongly recommend using a single display adapter that allows you to connect more than one monitor. I have found the Matrox Millenium (www.matrox.com) series of display adapters to be an excellent choice for both convenience and performance.

Keep in mind that on a Windows system you can't profile both monitors in a multiple-monitors arrangement. However, the second monitor wouldn't be used for critical image-editing work, so the accuracy of that display isn't critical.

Calibrating and Profiling Your Monitor

The process of profiling your monitor actually involves two steps. The first is calibrating your display, and the second is profiling (or "characterizing") it. Many people refer to the full process as "monitor calibration," but technically this is a misnomer.

Calibration involves adjusting the actual output of your monitor to get it as close as possible to known standards. For example, you would adjust the brightness, contrast, and color balance settings provided by your monitor to get it as accurate as possible before you profile it. This is actually changing the behavior of the monitor, not just providing software compensation. It is important to get the monitor calibrated as accurately as possible before profiling, so that the profile you generate doesn't result in significant changes to the display to produce accurate color. Doing so would restrict the range of tones and colors the monitor is able to produce, much like aggressive adjustment of your image in Photoshop can cause posterization in the final print.

> **Note:** Many LCD monitors do not offer color balance and contrast controls, offering only a brightness adjustment. This is because the signal that produces the image on the monitor remains digital all the way from the display adapter to the monitor. The digital signal can be counted on to be very accurate, provided the LCD is using a digital connection to the computer. Even with such a display, you should calibrate to ensure an optimal brightness setting. Also, it is still important to profile such a digital display to ensure the colors are completely accurate.

Once the monitor is calibrated, it is time to characterize (build a profile for) the monitor. This profile will ensure that the monitor displays an accurate representation of the color values in your image files. The profile provides a table of translation values, so that when the display adapter requests that a particular color be displayed, it uses the correct numbers to render the desired color.

Target Values

In order to produce a profile for your monitor, you need to know what target values you want to use for the gamma and white point settings.

Gamma refers to the brightness of midtones in the display. The general standards in use are 1.8 and 2.2. You may have heard that the standard for Macintosh is 1.8, and the standard for Windows is 2.2. While there is a historical reason for this, I don't recommend using these targets. Instead, I recommend using a target gamma value of 2.2 regardless of your operating system. However, if you will be sharing image files with others who have calibrated their monitors to a gamma setting of 1.8, then I suggest following suit to help ensure the highest degree of accuracy in the appearance of those images. A gamma setting of 2.2 will produce an image that has slightly more contrast than 1.8, with less shadow detail, but this will typically produce a more pleasing image that better matches the final printed output you can expect.

White point defines the "color" of white on your monitor. If you are familiar with the printing industry, you would probably assume that the white point should be set to 5000 Kelvin. That is because a 5000 Kelvin illumination source is the standard for color management when it comes to evaluating prints. However, a setting of 6500 Kelvin is much closer to the native white point for most monitors, and is the setting I recommend (see Figure 3.8). Using 5000 Kelvin will result in a monitor display that is a bit yellow and dingy. I always recommend using 6500 Kelvin as the target white point when calibrating your monitor.

Figure 3.8 I strongly recommend using a target white point of 6500 K when calibrating your monitor. A 5000 K white point (left) produces a display that looks yellow and muddy compared to a white point of 6500 K (right).

The Kelvin temperature scale is measured in degrees, but represented with just the letter *K* (e.g., 6500 K).

Preparing to Profile

Almost as important as actually profiling your monitor is profiling it under appropriate conditions. In order to have an accurate profile, you'll want to be sure that the display on your monitor has had a chance to stabilize. For a CRT monitor, that includes giving the monitor time to warm up. I recommend being sure it is on for at least half an hour before you attempt to calibrate and profile the display. LCD monitors don't typically need any significant amount of time to warm up.

It is also important that the monitor settings be established to those you are going to use, such as resolution, color depth (which should always be at the maximum value), and other adjustments. Changing any of the display properties for your monitor, either on the monitor itself or through your operating system or display adapter utility, can cause changes in the tone and color of the display. Any time you change these settings, you should recalibrate your monitor. Therefore, be sure the settings are where you want them before you start the process.

If you are using a package that includes a sensor to read values from your monitor (and you definitely should be) then take a moment to clean the monitor screen. I often use a micro fiber lens cloth—like the one you would use to clean a camera lens—to clean fingerprints and other smudges from the screen. If you need to use a cleaning solution to eliminate stubborn smudges, be sure to use one that is designed specifically for this purpose to avoid damaging the antiglare coating applied to most screens. Be particularly cautious when cleaning LCD monitors, which have a plastic film rather than glass on the surface, which makes them more susceptible to damage.

Tools for Calibrating and Characterizing

Many tools are available for calibrating and characterizing your monitor. In this section, I'll take a look at some of the more popular solutions, providing information on the benefits of each package and how to use them most effectively.

The best solution for monitor calibration is specialized software used with a calibrated sensor that reads the actual values produced by your monitor. Options include the Color Vision Spyder and Spyder Pro products, Gretag Macbeth Eye-One Display, and MonacoOPTIX from Monaco Systems. Any of these products represents an excellent solution that will ensure a consistently accurate display on your monitor if you recalibrate regularly.

The packages reviewed here that include a sensor and software for calibrating and profiling your monitor are all excellent. You'll have to decide which is best for you. I consider the Color Vision Spyder package to be the most user-friendly, and I highly recommend it to those who are new to monitor profiling. The Gretag Macbeth is the most advanced option, and it is a great choice for experienced users who don't mind spending a little more to possibly get a slightly more accurate profile.

If you don't want to spend the money on one of these solutions, you can also use software—such as Adobe Gamma or DisplayMate, as discussed later in this chapter—to perform a basic calibration. These solutions depend on your eyes rather than a calibrated sensor and are, therefore, not as accurate, so they're not solutions I recommend for a color-managed workflow.

Note: Make sure that no other software, such as Adobe Gamma, interferes with the display of your monitor after you have profiled. Also, be sure to leave the monitor controls alone and don't adjust them. If any changes occur, recalibrate your monitor.

Monitors with Included Tools

Some high-end monitors include calibration tools as part of the package. These options are more expensive, but they are incredibly convenient. Options include the very high-end Calibrator line of monitors from Barco (www.barco.com) and the Artisan series from Sony (www.sony.com).

For example, I currently use a Sony Artisan 21" monitor in my digital darkroom. This monitor connects to the display adapter in the normal manner, but it also includes a connection to the computer via a USB port. In addition, a sensor is included that connects to another USB port. With this arrangement, the included software can read monitor values from the sensor and make adjustments to the monitor with the control connection. The result is an elegant system for calibrating my monitor. I simply launch the software, attach the sensor, click a button to begin calibration, and walk away from the computer. After about ten minutes the process completes and my monitor is calibrated.

You might want to duplicate my setup. Besides the convenience of having the necessary hardware and software included with your monitor, this would also provide the benefit of an automatic calibration process. Therefore, you would be far more likely to calibrate your monitor on a regular basis, ensuring the most accurate display possible.

Color Vision Spyder

The Spyder package from Color Vision (www.colorvision.com) includes their Monitor Spyder sensor along with PhotoCAL software for calibrating your monitor. It is very user-friendly, providing a simple wizard interface where you perform one task at a time until the process of calibrating and profiling is complete. It lists for around $200, but can it be found at a lower price from a variety of sources. The package is cross-platform, providing an excellent solution for both Windows and Macintosh users.

To calibrate your monitor using PhotoCAL, perform the following steps:

1. Launch PhotoCAL, which will bring up the introductory screen. This screen reminds you what tasks will be performed as you step through the wizard. Click Next to get started.

2. Select the type of monitor (CRT or LCD) you are calibrating, and click Next.

3. Select target gamma for the calibration. I recommend using 2.2 unless you have a good reason to do otherwise. Click Next.

4. Select your target white point, which I recommend setting to 6500 Kelvin (see Figure 3.9), and click Next.

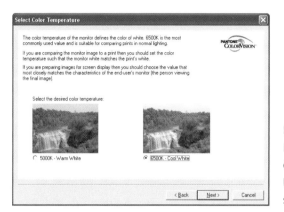

Figure 3.9
I recommend using a target white point of 6500 Kelvin when calibrating your monitor. PhotoCAL provides an excellent preview that supports this recommendation.

5. Reset all monitor controls to their factory default settings if you are calibrating an LCD monitor, and click Next

6. Maximize the contrast setting if you are calibrating a CRT monitor, and click Next.

7. Adjust the brightness if you are calibrating a CRT monitor. The adjustment is made by viewing a block of four rectangles (see Figure 3.10). You want to set the brightness so that you can just barely see a difference between each box. I recommend reducing brightness until the boxes blend into one black rectangle, and then slowly increase brightness until you are able to just make out the individual boxes. When you have the brightness adjusted, click Next.

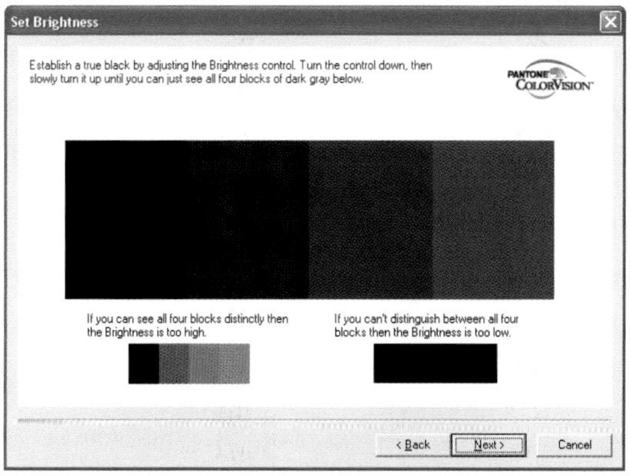

Figure 3.10
PhotoCAL uses a series of dark boxes to help you determine the best brightness setting. I recommend reducing the brightness until the boxes disappear into a single black rectangle, and then increasing it until you can just barely distinguish all four boxes.

8. Select whether your monitor has RGB controls or preset options for specific white point settings, and click Next.

9. Adjust the monitor controls for white point. If your monitor only has presets, select your target white point value (or the next highest value if the target value is not available). If your monitor has RGB controls, attach the sensor when prompted, and then adjust the individual gain controls for each RGB channel until the vertical bars for each channel are the same height within the box, clicking the Update button after each adjustment.

10. Attach the sensor to your monitor. Be sure to use the appropriate attachment method based on the type of monitor you are using. For CRT monitors, the baffle should be installed and suction cups used to attach the sensor to the monitor. For LCD monitors, the "honeycomb" filter should be attached in place of the baffle, and the attachment for mounting to LCD monitors should be attached to the sensor. Then hang the weight over the back of the LCD monitor and position the sensor in front of the monitor. Regardless of the monitor type, ensure that the center of the sensor is within the white area on the left of the dialog box, and that it is flat against the front of the monitor.

 Note: When calibrating an LCD monitor, be sure to use the appropriate accessory for placing the sensor on the front of the display. Attaching with suction cups used for CRT displays can damage your LCD monitor.

11. Adjust the luminance for CRT monitors. An initial luminance measurement will be displayed, which will likely be higher than the target luminance of between 85 and 95 cd/m². Reduce the contrast to bring the white luminance down, clicking the Update button with each adjustment. Continue to adjust the contrast setting on your monitor until the luminance value shown when you click Update is within 85 and 95. I generally target a value of 95, so that I'm maintaining a high luminance that is still within the target range. When you have achieved the desired luminance, click Next.

12. Measurements will be taken by the sensor (see Figure 3.11). Make sure the sensor remains flat against the monitor during the entire process to ensure accurate results.

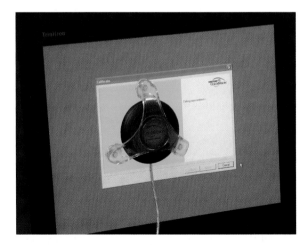

Figure 3.11
Once you have calibrated and set your preferences, PhotoCAL will take measurements of your monitor display to build a profile.

13. Remove the sensor from screen when prompted to do so, and click Next.

14. Enter a name for the profile that has been created. I recommend using "Photo-CAL Profile" so you'll know how this profile was created in the future.

Note: With this and other tools for creating monitor profiles, there is no benefit to saving a profile with the date as part of the name. You don't need old profiles that have been superseded, so simply save the profile with the same name each time you calibrate.

15. Click OK when the message appears indicating that the profile has been saved and set as the default profile.

16. Click Finish on the final screen, which reminds you to calibrate frequently and not to adjust monitor settings in the meantime.

Color Vision Spyder Pro

The Spyder Pro package from Color Vision (www.colorvision.com) includes their Monitor Spyder sensor along with OptiCAL software for calibrating your monitor. This is more advanced software, providing additional controls and a method for fine-tuning the profile after it is created. It sells for around $300, and it is cross-platform, with Windows and Macintosh support in a single package.

Note: Although the Spyder Pro package is an excellent tool for calibrating your monitor, it doesn't include anything you need that the standard Spyder package doesn't include. You'll save a little money and get identical results.

The main advantage of OptiCAL is that it allows you to fine-tune the profile it creates through the use of a Curves control. Frankly, if your monitor requires this level of adjustment, it is probably time for a new monitor. Therefore, I recommend PhotoCAL over OptiCAL. If you are already using OptiCAL, it does provide an excellent solution for calibrating your monitor. However, it doesn't offer you anything you need and costs more than PhotoCAL.

OptiCAL splits the calibration and profiling process into two steps, with the inclusion of their PreCAL utility. If you are calibrating an LCD monitor, you don't need to use PreCAL, but rather simply need to reset the monitor to the default settings. I strongly recommend running PreCAL first if you are calibrating a CRT monitor.

To do so, just follow these steps:

1. Launch PreCAL, and select the target color temperature (I recommend 6500 Kelvin), then click Continue.

2. Maximize the contrast setting on your monitor to achieve the highest white luminance, and then click Continue.

3. Adjust brightness to set the black point for your display. PreCAL uses a black screen with a faint logo displayed (see Figure 3.12). Adjust the brightness so that the logo is just barely visible. I recommend reducing the brightness setting until the logo disappears, and then increasing brightness until the logo becomes visible. Click Continue when you have finished adjusting brightness.

Figure 3.12
PreCAL uses a black box with a faint logo in it for setting the black point. Reduce brightness until the logo disappears, and then gradually increase brightness until it is just barely visible.

4. Set the color temperature preset for your monitor using the menu system on your monitor, and then click Continue.

5. Attach the sensor to your monitor.

6. Measurements will be taken by the sensor. Be sure the sensor remains flat against the surface of the monitor throughout this process.

7. Adjust the monitor RGB controls if available until each of the red, green, and blue bars are the same height within the displayed box (see Figure 3.13). Click the Update button after each adjustment to check the results.

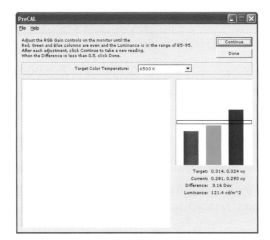

Figure 3.13
If your monitor provides RGB controls, you'll want to adjust them until the bars align within the black box when using PreCAL.

8. Click Done to close PreCAL.

Now it's time to run OptiCAL:

1. Launch OptiCAL, which will present a small dialog box where you set the parameters for the profiling of your monitor (see Figure 3.14). Select the type of monitor you are profiling (CRT or LCD), set the target gamma setting (I recommend 2.2) under the Curve option, and select the white point you want to target (I recommend 6500 Kelvin).

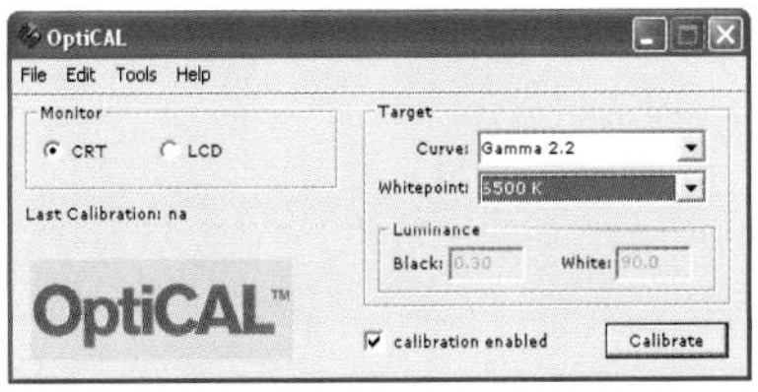

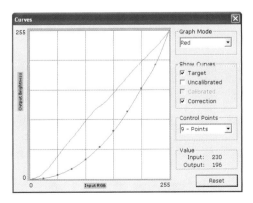

Figure 3.14

OptiCAL begins by asking you to specify the target values you want to use when calibrating your monitor.

2. Click the Calibrate button to begin the process of profiling your display.

3. Click Continue to pass the contrast and brightness adjustments, since you should have already made those adjustments by using PreCAL. If you are using an LCD monitor you should not need to make any adjustments here.

4. Attach the sensor to the monitor, and click Continue to begin the process of taking measurements. Be sure to use the appropriate attachment method based on the type of monitor you are using. For CRT monitors, the baffle should be installed and suction cups used to attach the sensor to the monitor. For LCD monitors, the "honeycomb" filter should be attached in place of the baffle, and the attachment for mounting to LCD monitors should be attached to the sensor. Then hang the weight over the back of the LCD monitor and position the sensor in front of the monitor.

5. Measurements will be taken by the sensor. Ensure that the sensor is flat against the front of the monitor during the full process.

6. Enter a name for the profile, and click OK. I recommend using "OptiCAL Profile," so you'll know what tool was used to create this profile.

7. Click OK on the alert messages that let you know what actions have been taken, and the process is complete.

After you have calibrated and profiled your monitor with OptiCAL, you can fine-tune the results using the Curves control. To do so, just follow these steps:

1. Check the Control Points In Curves Window checkbox found under Edit > Preferences in the main OptiCAL window.

2. Select Tools > Curves Window from the menu to view the adjustment curves being applied to your monitor display.

3. Select Red, Green, or Blue from the Graph Mode dropdown to select the color channel you want to adjust (see Figure 3.15).

Figure 3.15

OptiCAL allows you to fine-tune the profile for your display to achieve the most accurate results possible.

4. Adjust the curve control points to achieve the desired color balance.

5. Close the Curves window to apply the changes.

Note: If you are going to use the Curves control in OptiCAL to fine-tune the display on your monitor, I recommend having an image open in Photoshop in the background that you can use as a reference. You can download the PhotoDisc target image from my website, www.timgrey.com.

Gretag Macbeth Eye-One Display

The Eye-One Display package from Gretag Macbeth (www.eyeonecolor.com) provides a sensor and software solution for calibrating and profiling your monitor. It is the most thorough tool, offering exceptional control and fine-tuning to ensure accurate calibration and produce the best profile for your monitor. It supports both Windows and Macintosh, and sells for under $250.

1. Launch the Eye-One Match software.

2. Select the monitor from the display of devices you can profile (see Figure 3.16).

Figure 3.16 The Eye-One Match software allows you to profile a variety of devices if the appropriate modules have been purchased.

3. Select Advanced mode and click the right-arrow button.

4. Select the type of monitor you are calibrating (CRT or LCD), and click the right-arrow button.

5. Calibrate the sensor by placing it on the calibration dock and clicking the Calibrate button. This is an excellent feature that helps to ensure the most accurate results possible. When calibration is complete, click the right-arrow button.

6. Select the target calibration settings. I recommend using a gamma of 2.2 and color temperature of 6500 Kelvin. Click the right-arrow button when you have set your target settings.

7. Attach the sensor to monitor. For CRT monitors, use the suction-cup attachment and attach it at the top-center of the monitor. For LCD monitors use the attachment with the lead weight, hanging the weight over the back of the monitor. Be sure that the sensor rests flat against the surface of the monitor, and click the right-arrow button.

8. Maximize the contrast control for your monitor (see Figure 3.17) to achieve the brightest white point and click the right-arrow button.

Figure 3.17 Eye-One Match guides you through the process of calibrating your display with detailed instructions.

Figure 3.18
Watch the Contrast dialog box on the monitor (left) until the indicator shows that you have achieved the optimal setting (right).

9. Click Start to fine-tune the contrast setting. A white screen with a dialog box showing the target (black) and current (green) values will appear (see Figure 3.18). Adjust the contrast until the current value aligns with the target value. Be sure to pause between adjustments of the contrast control to allow the display to refesh. When the current value marker aligns with the target value, click the Stop button, and then click the right-arrow button.

10. Set brightness to 0% to minimize the black point, and click the right-arrow button.

11. Click Start to fine-tune the brightness setting. A black screen with a dialog box in the top right showing the target (black) and current (green) brightness values will appear. Click the Measure button to measure the current setting and update the display, following the instructions for the brightness setting to use. First, you will be prompted to set specific brightness values to achieve a baseline, and then you will be instructed to set specific values while the software attempts to achieve the appropriate black point. When the "Brightness reached" message is displayed, click Stop and then click the right-arrow button.

12. Select the type of controls offered by your monitor, whether they are individual RGB controls or color temperature presets. Click Start to make precise adjustments if your monitor includes RGB controls. This will display a white screen with a dialog box showing the target and current values for red, green, and blue. Adjust the RGB controls on your monitor until all three align with the target value, click Stop, and then click the right-arrow button.

13. Measurements will be taken by the sensor (see Figure 3.19). Note that unlike other packages that only read red, green, blue, and gray values, the Eye-One Match software measures a wide range of hues to achieve the most accurate results possible.

Figure 3.19
The Eye-One Display package measures a variety of hues from your monitor, helping to ensure the most accurate results possible.

14. Enter a name for the profile that was created. I recommend saving it as "Eye-One Display" or another name that will remind you of what tool was used to build the profile. The profile will then be set as the default for your operating system, and you're done.

Note: If you plan to purchase the Gretag Macbeth Eye-One Display package to calibrate your monitor, consider purchasing the Eye-One Photo package that includes all the capabilities of Eye-One Display along with the ability to create RGB output profiles, which I'll discuss in Chapter 7, "Output."

MonacoOPTIX

MonacoOPTIX from Monaco Systems (www.monacosys.com) is a sensor and software package for calibrating and profiling your monitor. A step-by-step wizard interface guides you through the process of adjusting your monitor and building a display profile. It supports both Windows and Macintosh, and sells for under $300.

Follow these steps to calibrate and profile with MonacoOPTIX:

1. Launch the MonacoOPTIX software.

2. Select the type of monitor (LCD or CRT) you are calibrating.

3. Review the instructions in the Before You Begin dialog box and click the right-arrow button (see Figure 3.20).

Figure 3.20
MonacoOPTIX reminds you of key steps in getting the best results with your monitor calibration before the process is started.

4. Select the target White Point. I recommend using a target color temperature of 6500 Kelvin. Adjust the white point setting on your monitor if such controls are provided. Click the right-arrow button to continue.

5. When prompted to do so, place the sensor flat against a completely opaque surface such as the top of your desk and click the Calibrate button (see Figure 3.21).

Figure 3.21
Calibrating the sensor by blocking all light while a reading is taken helps to ensure the most accurate results.

6. Adjust brightness and contrast on your monitor to their maximum settings, position the sensor on the monitor as shown, and click Measure (if your monitor does not include these controls, click Skip). Click the right-arrow button when the measurements are completed.

7. Set the brightness on your monitor to the minimum setting and click Measure. When the measurements are completed, click the right-arrow button.

8. To set the brightness, click the Measure button to begin taking readings. The blue bar shows the current brightness setting, with the red and green bar showing bad and good readings, respectively. Adjust the brightness on your monitor until the right edge of the blue bar is in the middle of the "good" zone (see Figure 3.22). Then click the Done button and click the right-arrow button to continue.

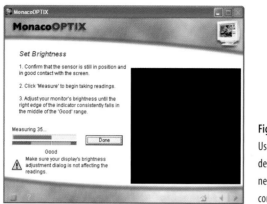

Figure 3.22
Use the blue "meter" bar to determine when the brightness setting is established correctly for your monitor.

9. Click the Measure button to begin reading the color patches. These readings will be used to generate the monitor profile. When measurements are complete, click the right-arrow button.

10. Select the desired target gamma setting. I recommend using a setting of 2.2.

11. Click the Save Profile button to save the resulting monitor profile. I recommend that you use a name for this profile that will reflect the monitor and tool used to create the profile.

12. Click the right-arrow button to return to the main screen, and then close MonacoOPTIX.

Confirm Windows' Default Profile

All of the tools for calibrating and profiling your monitor are usually pretty good about setting the profile they create as the default profile for your monitor. However, you should confirm the profile just to be sure your monitor display will be as accurate as possible if you are a Windows user, because sometimes Windows seems to interfere with this process.

To confirm the default profile for your monitor, select Display Properties from the Control Panel, or simply right-click on the Desktop and select Properties. Select the Settings tab, and then click the Advanced button to display the advanced properties dialog box. Select the Color Management tab from this dialog box, and then check the Default Monitor Profile setting. If the appropriate profile is not selected, but is listed in the box below, select it and click the Set As Default button. If it isn't listed, click the Add button, locate the profile, and click Add. Then select it from the list and click Set As Default. The profile should then be listed as the default profile, so you can click OK on both of the dialog boxes you have opened.

Adobe Gamma

Although you trust your eyes when you are making adjustments to your images, I strongly recommend that you *not* trust your eyes when it comes to calibrating your monitor. That is exactly the method used by Adobe Gamma, which is why I don't recommend that you use Adobe Gamma. You may be wondering why I've included this section in the book if I don't recommend using this option. Using Adobe Gamma is better than using nothing at all. If I can't convince you to spend money on a better alternative, I'd at least like you to know how to use Adobe Gamma (which is included free with most of Adobe's applications).

Note: If you're a Macintosh user, the ColorSync Calibrator utility takes the place of Adobe Gamma. In fact, Adobe Gamma has been discontinued on the Macintosh platform, likely because it is redundant. The options in the ColorSync Calibrator utility are virtually identical to Adobe Gamma, so Macintosh users can simply use the Adobe Gamma information here as a guide on how to work with the ColorSync Calibrator utility. To get started with ColorSync Calibrator, choose Monitors from the Control Panel and check the box to use Expert Mode.

To do so, just follow these steps:

1. Launch Adobe Gamma by double-clicking its icon in the Control Panel. This will present an introductory screen that allows you to select the Step By Step option or Control Panel. I recommend that you select the Step By Step option and click Next.

2. Provide a description for the profile that will be created. You'll want to give the profile a descriptive name that will be meaningful if you see it later, or you need to select the appropriate monitor profile from a list. I suggest naming it "Adobe Gamma Profile." If you have an existing profile for the monitor, you can use that as the starting point by clicking the Load button and locating that profile. If you're using Adobe Gamma, chances are you don't have an existing profile for your monitor that can be trusted to be accurate. Click Next to continue.

3. Set the black and white points for your monitor using the brightness and contrast controls, respectively. You'll be instructed to adjust the contrast control to the highest setting, so that the monitor will produce the brightest white possible. A graphic showing a gray box within a black box within a white box is provided to allow you to adjust the brightness control (see Figure 3.23). The idea is to make the interior gray box as dark as possible while still being able to distinguish it from the surrounding black box. Remember that if you adjust the monitor controls in the future you'll need to run through Adobe Gamma again to produce a new profile. When you have adjusted the monitor controls, click Next.

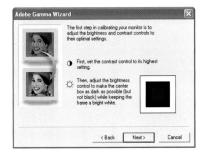

Figure 3.23
When using Adobe Gamma, set the contrast to the maximum value and then adjust brightness until the center gray box is barely visible inside the black box, with a bright white box surrounding.

4. Select the phosphor type, if known. Unfortunately, chances are you don't know what type of phosphors are used in your monitor. You might check to see if that information is available in the manual that came with your monitor (you did keep it, right?) or on the Internet. If you don't know what type of phosphors your monitor uses, accept the default option and click Next.

5. Adjust gamma settings to obtain the most accurate monitor display. First, turn off the View Single Gamma Only checkbox, so that you can adjust the gamma setting for each of the three color channels independently (see Figure 3.24). The controls display a central box with stripes surrounding it. The idea is to adjust the slider until the box blends into the stripes. The problem I have with this is that I always see stripes rather than a blended color, so I find it challenging to get a good adjustment. If you have poor vision, try taking off your glasses so the stripes blend into a single tone. If you have good eyesight, try squinting to put the stripes out of focus. Adjust all three sliders to get as close a match as possible. Then select the desired target gamma (I recommend using 2.2) and click Next.

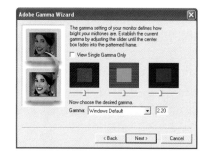

Figure 3.24

The gamma adjustments in Adobe Gamma are the trickiest to get right. Try removing your eyeglasses or squinting your eyes to help make a better decision about when the center boxes blend with the surrounding stripes.

6. Set the hardware white point for your monitor. This is the actual setting you have used on the menu for your monitor, if it offers this adjustment. I would usually recommend setting this value to 6500 Kelvin. If your monitor only offers preset values for the white point, but doesn't have a 6500 Kelvin option, select the next higher value (9300 Kelvin). After selecting the option you have used for your monitor (or 6500 Kelvin if your monitor doesn't have this adjustment), click Next.

7. Set the adjusted white point you would like to target for the profile. I always recommend using a target white point of 6500 Kelvin.

8. Confirm display quality by selecting the Before and After options, in turn. If you are happy with the "after" version, keep that option selected, check the box to Use As Default Monitor Profile, and click Finish. You will be prompted for a name to use to save the profile, and I recommend using "Adobe Gamma Profile," and then click Save.

Note: If you start off working with Adobe Gamma, but then move on to a better tool for calibrating and profiling your monitor, be sure to disable Adobe Gamma. You must remove Adobe Gamma Loader from the Startup group to ensure that it won't run at startup, interfering with the adjustments you have made with your new calibration tool.

DisplayMate

DisplayMate is a software utility (Windows only) that helps you evaluate, optimize, and calibrate the display on your monitor to help you achieve the most accurate results with the highest quality display. It isn't as accurate as the software tools that use a sensor, because it depends on your own evaluation using your eyes. It is better than using Adobe Gamma, so it falls somewhere in between. The Video Edition, which includes many tools for fine-tuning your display, sells for about $100 and is available at www.displaymate.com.

Although a system that uses your eyes to evaluate the monitor isn't the best solution, DisplayMate provides an innovative way to ensure the most accurate results possible within the inherent limitations. It provides a series of test images that are displayed on your monitor while you adjust the appropriate settings (see Figure 3.25). Before showing you each test image, a detailed description of what you will see, what to look for, and what action to take, is provided. This allows you to provide very good results without using a sensor. Note that using DisplayMate does not actually create a profile for your monitor, but rather just helps you ensure as accurate a display as possible without a sensor.

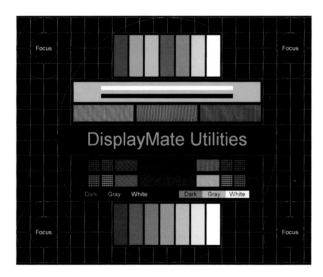

Figure 3.25

DisplayMate provides a good way to adjust and evaluate your display, but it is no replacement for actually calibrating and profiling.

The most helpful portion of the Set Up Program portion of DisplayMate is for setting your black and white points on the monitor, and adjusting the brightness and contrast. The color adjustments aren't quite as helpful, because they don't offer variable displays to allow you to see when the white point is less than accurate.

Overall, DisplayMate provides a solution for adjusting your monitor that is better than Adobe Gamma but not as good as the options using sensors that are discussed in the earlier sections. However, it is an excellent set of utilities that help you evaluate the overall accuracy and quality of your monitor display. Although I don't recommend it as the best solution for monitor calibration, I strongly recommend it for evaluating the display on your monitor.

Evaluation

If you are using one of the solutions outlined above that utilizes a sensor to build an accurate profile for your monitor, you can probably trust that your display is now highly accurate. However, it is a good idea to perform a "reality check" to confirm the accuracy of the display. The DisplayMate software described earlier in this chapter provides many test images that allow you to do this, but I usually use the PhotoDisc target image (see Figure 3.26). This image includes many "memory colors" that you can judge based on your experience, so that you can make an evaluation of the accuracy of your monitor quite easily. Simply open the image (or a similar image that you know to be accurate) using Photoshop or other software that supports color management, and check to be sure that the colors appear accurate. If not, try profiling your monitor again, or use a more advanced tool such as OptiCAL to fine-tune the display properties of your monitor.

Figure 3.26
The PhotoDisc target image is an excellent tool for evaluating the accuracy of your monitor display.

Note: You can download the PhotoDisc target image described here from my website, www.timgrey.com.

Frequency

Once you have successfully calibrated your monitor, it is easy to put the sensor aside and forget all about calibrating again. Of course, some of the software reviewed in this chapter will automatically warn you to recalibrate every two weeks to a month. To ensure the most accurate display on a long-term basis, it is important to repeat the process on a regular basis.

It is important that you recalibrate regularly, particularly with CRT monitors. That is because the phosphors that produce the image you see, as well as the guns that fire electrons at these phosphors and other components in the monitor, get weaker with time. This causes a gradual shift in the brightness and color of the monitor, making it important to recalibrate regularly. While LCD monitors don't fade as quickly, calibrating on a regular basis is still a good idea.

This brings up the issue of how frequently you should calibrate your monitor. With a highly stable monitor, you could probably get away with calibrating every six months without any significant problems. However, I wouldn't take that chance. I recommend calibrating at least every month. Ideally, you should try to calibrate every two weeks. More often is fine. I know many photographers who calibrate their monitors every day. I certainly wouldn't consider this necessary, but it isn't doing any harm either.

The important thing is that you set a regular schedule to calibrate your monitor so that you never allow too much time to pass between calibrations. If your software provides a "nag" feature to remind you, make use of it with a reminder every two weeks. If it doesn't provide this option, mark your calendar or get in the habit of calibrating at a particular time of the month, every Monday, or on whatever schedule works for you, provided you consistently calibrate your monitor with reasonably frequency.

Display Conditions

If the image displayed by your monitor is accurate, you're off to a good start. However, if the environment in which you view your monitor isn't ideal, it can have a considerable impact on the displayed image.

When I teach a course on digital imaging at the Lepp Institute of Digital Imaging (www.leppinstitute.com), I like to have a little fun with the students when I guide them through the process of calibrating the monitor they'll be working in front of for the week. In the digital darkroom lab at the Lepp Institute, we use PhotoCAL to calibrate the displays, so during the process each student needs to adjust the brightness so that the four boxes displayed are "just barely" distinguishable from each other. If the brightness is set too low, the boxes will all blend into a single black rectangle. If it is set too high, the boxes will appear slightly washed out and the difference between them will be too significant.

When all of the students have the display configured so that the four boxes are distinguishable, I turn on the overhead lights. Besides groans from the students that they've been temporarily blinded, they notice a profound change in the display on their monitors. Instead of four boxes that are just barely discernible, they see a single rectangle, or perhaps a couple of the four boxes. This drives home the point that your working environment has a profound effect on the appearance of the image on your monitor.

To ensure the most accurate and consistent display on your monitor, I recommend the following:

Keep the lights dimmed.   A number of photographers have asked me why I refer to the "digital darkroom," instead of calling it the "digital lightroom." Their reasoning is that with digital tools you don't have to worry about excess light the way you did when processing prints or (especially) film in the wet darkroom. My response is that while we don't need to keep the room quite as dark, keeping it dark is beneficial. The display on your monitor is produced with emitted light. Just as a flashlight doesn't cast a light on the ground in daylight, the monitor is influenced (to a lesser degree) by ambient light. It is best to keep the light to a minimum so that you are seeing only the light from the monitor with no outside influence.

Close the blinds.   Besides the influence of excess ambient light, the color of that light is a factor to consider. For reasons described in the previous point, covering the windows in the room where you are working on your images is obviously a good idea. In addition, this helps to eliminate any variations in the color of that light throughout the day. As photographers know, the light is much warmer early and late in the day, and more neutral at mid-day. These changes throughout the day can affect the accuracy of the colors in your image. For example, if you adjust an image with warm light being cast on your monitor at sunrise, you may over-compensate for that warmth and produce an image that is too blue. Keeping the blinds closed will help eliminate these potential problems.

Use neutral colors for the walls.   OK, I don't expect you to paint your walls to match an 18% gray card (though that isn't a bad idea), but you don't want to paint the walls with a bright color that will influence the display on the monitor. The more subtle and neutral the colors in your digital darkroom, the better.

Don't wear bright clothing.   This is actually even more important than having neutral walls and other decorations, because you'll be sitting right in front of your monitor. If you wear a bright white shirt, the reflection in the monitor can be distracting at best and cause an inaccurate display at worst. Also, vibrant colored clothing can influence the color appearance of the monitor. Although these influences may be minor, they can make a difference. Of course, if you have dimmed the ambient light in your digital darkroom, this will be even less of an issue!

Use a neutral desktop wallpaper.   In general you'll want to be sure there aren't strong colors elsewhere on your monitor when you are adjusting or evaluating an image, as these can most certainly influence the display. A common problem here is using a very colorful desktop wallpaper. This is a particular concern for Macintosh users, because the Macintosh applications don't have a backdrop, meaning you are able to see the desktop wallpaper behind your image windows. This can also be an issue on Windows computers if you don't keep Photoshop (or other software) maximized to fill the full screen.

Add a monitor hood.   In many situations, blocking out all of the ambient light in your digital darkroom is difficult or impossible. In these cases, I would strongly recommend using a monitor hood (see Figure 3.27) to help block that light. Some high-end monitors come with a monitor hood, but you can also purchase them separately from sources such as www.hoodmanusa.com. For a more frugal solution, you can make your own monitor hood with cardboard or other material, painting the inside that will face your monitor display with a flat black paint.

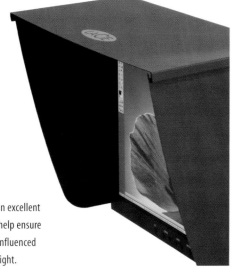

Figure 3.27
A monitor hood is an excellent accessory that will help ensure your display is not influenced by excess ambient light.

Scanning

It is most certainly a digital world. Digital photography is supplanting film at a phenomenal rate, accelerating as new and better digital cameras become available at lower prices. Most photographers are making the switch with enthusiasm. Others are sticking with film for a variety of reasons. In both cases, today's photographer needs to include film scanning in the color-managed workflow.

4

Chapter Contents

Choosing a Scanner

Before you can start scanning your existing film images, you'll need to get a film scanner. That means considering a variety of specifications to ensure the scanner will meet your needs. Some of the important factors relate more to output size and image quality than color management, but I'll still address those issues here so you'll know how to ensure the very best quality in addition to accurate color (see Figure 4.1).

Figure 4.1
The right scanner will allow you to capture maximum detail with accurate color from your original transparencies. (Photograph by Linda F. Peterson.)

Note: If you already have a scanner, you may not be looking to buy a new one. However, you should still review the specifications in this section to help you determine if your current scanner is the best for your needs and to help you decide what features to look for if you decide to replace your current scanner.

Flatbed versus Film Scanner

The first decision you need to make when purchasing a new scanner is whether to get a flatbed scanner or a dedicated film scanner (see Figure 4.2). Flatbed scanners are designed for scanning prints, but they are able to scan film by using an attached or accessory transparency adapter. Film scanners, as their name implies, are only able to scan film. Because they are specifically designed for this purpose, they generally offer better quality than flatbed scanners. I, therefore, strongly recommend that you use a film scanner rather than a flatbed for scanning your film for high-quality output (see Figure 4.3).

Figure 4.2
One of the first decisions you need to make when buying a new scanner is whether you want the flexibility of a flatbed scanner or the higher scan quality of a dedicated film scanner.

Figure 4.3
I highly recommend the latest scanner models from Nikon. The Nikon Super Coolscan 5000 ED (center) offers a resolution of 4,000 dpi, DMax of 4.8, and 16-bit analog-to-digital (A/D) conversion.

Flatbed scanners allow you to put your film down on the glass surface, illuminating the film from above with a transparency adapter. This means the film is actually being scanned through glass with most flatbed scanners. A few models use special film holders to place the film under the glass, but these are the exception.

Another issue with flatbed scanners is that they generally offer a much lower dynamic range than film scanners. This means that—in most cases—they capture less information from the film than a film scanner would. Dynamic range will be addressed later in this section.

> **Note:** If your budget allows, you'll get the best utility by having both a dedicated film scanner and a flatbed scanner. This means spending more money, but it will provide greater convenience and flexibility. Use the film scanner to scan film for images that will be printed and need to be of the highest quality. Use the flatbed scanner when you need to scan prints for which you don't have the original transparency and for quickly scanning a series of slides or negatives for contact sheets or other purposes.

Flatbed scanners do offer better utility than film scanners, because they can scan a broader variety of film sizes, as well as prints. They are also less expensive than film scanners of equal or better specifications. This makes them very attractive to many photographers. If your budget won't allow you to purchase a high-quality film scanner, you can choose from many flatbed scanners that will produce acceptable results. However, I strongly recommend using a dedicated film scanner for the very best results.

Note: Keep in mind that film contains considerably more information than a print. Therefore, you will want to scan the original film whenever it is available. Only scan prints when quality isn't your primary concern or when you don't have access to the original film.

Resolution

Resolution directly relates to how large you are able to reproduce the image, which is usually a consideration primarily for potential print sizes. The higher the resolution of the scanner, the more information is gathered from the film. That translates into finer detail and larger prints.

Note: The terms dpi (dots per inch) and ppi (pixels per inch) are a common source of confusion, particularly because they are often used interchangeably. More often, dpi is used under all circumstances. The distinction is generally one between dots on paper or pixels on your monitor. Scanner resolution is measured in dpi because it is reading a piece of film or print, effectively reading the original as a series of dots. The result is an image file that would more appropriately be referred to with ppi, but scanner resolution focuses on the media being scanned, and therefore dpi is the term in common use.

Most film scanners fall into two general categories. At the lower end are scanners that offer resolutions somewhere around 2,700 dpi, which produces an image from a 35mm original that could be printed at around 9"×12" without interpolation. Higher-end scanners typically offer 4,000 dpi or more (see Figure 4.4). At 4,000 dpi, a 35mm original would produce an image file that could be printed at about 12"×19" without interpolation.

Figure 4.4
The Minolta DiMAGE Scan Elite 5400 offers a particularly high resolution of 5,400 dpi, along with 16-bit-per-channel bit-depth and a 4.8 DMax. It produces excellent scans, although the Nikon scanners offer better DIG-ITAL ICE (for automatic dust and scratch cleanup) performance.

Naturally, images scanned from a scanner in either resolution category could be interpolated up to produce larger output. However, to achieve the best quality, you'll want to start with an image file that is as close to the final output size as possible.

My recommendation is to get a scanner that offers a resolution that will give you a scan large enough to produce the output size you anticipate producing. Assuming you are scanning 35mm film, scanner resolution of 2,700 to 2,900 dpi is more than adequate for prints up to about 13"×19". Some interpolation will be required to achieve that print size, but the quality will still be excellent assuming an original of the best quality. If you need to produce prints larger than 13"×19", I definitely recommend a scanner that offers 4,000 dpi or higher resolution.

You may have noticed that the recommendations up to this point were based on scanning a 35mm original. If you are scanning medium-format film sizes, the larger original doesn't require a particularly high resolution to produce large output. However, if you need a film scanner that scans medium format, you don't really need to think about resolution, because medium-format scanners as a general rule offer 4,000 dpi or higher.

If you will be using a flatbed scanner with a transparency adapter to scan film, then the same recommendations for resolution apply as offered for film scanners. For prints, resolution really isn't something you'll need to consider. That is because a print is usually much larger than a piece of film, so you don't need as much resolution to be able to produce a large image file. Furthermore, because prints don't include nearly as much information as the original film would contain, scanning at a higher resolution won't extract more detail. The detail simply isn't there to begin with. Again, this means that you don't need as much resolution.

In general, I don't scan prints at more than 600 dpi. Because standard output resolution is 300 dpi, that means you would be able to produce a print that is twice as tall and twice as wide as the original (four times the total area). You'd have a difficult time finding a flatbed scanner that didn't offer more than 600 dpi, so virtually any flatbed scanner would work well from the standpoint of resolution. Keep in mind that this resolution needs to be an optical resolution, not interpolated resolution. The resolution presented by the scanner manufacturer often includes two numbers (i.e., 1200/2400). While the optical resolution may not be presented, it will never be more than the lower of the two resolution numbers.

> **Note:** Experts have different opinions about how much information is contained within a piece of photographic film, and the actual amount will depend to a degree on the specific grain structure of the film being scanned. The consensus seems to be that anything over 4,000 dpi doesn't provide any real benefit. My testing tends to support this conclusion, so I consider 4,000 dpi to be an acceptable "top end" in resolution when you're looking for a new scanner.

Dynamic Range

The dynamic range of a scanner is one of the most important factors affecting how much detail and information is captured in the final image file. It is also the feature that seems to cause the most confusion, and it seems scanner manufacturers take advantage of that confusion in their marketing efforts.

Dynamic range is a measure of the difference between the minimum and maximum values a scanner is able to read. A higher dynamic range means that more subtle detail will be recorded by the scanner. This range is most important in the high-density areas of the original image. Low-density areas of the film are easy to record, because those areas don't obstruct the light passing through the film to the sensor. The dense areas of a slide or negative don't allow very much light from the scanner's illumination source to pass through the film and be read by the sensor. In effect, higher dynamic range relates to higher sensitivity to light, so that the sensor is able to measure even the minimal amount of light that reaches it through the dense areas of the film.

Technically, the figure quoted as dynamic range by most scanner manufacturers isn't actually a range at all, but rather a maximum density that the scanner is able to read. It is reported as a DMax value.

Obviously, a high dynamic range is desirable because it means more detail will be captured in your image. Because the key issue is being able to record values in the highest-density areas of the original, the key factor is the DMax value. The higher the number, the broader the range the scanner will be able to record (see Figure 4.5). Note that for positive images, such as prints or slides, a higher DMax indicates that more shadow detail will be recorded. For negatives, the higher-density areas represent the highlights, so a high dynamic range will affect how much highlight detail can be recorded.

Figure 4.5 The foreground detail in this image adds an interesting element of texture, which would have been lost if the film scanner didn't have a high enough dynamic range. (Photograph by Jeff Greene, www.imagewestphoto.com.)

Theoretically, a DMax of 4.0 represents black, or maximum density. In practice, the scale doesn't have an absolute upper limit. However, film is generally considered to have a DMax of no more than 4.0 (it varies with different types of film), so a scanner with a DMax higher than that probably doesn't offer a real benefit. However, having more than you would expect to need is a good idea.

I recommend that you look for a DMax of 4.2 or higher in a film scanner to get the very best results. You can still get very good scans with a DMax of 3.6 or higher, but when you need to extract maximum details from the high-density areas of an image, a higher value will be very helpful.

For flatbed scanners, the DMax value is generally more limited. Typical DMax values for the best flatbed scanners are around 3.4, which represents considerably less detail than a typical film scanner. This is one of the major reasons I don't recommend flatbed scanners for film scanning, as indicated earlier in this chapter. However, if you limit your flatbed scanning to prints, dynamic range is again not a major consideration. Most prints have a maximum dynamic range of around 2.0 to 2.5, which is well within the range of all current flatbed scanners that are otherwise adequate for scanning photos.

Note: Some of the scanner specifications presented in this section may not seem to have anything to do with color management. However, consider that if you are putting forth the effort to ensure the most accurate color in your prints and other output, beginning with images of the very best quality makes sense.

Bit-Depth

Dynamic range and bit-depth are closely related, because they are both factors in the amount of detail available in the final image. The dynamic range relates to the range of values the scanner is able to read from the original, bit-depth is a measure of how many discrete values the image file will contain.

A scanner's primary function is to translate analog values in the original to digital values in an image file. Analog data is represented by continuous variations, with no limit on the possible values that can be stored. Digital data must contain discrete values. That means that there will be a finite limit to how many actual values are available. The number of possible values determines how many possible tones or colors can be contained within the image. Bit-depth defines how many values are actually available.

An 8-bit per channel image contains 256 tonal values per channel, for a total of over 16.7 million total possible color values. If the original is of excellent quality, with good contrast and proper exposure, this is adequate to produce images of photographic quality. In fact, photo inkjet printers only use 8-bits per channel of information to produce a print, even when the file contains more information.

Higher bit-depths are primarily helpful when significant adjustments will need to be made to the image to get it ready for print. When any adjustment is made to an image, some amount of information is lost. If you start with far more information than is needed for the final print, the information lost through adjustments is of no consequence. Scanners that offer more than 8-bits per channel of bit-depth, therefore, provide more detail in the final image, with less risk of posterization, which is represented by the loss of smooth gradations in the image (see Figure 4.6).

Figure 4.6 High bit-depth ensures that smooth gradations of tone and color will be maintained in the image. If you scan at a minimal bit-depth and then need to make major adjustments to your image, posterization may occur, as shown here.

For film scanners, bit-depth is usually referred to based on how many bits per channel it is able to record from the original. A 12-bit scanner would be able to record 4,096 tonal values per channel. At 14-bits per channel, that number goes up to 16,384 tonal values per channel. I recommend purchasing a scanner that is capable of 14-bits per channel or more.

With flatbed scanners, bit-depth is provided based on the full bit-depth of the final image, rather than a per-channel value. A 24-bit scanner is the equivalent of 8-bit per channel. Therefore, a 14-bit per channel flatbed scanner would be referred to as a 42-bit scanner. I recommend that you look for a flatbed with 42-bit color or higher.

Maximize Bit-Depth

If your scanner offers an option to scan an image using more than 8-bits per channel (24-bit), I strongly recommend that you take advantage of this option, at least for your most challenging images. Scanning with the highest bit-depth possible maximizes the total number of possible tonal and color values in the image, and virtually guarantees that you will be able to maintain smooth gradations within the image.

High-bit scans produce files that are twice as big as you would obtain with 8-bit per channel scans, so you'll want to be sure you have the processing power, memory, and hard drive storage space available before you start producing high-bit scans. Also, I encourage you to upgrade to Adobe Photoshop CS, which offers extensive support for high-bit files, including the ability to use adjustment layers on them.

Software Issues

In addition to the capabilities of the scanner itself, you'll want to consider issues related to the software provided with the scanner for producing the best scan for a color-managed workflow.

Unfortunately, it can be difficult to determine the quality of the scanner software before you buy it. Scanner manufacturers provide excellent detail about the scanner specifications, but very little information about the software that will control the scanner in most cases. I recommend reading reviews in magazines and on websites to get a better idea of how good the software is for a particular scanner.

The best scanner software allows you to configure it to meet the needs of your color-managed workflow, including the ability to set a specific working space for the scanned image (see Figure 4.7). It also includes excellent control over the scan itself, so that you can fine-tune the scanner settings to produce the best image possible.

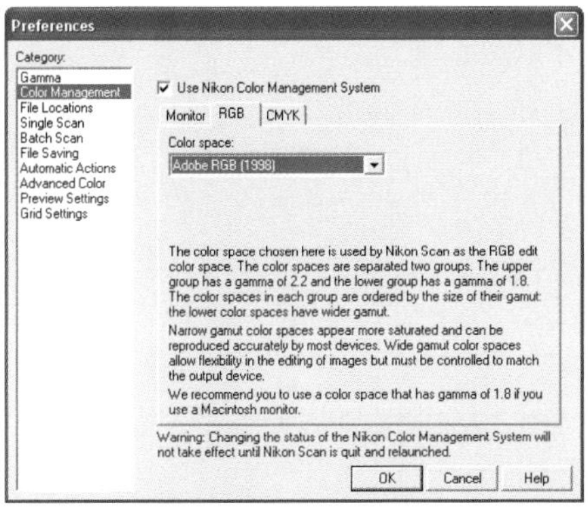

Figure 4.7

Advanced scanners, such as those from Nikon, allow you to adjust color management settings in the scanner software, with options such as the color space the image should be converted to after scanning.

Many third-party scanner software applications that support a wide range of scanners are available. If you aren't sure of the quality of the software included with a scanner you are considering, you may want to check if third-party software will support your scanner. For example, SilverFast from LaserSoft Imaging (www.silverfast.com) provides excellent control over the scanning process and support for custom profiles for your scanner. I highly recommend this software if your scanner supports it. In fact, whether SilverFast supports the scanner you are considering may be a factor to consider in your final decision.

Approaches to Scanning

Scanning is a process of gathering information. When you are doing your own scanning, you are able to exercise control over the process of gathering information from your original, ensuring the best scan possible.

Of course, accurate color is also important, but it may not be as important as you think. There are two basic approaches to scanning: the "information" method and the "accuracy" method.

Information Method

Scanning for information means that you are attempting to capture as much information out of the original as possible. This ensures the maximum amount of information possible in your image, so that fine details are preserved. That information also allows you more latitude to make fine-tuning adjustments to your images, allowing you to achieve exactly the results you are looking for (see Figure 4.8).

Figure 4.8 When Dewitt Jones creates a unique interpretation of an image from a photographic original, the accuracy of the initial scan becomes less important. In such cases, the information method of scanning provides the best solution. (Photograph by Dewitt Jones, www.dewittjones.com.)

By emphasizing a scan with maximum information, you will probably have to sacrifice total accuracy in that scan. This is because a profile will often shift the values in your native scan so much that detail is lost in the process. You can generally optimize the image with photo-editing software to achieve excellent results, with more detail than you may have ended up with by using the accuracy method.

 Note: Emphasizing the capture of as much information as possible doesn't mean that you allow the scan to be extremely different from the original. It simply means that you are more focused on information than on specific colors and tonal values.

Another advantage of the information method is that you don't need any additional software or tools to be able to use this method. That means you don't need to spend any additional money to implement this method.

Of course, there is a downside. For one thing, the scan won't be as accurate as you would obtain with the accuracy method. By using the information method you are giving up that accuracy. In general, that isn't a major problem because you can optimize the image with your photo-editing software to achieve the results you are seeking. However, the relationships between colors in the image may not be accurate when you don't use the accuracy method. As a result, you'll need to make relatively complicated adjustments to achieve an image that matches the original. You may need to target specific adjustments to particular colors or areas of the image.

Implementing the information method of scanning is relatively simple. No special settings need to be used, but you'll want to make adjustments in the scan with a workflow along the lines of the following:

1. Perform a preview scan with the scanning software.

2. Crop the image so that the scan will include only the actual image area.

3. If the scanner software includes a histogram display or other method for reviewing the values in the image, use it to determine if you are clipping any highlight or shadow detail in the image (see Figure 4.9).

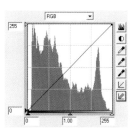

Figure 4.9

A histogram display in the scanner software can help you determine if you are losing any detail in the highlights or shadows of your image.

4. Adjust the brightness control in the scanner software so that the maximum amount of information is captured. In general, you will want to keep the adjustment at a setting that will produce an image that is as bright as possible without losing any highlight detail. This is often referred to "as achieving maximum density" in the image file.

5. Adjust the contrast, but only to reduce contrast in the scan. Increasing contrast will, by definition, result in a loss of detail in the highlights and shadows of your image. Start with the contrast control at a neutral setting. If the histogram or other information display shows that you have lost detail in the image, reduce contrast in an effort to keep the information within the range the scanner is able to record. This underscores the importance of a scanner with an adequate dynamic range to record all of the information in the original.

6. Adjust the color balance to bring the image as close as possible to accurate color. Remember that the focus with this method is to capture as much information as possible. If the color balance in the scan is off by a significant amount, detail may be lost in the highlights or shadows of certain color channels. Adjusting the color balance to bring it as close to accurate as possible will ensure that maximum information is recorded.

7. Apply a very small amount of sharpening in the scan if the scanner software provides an Unsharp Mask feature with a high degree of control over the sharpening applied (see Figure 4.10). It is helpful to apply minimal sharpening in the scan to compensate for the loss of sharpness that occurs when you digitize the original. If this level of control is not provided in your scanner software, do not apply any sharpening until you open the image in your photo-editing software.

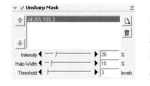

Figure 4.10
A very small amount of Unsharp Mask applied in the scan will help compensate for the loss of sharpness that occurs in the digitization process, allowing you to produce better scans.

8. If your scanner offers a multiple-pass scanning option, you might consider using this for particularly dense images. This feature causes the image to be scanned more than once, with the pixel values compared between scans. If the values are different between each pass for some pixels, the software knows that this is noise and deals with the pixels accordingly. Noise occurs in the dense areas of an image, where the scanner has to work harder to see information. For example, a dark night scene captured on slide film would have a higher potential for noise in the dark night sky (see Figure 4.11).

9. If your scanner offers a high-bit scan option, I recommend using this option to ensure the maximum amount of information in the image file. It will also allow you to make much broader adjustments to the image without a loss of smooth gradations, making it particularly helpful for your most difficult images.

10. Scan the image and save the resulting file in a format such as Photoshop PSD or TIFF with no image compression applied.

Because most scanner software only allows you to see a low-resolution preview of the image, ensuring that the settings you have used are the best is difficult. Once you have the image open in your photo-editing software, zoom in to critical areas of the image at 100 percent scale (so that one pixel on your monitor is equal to one pixel in the image) to determine if you have achieved the best scan possible in terms of information recorded (see Figure 4.12). If not, rescan the image with revised settings.

Figure 4.11 High-density areas of an image will benefit from multiple-pass scanning. This is an ideal way to avoid noise in images that contain very dense areas, such as a nighttime cityscape. (Photograph by Jeff Greene, www.imagewestphoto.com.)

Figure 4.12
Using the information method of scanning will result in an image that is slightly "muddy," but that contains maximum detail to allow you to optimize the image with photo-editing software.

Accuracy Method

The accuracy method of scanning focuses on getting a scan that matches the original image as closely as possible. Obtaining an accurate scan with the information method presented in the previous section is possible, but it can be more of a challenge. The accuracy method allows you to produce accurate results with minimal effort.

As mentioned in the previous section, using the information method requires that you adjust the image after the fact to achieve the desired results, because the initial scan will most certainly not be a final image. The accuracy method, because it focuses on achieving a scan that is as close to the original as possible, will require much less adjustment. For this reason, it is the preferred scanning method for those who need to process a large number of images. If you are producing fine-art images in relatively low numbers, the information method may make the most sense. But large-volume work, such as scanning many images to include in a catalog, most certainly benefits from the accuracy method of scanning.

The cornerstone of the accuracy method is producing an accurate scanner profile, which will ensure an accurate scan. Each scanner has a particular bias, producing varying results. If you scan the same image with a variety of scanners—even more than one scanner of the same make and model—each image will be unique. The differences may be subtle, but there will be differences. A scanner profile "normalizes" the result of a scan, compensating for any inaccuracies in how the scanner records the information in the original.

A scanner profile is created by scanning an image with known values, and then comparing the known values to what the scanner actually recorded. The differences can then be translated into the amount of compensation required to adjust the scanned image to produce an accurate result.

Note: Don't focus too much energy on getting scans that perfectly match the original you are scanning. Although a high-quality scanner profile will give you a very accurate scan, I recommend that you focus on making the final image look its very best, rather than getting caught in the trap of trying to match the original too closely. You can often produce a much better image by taking it beyond the limitations of the original.

Scanning for accuracy involves the following steps:

1. Perform a preview scan with the scanning software.
2. Crop the image so that the scan will include only the actual image area.
3. Make sure any color management options are turned off.

Note: Nikon Scan software, included with Nikon's line of film scanners, includes a color space option in the Color Management settings called Scanner RGB. This color space is intended to simulate the results of using no color management, while still allowing you to apply Unsharp Mask to your image. If you are using a Nikon scanner, I recommend leaving Color Management turned on with the color space set to Scanner RGB when creating a profile and scanning images with the accuracy method.

4. Make sure all adjustment options are reset to their default values.

Note: Steps 3 and 4 ensure that the scanner software doesn't apply any adjustments to the scanned data and that the settings are the same ones you used when you actually created the scanner profile.

5. Scan the image.
6. Assign the custom profile to the image, as described later in this chapter.

7. Scan the image and save the resulting file in a format such as Photoshop PSD or TIFF with no image compression applied.

As you can see, scanning with the accuracy method is much simpler, and it results in an image that is a much closer match to the original.

Scanner Profiles

Whenever you scan an image, a scanner profile is used to translate what the scanner recorded into actual color values in the image file. If you are using the information method to scan your image, then you are using a generic profile that is included with the scanner for this translation. Because it was not created for your specific scanner, it may not be completely accurate. A scanner profile is used to provide a translation between the values the scanner actually records and the final color values in the image. A custom profile for your scanner allows the image data acquired by the scanner to be adjusted accurately.

> **Note:** Remember that in order to ensure the most accurate results possible, whenever you scan an image that will utilize a custom scanner profile, you should configure the scanner settings exactly the same as you had them when scanning the target during the profile creation process.

A custom profile specifically created with your scanner ensures the most accurate results possible, as outlined in the "Accuracy Method" section earlier in this chapter. Fortunately, producing a custom profile is quite simple. The basic process involves scanning an image with known values, and then comparing the known values with what the scanner actually recorded. This target image can be anything that the profiling software has established values for, but it is most often a target known as an IT-8.

If you perform a large number of scans, I strongly recommend that you obtain a package that will allow you to generate a custom profile. The time saved will more than pay for the cost of the package in no time.

> **Note:** Due to problems caused by the "orange mask" included in the emulsion of negative film, producing reliable profiles for scanning negatives is not possible. For those images, you'll need to use the information method of scanning presented earlier in this chapter.

MonacoEZcolor

MonacoEZcolor from Monaco Systems (www.monacosys.com) provides a very easy-to-use package for creating monitor, scanner, and printer profiles. It supports both Windows and Macintosh, and sells for under $300. However, it doesn't include everything you'll need for all of these purposes. For example, it does not include a sensor for creating monitor profiles. For scanner profiles, it includes IT-8 targets for reflective and transparency profiles for flatbed scanners, so that you can build a profile for both reflective and transparency scanning. To create a custom profile for a film scanner, you'll need to purchase a 35mm IT-8 target, which is available from Monaco Systems for about an additional $40.

Follow these steps to create a custom scanner profile using MonacoEZcolor:

1. Launch MonacoEZcolor.

2. Select the type of profile you would like to create (see Figure 4.13). In this case, you should select Create Input Profile because a scanner is considered an input device.

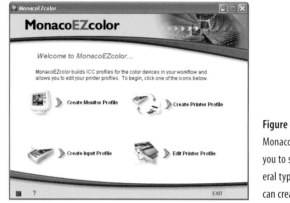

Figure 4.13
MonacoEZcolor allows you to select from several types of profiles you can create.

Note: If you are using a flatbed scanner to scan both prints and film, you'll need to create two separate profiles: one for reflective targets (prints) and one for transmissive targets (film).

3. The Before You Begin screen provides some important reminders (see Figure 4.14). Be sure that the scanner you will be profiling has been turned on for at least 30 minutes to ensure it has stabilized. It reminds you to turn off the automatic adjustment options provided in the scanner software, and it reminds you to turn off any color management options. Review the reminders, and click the Next button (the right arrow) to continue.

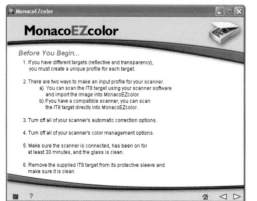

Figure 4.14
The Before You Begin screen in MonacoEZcolor offers some important reminders about the profile-creation process.

4. Select the type of IT8 target (see Figure 4.15) you will be scanning to produce a profile. For profiling a flatbed scanner for prints, you will select the 5×7 Reflective

option. For a flatbed scanner while using a transparency adapter, you will select the 4×6 Transparency option. If you are profiling a dedicated film scanner, you will use the 35mm Transparency option.

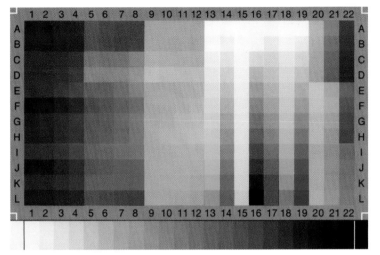

97

Figure 4.15
An IT-8 target is a standard target for creating custom scanner profiles.

Note: The standard MonacoEZcolor package does not include a 35mm transparency IT8 target, so you'll need to buy that separately. It is available from Monaco, as well as other sources.

5. Position the target to be scanned as appropriate for the type of scanner you are profiling. For flatbed scanners, be sure the glass is clean and place the target on the glass. If you are using the transparency target for your flatbed, be sure it is aligned under the area that the transparency adapter actually illuminates. For film scanners, insert the 35mm target into the scanner as you normally would to scan a slide.

6. Select the option to directly scan into the MonacoEZcolor software if your scanner supports TWAIN, or select the Load An Image option if you have already scanned and saved the target. I recommend using the TWAIN option to scan at this time, as it avoids any possible application of other profiles, such as your working space, when you scan the image and save it using your image-editing software. If you decide to load an existing scan, skip to Step 10.

7. Configure the scanner settings using the resolution recommended by MonacoEZcolor in the previous step. Reset all controls to their neutral values, and turn off any automatic adjustment or color management options.

8. Crop the target so it is the only item being scanned, and click the Scan button to acquire the image. Close the scanner software when the scan is complete.

9. Verify the scan to confirm it is properly cropped and oriented. The screen displayed will show a thumbnail of the scan you created, along with a series of samples showing you a good scan and examples of incorrect scans (see Figure 4.16). If your

scan is not correct, click the Back button (the left arrow) and rescan the target. Otherwise, click Next.

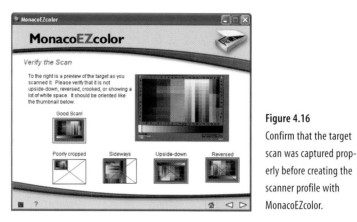

Figure 4.16

Confirm that the target scan was captured properly before creating the scanner profile with MonacoEZcolor.

10. Select the appropriate reference file for the target you are scanning. This information is shown on the target itself. Click the Select Reference button, choose the appropriate reference file, and click Open.

11. Click the Save Profile button, and type a name for the profile you have created. I recommend naming the profile to reference the specific scanner you are using as well as the type of profile if you are profiling a flatbed scanner.

12. The final dialog will confirm that the profile was successfully created. When you click the Next button, you will return to the Welcome screen from Step 2.

Gretag Macbeth Eye-One Publish

The Eye-One Photo package from Gretag Macbeth (www.eyeonecolor.com) provides a complete solution for producing very accurate monitor, scanner, digital projector, and printer profiles. It is an all-inclusive package, with the exception of a target for creating custom profiles for a film scanner, which will require a 35mm IT-8 target. It supports both Windows and Macintosh, and it sells for around $2,700. To be sure, this is an expensive package, but it includes everything you need (except for the 35mm IT-8 target) to produce profiles for all of the devices in your color-managed workflow.

Eye-One Publish takes a unique approach to creating custom profiles for flatbed scanners. Instead of simply scanning a target that consists of known values, this package actually has you measure the values for the scan target in the process of creating your scanner profile. This helps you produce the most accurate profile possible. Instead of using data that tells the software what the target values should be, you are measuring what they really are. You can save this data for future use, but you can also remeasure the target at any time to ensure you are getting the most accurate profile possible. This is one of the features that make this package worth its relatively high price, if you can fit it into your budget.

To create a custom profile for a flatbed scanner with the Eye-One Publish package:

1. Scan the flatbed target with your scanner, making sure that all controls are set to their default value and any color management options are turned off. Save this file as a TIFF image without assigning a profile.

2. Launch the Eye-One Match software.

3. Select the Scanner option from the list of devices you can profile, and click Next.

4. For the Select Reference File option, choose to Measure The Reference Chart, and click Next.

5. Place the sensor on the calibration stand, and click the Calibrate button. When calibration is complete, click Next.

6. Select the method you want to use to measure the target values. I strongly recommend using strip mode, which allows you to scan across the target one row at a time. Patch mode requires you to place the sensor over each individual target one at a time.

7. Follow the instructions on the screen to measure the target values with the sensor (see Figure 4.17). When all patches have been read, click Next.

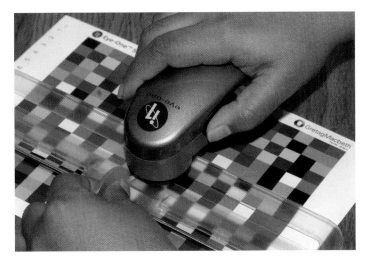

Figure 4.17
The Gretag Macbeth Eye-One Publish package has you measure the values of the target before scanning it to create a profile, ensuring the most accurate results possible.

8. You will be given an opportunity to save the data you have measured. Click the Save The Data button, and enter a name for the saved file. I recommend using a filename that references the scanner you are profiling, as well as the date the measurements were taken. After you have saved the measurement data, click Next.

9. Click the Load button, and select the image you saved in Step 1.

10. Crop the scanned target to include only the color patches. Tools are provided to rotate the image if necessary (see Figure 4.18). A magnifier tool helps you crop the target image as accurately as possible. When you have cropped the image properly, click Next.

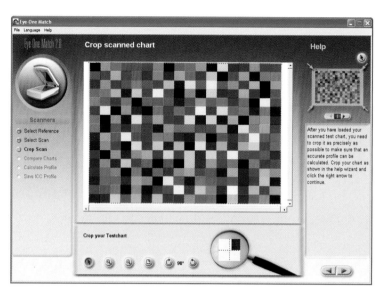

Figure 4.18 The scanned target image must be cropped properly to ensure the profile is built properly.

11. Confirm the layout of the measured data file provided and the target you scanned (see Figure 4.19). If they don't match in terms of overall layout, click Previous and recrop the image or rescan the target if the scan was performed incorrectly. If they match, click Next.

Figure 4.19 Before generating your custom profile, be sure that you have scanned and cropped the target properly by comparing it to the sample displayed.

12. A profile will be generated. When the process is complete, enter a name for your profile. I recommend using a name that identifies the specific scanner you are profiling, as you'll need to reference this profile for future scans. Click Next to return to the main Eye-One Match screen.

The Eye-One Publish package does not include a 35mm target for use in creating a custom profile for a film scanner. Therefore, you'll need to purchase an IT-8 target to use Eye-One Publish to profile your film scanner. These are available from a variety of sources for around $40.

To create a custom profile for a film scanner with the Eye-One Publish package, follow these steps:

1. Scan your IT-8 target with your scanner, making sure that all controls are set to their default value and any color management options are turned off. Save this file as a TIFF image without assigning a profile.

2. Launch the Eye-One Match software.

3. Select the Scanner option from the list of devices you can profile, and click Next.

4. For the Select Reference File option, choose to Load A Reference Chart and click Next.

5. In the Open dialog that appears, navigate to the location that contains the measurement information for your IT-8 target. This file should have been included with the target itself.

6. Click the Load button and navigate to the location that contains the scanned IT-8 target from Step 1. Select the file, and click the Open button.

7. Crop the image to include only the actual target area, identified by white brackets near the corners of the overall image. Tools are provided to rotate the image if necessary. A magnifier tool helps you crop the target image as accurately as possible. When you have cropped the image properly, click Next.

8. Confirm the layout of the measured data file provided and the target you scanned. If they don't match in terms of overall layout, click Previous and recrop the image or rescan the target if the scan was performed incorrectly. If they match, click Next.

9. A profile will be generated. When the process is complete, enter a name for your profile. I recommend using a name that identifies the specific scanner you are profiling, as you'll need to reference this profile for future scans. Click Next to return to the main Eye-One Match screen.

Integrated Profiles with SilverFast

SilverFast is specialized scanning software from Lasersoft Imaging (www.silverfast.com) that provides exceptional control over the scanning process. It supports a wide variety of scanners, and I highly recommend this software for those who want to produce the best scans possible. In addition, an option is offered that allows you to create custom profiles for your scanner using a standard IT-8 target. SilverFast even allows you to apply that custom profile to the scan directly, which is very convenient. Pricing for SilverFast varies with the particular scanner supported, but for a typical film scanner the price is under $350 including an IT-8 target for profiling. For more information about SilverFast, look for *SilverFast: The Official Guide* (Sybex, 2003).

Assigning a Scanner Profile

A custom scanner profile provides the information needed to translate the data from your scans into accurate color information in the image file. However, that translation doesn't happen automatically because most scanning software doesn't allow you to assign custom profiles directly to your images. Instead, you'll have to assign the image to the file after opening it in your photo-editing software.

Note: The instructions in this section are specific to Photoshop. If you are using different software, you'll need to investigate how to assign a custom profile to your image files using that software.

The color value for each pixel in an RGB image is stored as values of red, green, and blue that together define the exact color of the pixel. However, by themselves these values don't mean anything. They are just numbers. To assign a color to them, a translation table must define what the values mean in a device-independent color space. In the absence of a profile, the colors will be interpreted by Photoshop based on the current RGB working space.

Obviously, that RGB working space does not accurately represent the color values in our scanned image. That's why we created the custom profile. All we need to do is tell Photoshop to translate the color numbers in our image based on the translation information in the custom scanner profile that was used to scan the image (see Figure 4.20).

Figure 4.20 When you assign your custom scanner profile to a scanned image, the color values will be interpreted properly. The image on the left shows the appearance before assigning the profile, and the image on the right shows the image after assigning the profile. (Photograph by John Shaw, www.johnshawphoto.com.)

Understanding the difference between *assigning* your custom scanner profile to the image and *converting* the image to that profile is important. Assigning a profile does not cause the color values in the image to be changed. Rather, it causes them to be interpreted based on the information in that profile. The color values remain the same, but their meaning changes.

Converting an image to a profile is very different. Instead of changing the way the color values are interpreted, it changes the numbers in the image data file so that each pixel will have the same color appearance (as closely as possible) when interpreted based on a different profile. When using a custom scanner profile, you most certainly don't want the colors in our inaccurate scan to remain the same. This is why the custom scanner profile will be assigned to the image, rather than converting the image to that profile.

In order to obtain the best results, it is important that the color values in the original scan do not change before assigning the custom profile to the image. If you are opening a scanned image, it is therefore important that you not allow the image to be converted to your working space when it is opened. If you followed my recommendations from Chapter 2, you will have the box checked in Photoshop's Color Settings dialog box so that you will be alerted before an image without an embedded profile is automatically converted to your working space. If not, I recommend either checking that box before opening scanned images that need to have a profile assigned or selecting the option to Preserve Embedded Profiles.

To assign your custom scanner profile to an image, use the following steps:

1. Open the image. If the Missing Profile dialog box is displayed, select the option to Assign Profile (see Figure 4.21). Select the appropriate profile for your scanner from the dropdown list. I also recommend that you check the box to convert the image to your working space after assigning the profile. Click OK, and the profile will be assigned to the image. You can then skip the rest of the steps here.

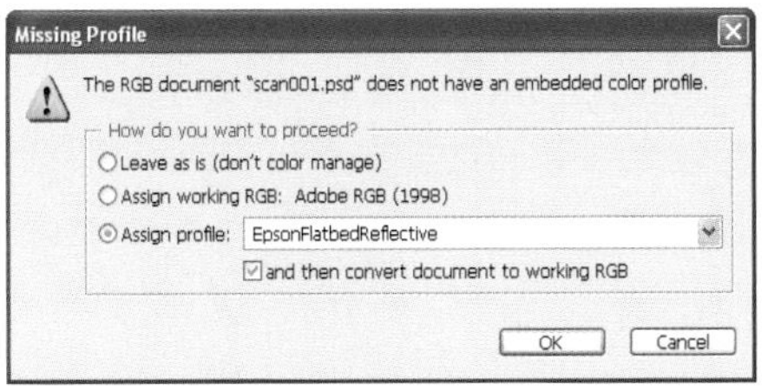

Figure 4.21
If the Missing Profile dialog box is displayed when you open an image, you can simply assign the scanner profile here and you are done.

2. If the Missing Profile dialog box was not displayed, select Image > Mode > Assign Profile from the menu (see Figure 4.22).

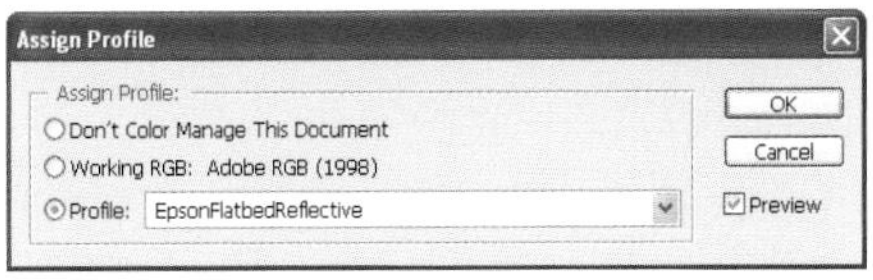

Figure 4.22
The Assign Profile dialog box allows you to select the custom scanner profile that should be used to interpret the color numbers in the scanned image.

3. Select the Profile option.

4. From the dropdown list of profiles, select the custom scanner profile you created for the scanner that was used to scan your image.

5. Click OK. The colors in the image will now be interpreted based on your custom profile, resulting in more accurate colors assuming a high-quality profile.

Automated Assignments

If you scan a large number of images with the same scanner, it can become laborious to assign your custom scanner profile to each image. You can automate the process by creating an action in Photoshop:

1. Open an image that has been scanned but doesn't yet have the custom scanner profile assigned to it.

2. Select the Actions palette. If it isn't visible, you can select Window > Actions from the menu.

3. Select the folder on the Actions palette that you would like to use to save your action. You can also create a new folder by clicking the Create New Set button at the bottom of the Actions palette, typing a name in the New Set dialog box, and clicking OK.

4. Click the Create New Action button at the bottom of the Actions palette.

5. Type a name for the action. If you are going to assign a function key to use as a shortcut (which I strongly recommend), you should include that keystroke in the name for the action. For example, you might name the action "AssignNikonScanner - F12."

6. If you want to assign a shortcut key to the action (which, again, I strongly recommend doing), select it from the Function Key dropdown, checking the boxes for Shift and/or Control (Command on Macintosh) if you would like to include those modifier keys as part of the shortcut.

7. Click Record, and Photoshop will record the steps you take from this point forward until you stop recording.

8. Select Image > Mode > Assign Profile from the menu. Select the Profile option, and then select the custom profile for your scanner from the dropdown list and click OK.

9. Click the Stop button at the bottom of the Actions palette to stop recording the action.

In the future, you can assign a profile to the image by running the action you have recorded from the Actions palette after opening the image. Even better, if you followed my suggestion to assign a keyboard shortcut to the action, you can simply press that key any time you need to assign your custom scanner profile to an image or process a folder full of images with the File > Automate > Batch menu option.

Evaluating Scans

After you have scanned an image, you'll want to evaluate it to confirm that you have achieved the best results possible. If you are using the information method of scanning, the scan probably will not be very accurate compared to the original. Rather, it will contain the maximum amount of information, so that you can optimize the image after the fact as part of your imaging workflow. Still, you should evaluate this image carefully to confirm that you have indeed captured as much information as possible.

I recommend zooming in on your image to 100 percent, so that one pixel on your monitor equals one pixel in the image file. Check for fine detail, particularly in the highlights and shadows of the image. Often, it can be difficult to determine if there is adequate detail in the image simply by looking at it on your monitor. Therefore, I recommend that you examine the original image with a loupe, comparing how much detail is in the original to how much appears in the scanned image. If the results aren't what you expected, rescan the image with more care to the settings used in the scanner software.

If you are using the accuracy method of scanning, you'll want to examine the overall image for color accuracy after assigning your custom scanner profile to the image. This can present a challenge, because you will be comparing images displayed on two different mediums. You'll have to compare the luminous image on your monitor with either a print or transparency. To compare the images, you'll need to be sure to compare the images accurately. For prints, that means viewing the image under a 5000 Kelvin illumination source, comparing it to the monitor display with as little light as possible. For transparencies, you'll want to evaluate the image under a loupe using a light table with a 5000 Kelvin illumination source.

While this evaluation can be done with any image, you may want to initially evaluate the results you obtain using an IT-8 target, because it contains a range of various hues. It also doesn't have any context as far as content in the image, which can help to ensure that your evaluation isn't biased based on what you think the image "should" look like. The IT-8 target also includes a grayscale step wedge that helps you evaluate the tonal range you are able to record in your scans.

Using the methods presented in this chapter, you should be able to produce scans that more than meet your expectations when you evaluate them closely.

Digital Capture

Digital cameras have rapidly evolved over the years, now offering professional-level image quality, large potential output sizes, excellent color fidelity, instant review and other conveniences, and increased flexibility for photography. The latest cameras make it easier than ever to get accurate color in your images, and a color-managed workflow that includes your digital camera can ensure consistently pleasing color.

5

Chapter Contents

Digital Cameras

Back when film photography was king, before digital photography started its meteoric rise in popularity, most photographers didn't have to give very much thought to color accuracy when they took pictures. For example, an outdoor photographer using daylight-balanced film didn't have to make any adjustments in the camera to produce relatively accurate color. Film processing could obviously play a role in the final color of the image, but this was outside the photographer's control. By and large, the photographer didn't have to think about color accuracy in the "capture," and in many cases didn't control the color for the final output either.

Digital has changed this in a couple ways. For one thing, most photographers who have made the move to digital have also taken control over the optimization and printing process. This obviously includes a considerable investment of time, but the payoff is complete control over the final image. The other difference is that the photographer must take responsibility for accurate color in the original capture when using a digital camera (see Figure 5.1).

Figure 5.1
Understanding the options available to you for controlling color in your digital captures will help you achieve the most accurate images possible. (© Corbis)

Of course, for both film and digital photography, there are some issues that affect the color of an image during capture. For example, studio photographers are very familiar with the use of gels to change the color cast created by their lights, to offset colors they don't want, or to add a desirable wash of color. Digital photography simply adds some extra work for the photographer in making sure that the captured colors are accurate.

It is easy to think of these added responsibilities as a problem. Instead, I think of them as opportunities. You need to take responsibility for accurate color because digital cameras maintain such tremendous flexibility. In fact, the flexibility is more in the way the data is processed, not in how the camera initially records the photograph. A digital camera actually records only brightness values for individual pixels, recording how much light of a particular color (red, green, or blue) contacts a given pixel on the imaging sensor.

Because the camera measures only the light levels for each pixel, you can modify how the final image appears by changing the way the information captured by the imaging sensor is processed. This control can be exercised by adjusting camera settings, using custom settings, or creating a custom camera profile. I'll cover each of these methods in this chapter.

Before implementing any of these procedures, you'll obviously need a digital camera. When buying a digital camera, you'll want to consider the features offered to be sure they meet your needs, both now and in the future. You'll also want to be sure that the digital camera offers the options that are important to you when it comes to optimizing the image being photographed.

Features to Look For

Even if you already have a digital camera that meets your photographic needs, chances are you'll be thinking about a new camera in the near future (see Figure 5.2). Besides the issues of ergonomics, compatibility with existing accessories, and the quality of the final result, you'll want to consider issues related to color management, and the ability to exercise control over the way the camera captures and processes the color in your images.

Figure 5.2

Even if you are working with the very latest digital SLR camera, you can count on new models coming out in the near future that may tempt you to upgrade. (Courtesy Canon USA)

Resolution

The issue of resolution in digital cameras has fueled the "megapixel wars" that are largely a marketing device. It is far too easy to get caught up in the hype and to forget that there are many other factors that affect image quality. High resolution isn't a panacea.

That isn't to say resolution shouldn't be considered. It simply needs to be taken into context. Quite simply, resolution relates to potential output size. The more pixels you capture, the larger you'll be able to reproduce the image while maintaining excellent quality and detail in the image (see Figure 5.3).

Figure 5.3 Besides allowing you to produce larger prints, a digital camera with higher resolution also ensures that you'll maintain fine details in the image. (Photograph by Peter Burian.)

Related to the issue of resolution is pixel size. The larger the pixel, the more light it is able to gather, and the less noise it will tend to exhibit in the final image. The smaller the pixel, the less sensitive each pixel will be to light, which will result in more noise because the sensitivity of the sensor must be amplified artificially.

Other factors also play a role in the final image quality, including the sensor type, the specific nature of the sensor array, the quality of the components in the sensor, and other issues. Unfortunately, evaluating each of these factors for a given camera is difficult, and camera manufacturers are not likely to include very much information to help you make such a decision. Furthermore, all of these factors can't be fairly evaluated in context. Rather than trying to evaluate a camera based on how many micrometers across each pixel is, try to arrange to test the cameras you are considering at a camera store, or read reviews that include detailed information about the quality of the pictures the camera is able to produce with sample images for you to evaluate for yourself.

Note: When researching various cameras to make a final decision, I strongly recommend reading the reviews posted at Digital Photography Review (www.dpreview.com). These reviews are incredibly thorough, and they include high-resolution sample images to help you make a more informed purchasing decision.

The decision about how much resolution will be enough depends on the size of the output you intend to produce. The problem is you can't always accurately predict the largest output you'll need to produce. Use Table 5.1 as a basic guide when considering how much resolution will be enough to produce prints of high quality and color fidelity.

Uninterpolated size is based on output at 300 dpi with no interpolation in the image file. Maximum size is the maximum output size recommended assuming the best quality image and subjective evaluation of optimal quality.

▷ **Table 5.1** Digital Camera Resolution and Output

Megapixels	Uninterpolated	Maximum
3	5"×7"	11"×14"
4	6"×8"	13"×19"
5	6"×9"	13"×19"
6	7"×10"	16"×24"
11	9"×14"	20"×30"
14	10"×15"	24"×36"

Note: The "Maximum" output size shown in Table 5.1 is only a guideline based on acceptable photographic output after *interpolating* an image (that is, changing size by adding pixels to it). You can actually enlarge a high-quality image to a much higher degree, particularly if the viewing distance will be more than normal.

White Balance Presets

Virtually all digital cameras include preset white balance settings, which allow you to effectively tell the camera what the lighting conditions are like, so that the processing of the image can be adjusted accordingly (see Figure 5.4). More to the point, the colors in the image are calculated based on the white balance preset, eliminating the color cast produced by that type of lighting. For example, a "shady" white balance setting would compensate for the strong blue component of the light found in shade, shifting the image more toward yellow. A "tungsten" (or incandescent) setting would compensate for the warm light produced by this type of lighting, shifting the image more toward blue and cyan.

All digital cameras offer an automatic white balance that determines what compensation is necessary based on the lighting conditions. Some lower-end cameras offer this as the only option, but most digital cameras include a variety of white balance presets. If you plan to use this option, be sure that the digital camera you purchase includes presets for the types of lighting under which you expect to photograph.

Some cameras even include the ability to fine-tune the in-camera presets. Simply select the white balance preset that represents the closest match, and then adjust the value up or down to fine-tune your results.

Tungsten

Fluorescent

Flash

Daylight

Cloudy

Shade

Figure 5.4
The white balance presets on a digital camera allow you to change the way the colors in an image are interpreted. This series of images (in order of Kelvin color temperature) shows you the wide range of interpretations possible when different white balance presets are used. (Photograph by Jeff Greene, www .imagewestphoto.com.)

Custom White Balance

A custom white balance option can be very helpful, particularly if you photograph under a variety of lighting conditions, or conditions that aren't covered by the white balance presets available on your camera. This option allows you to use a custom color temperature setting for white balance, based on a specific measurement. This provides much more accurate results than using the white balance preset that seems to be closest to the specific lighting conditions under which you are photographing. Studio photographers in particular would benefit from this option. I'll show you how to use a custom white balance setting later in this chapter.

RAW Capture

For maximum flexibility, control, and image quality, I strongly recommend using a camera that provides a RAW capture option. When using this mode, the camera will save the values recorded by the imaging sensor for each pixel, without applying any adjustments or optimizations to the image. The result is a RAW data file, which is not a standard image file. Instead, it is a data file that must be converted to an image format. This conversion process allows you to adjust the image to produce the best image possible with incredible flexibility.

The overall benefit of RAW capture is that you are in control of the post-processing of the image, rather than leaving those tasks to the camera. You are able to manipulate the same data that the camera normally processes internally. The result is that you can make adjustments to the image without the penalty in image quality that would occur if you captured in a normal image format (such as JPEG) and applied the same adjustments to an image after capture.

I'll talk more about working with RAW captures, and converting them to image files, later in this chapter. In the meantime, know that I strongly recommend using a digital camera that includes a RAW capture option, even if you don't use it for all of your photography.

Basic Camera Settings

The right camera settings can make all the difference in capturing the most accurate color, ensuring the highest image quality, and fitting into an efficient color-managed workflow.

Capture Mode

Capture mode refers to the type of image file the camera will produce when you take a picture. These options affect image quality, file size, and flexibility:

JPEG is the default option for most cameras, and for most photographers is also the most convenient. However, it does represent a compromise in quality and flexibility. With JPEG capture, the camera will do considerable image processing. This produces an image with excellent contrast and saturation, but it does potentially sacrifice some image detail in the process. At the highest-quality setting, JPEG capture will produce an image with virtually no compression artifacts in the image, and excellent color fidelity. However, if an incorrect white balance or other setting is used, it may be impossible to correct the image adequately (see Figure 5.5).

Figure 5.5 If an incorrect white balance preset is used for a JPEG or TIFF capture, achieving a final image you are happy with (left) may be nearly impossible, due to the complicated white balance compensation applied to the image (right).

TIFF is a higher-quality option than JPEG, but this option includes compromises of its own. It doesn't use any image compression, therefore eliminating the risk of compression artifacts. However, that lack of compression also results in a very large image file. The file size in megabytes will be three times the megapixel count for the camera, because each pixel requires three bytes to record the final color value. So, a 6-megapixel camera would result in an 18-megabyte image file (even larger than a RAW capture), which requires additional time for processing and writing to your digital media card, and will fill that card to capacity quickly. Although TIFF represents a high-quality option, it is not one I recommend for most photographers.

RAW capture mode represents the ultimate in quality and flexibility for the photographer. It isn't actually an image file format, but rather a data file that contains the information gathered by the sensor during exposure. The camera does not process that data to optimize the final result. This may sound like a bad thing, but it is actually a major benefit because it allows the photographer to make those decisions. No image compression is applied, ensuring that no artifacts appear in the image. One of the biggest benefits is that white balance adjustments aren't applied to the image data until RAW conversion, so that you can fine-tune the adjustment to produce the most accurate color possible. This is the format I recommend the most when a photographer wants to exercise maximum control over the image to produce the best final quality possible.

Note: Because no in-camera processing is applied to RAW captures, the settings for Color Space and Image Controls referenced in the following sections do not apply directly to the image data when you are using RAW capture, but rather become the default settings for the RAW conversion.

Color Space

Most cameras default to using the sRGB color space for the image files produced. As discussed in Chapter 2, "Photoshop Setup," the sRGB color space is excellent for monitor display or digital projection, but not ideal for print. You can still get very good results with sRGB, but it isn't as good a choice as Adobe RGB (1998).

My recommendation is to use the same color space in your camera that you use when working on your images in Photoshop. Therefore, if your camera includes your Photoshop RGB Working Space as a color space option, I recommend using that. My color space preference is Adobe RGB (1998), but not all digital cameras offer this option. Review the options provided by your camera to determine the best choice. You may not have any option other than sRGB, or you may have options for color spaces geared toward specific types of photography, such as nature or portraiture.

The color space you set in your camera determines what range of colors will be available in the final image file, and so using a space that matches your working space or output profile as closely as possible will result in the broadest range of colors that will be available in the final output. This helps to maximize output quality by maintaining smooth gradations with no posterization.

Image Controls

Besides the general options that affect how images are captured and stored, most digital cameras also offer a wide range of adjustments you can apply to the image within the camera after capture. These include adjustments for contrast, saturation, sharpness, and other settings.

Although these adjustments will usually result in an image that has better perceived quality, they also cause a loss of detail in the image. My recommendation is to leave all of these settings at their neutral values. The adjustments they apply to your images can easily be reproduced in Photoshop with much greater control while being sure not to lose significant detail in the image. Rather than attempt to mimic the behavior of a particular type of film in the camera, plan to make those adjustments in Photoshop to ensure that the images you capture will be of the highest quality with maximum detail (see Figure 5.6).

Figure 5.6

Even if you aren't a Photoshop expert like Jack Davis, you can still leave many of your adjustments for the photo-editing stage, rather than at the time of capture through camera settings. (Photograph by Jack Davis, www.wowbooks.com.)

Managing Digital Camera Color

Color management for digital photography starts with the original capture. You'll want to make sure you are using the best camera settings to ensure the most accurate color and best image quality. There are several methods you can use to manage the color of your digital captures. They range from simple camera settings, to custom white balance settings, custom camera profiles, and exercising control with RAW capture. Each option has its own benefits and compromises in terms of convenience, color accuracy, and flexibility.

White Balance Presets

Digital cameras allow you to set a specific white balance setting, so that you can tell the camera how to compensate for the lighting conditions. As discussed earlier in this chapter, a digital camera without any compensation simply measures the light from the scene, not taking into account the color of the light source. Changing the white balance preset allows you to determine how the camera will compensate for the lighting conditions. In effect, a white balance setting allows you to select an in-camera compensation that attempts to ensure that a white object will actually appear white, regardless of the color of the light illuminating the scene (see Figure 5.7).

Figure 5.7 A white balance preset allows you to compensate for the lighting in a scene, returning it to a neutral color. The image on the left was illuminated by incandescent lighting, which produces a yellow cast to the scene. Using the tungsten (incandescent) white balance preset, the color in the scene is neutralized in the image on the right.

In many situations, choosing the correct white balance preset to ensure accurate color is easy. When photographing outdoors on a cloudy day, choosing the "cloudy" or equivalent white balance preset on the camera makes sense. When photographing outdoors on that same cloudy day, but with the addition of fill flash, what setting will be best? The answer depends on the specific color of the light, and what the dominant influence of that light will be. This is only one example of a situation where choosing the right preset can be a challenge. Even worse, if you are capturing in JPEG or TIFF mode, that white balance setting will be applied to the image. If it is the wrong setting, the resulting color will be very incorrect, and it may be impossible to achieve a good color adjustment after the fact.

In my experience, most digital cameras do an excellent job of assigning the correct white balance setting when you use the Auto White Balance setting. By using the automatic option, you no longer need to try to figure out what the best setting really is, and you don't have to worry about forgetting to change the white balance setting, causing color problems in subsequent images when the lighting conditions change. Fortunately, the LCD review on the camera can often make it quite clear when the wrong setting was used.

If you prefer to use a specific white balance preset, carefully consider the lighting conditions when deciding which setting to use. If you aren't confident you're using the correct setting, take a few test shots, evaluating the results on the LCD display. There is no substitute for experience here. Many digital cameras also offer a white balance bracketing option, which you may want to take advantage of particularly in situations with mixed lighting or when you otherwise aren't sure what white balance preset will provide the most accurate results.

Also keep in mind that many cameras allow you to slightly fine-tune the white balance presets. For example, you can select a preset and then apply a slight compensation to it to either warm up or cool down the appearance of the final image (see Figure 5.8).

Figure 5.8 Some cameras allow you to apply a slight compensation to the white balance preset in the camera. The image on the left was set to an appropriate white balance preset, and the image on the right was photographed using a compensation to warm the image slightly.

In most situations, you may want to use the Automatic White Balance option, particularly if you are capturing in RAW mode where you can always fine-tune the white balance during the conversion without negatively impacting the quality of the image. However, understanding how the white balance presets work and what other options are available with your camera will help you deal with situations that don't seem to fit into the limited white balance presets available in your camera.

Custom White Balance

When you are photographing under a lighting situation that doesn't seem to fit into one of the white balance presets, a custom white balance option can save the day. This option is particularly helpful for studio photographers who employ a variety of mixed lighting, with different lighting setups for each shoot.

The custom white balance option is offered by many digital cameras, and it works about the same with most of them. Because white balance adjustments are intended to make white look white, so that all other colors also look accurate, the process of creating a custom white balance setting revolves around measuring the light reflected off a white object. Most commonly, you photograph a white piece of paper under the lighting conditions you'll be photographing, and then tell the camera to use that image as the basis of a custom white balance adjustments. You then set the camera to custom white balance, and the images captured will be adjusted based on the measurement you took.

For example, with Canon's EOS 10D digital SLR, the process of creating and using a custom white balance setting is as follows:

1. Select any white balance preset on the camera.

2. Choose an object to photograph that will show the camera the color temperature of the lighting being used. I recommend using a blank sheet of white paper.

Note: When creating a custom white balance setting, the intent is usually to eliminate the color cast produced by the lighting. Sometimes that isn't desirable. In those cases, you may want to select an object to photograph that isn't neutral. For example, products such as WarmCards (www.warmcards.com) provide a "cool" target, resulting in a warmer final image when using the custom white balance created from this target.

3. Photograph the selected object under the lighting you plan to photograph under using a normal exposure with no compensation. You aren't trying to render the paper as white, but rather use it to show the camera what the color of the lighting is.

Note: Remember that creating a custom white balance setting will effectively eliminate the color cast produced by the lighting. We often want to add specific lighting to produce a desirable color cast, but a custom white balance setting will eliminate this cast. If you are adding lighting in order to add a specific color cast (such as a warm glow), leave those lights off when photographing the white object to create your custom white balance setting. Turn the lights back on when you are actually photographing the subject using the custom white balance.

4. Press the Menu button to bring up the menu on the LCD display.

5. Turn the dial to select Custom WB, and press the Set button.

6. The LCD will show the current image on the card. Turn the dial to select the image of the white paper photographed under the current lighting setup and press the Set button (see Figure 5.9).

7. Press Menu to turn off the menu display.

8. Set the camera white balance preset to Custom.

9. You can now take pictures under the same lighting conditions, and the white balance will be compensated based on the custom setting calculated by the camera from your photo of the white object.

10. It is a good idea to do a "reality check" after the first couple pictures, checking them on the LCD display to confirm that the colors appear accurate.

11. Don't forget to return the white balance setting on the camera to Auto or a specific preset when you start photographing under different lighting conditions.

Figure 5.9

When creating a custom white balance setting, you'll need to select the image in the camera that was taken of the white object under the lighting conditions you'll be working with to photograph. Here you can see the image on the LCD of the camera as it is selected to establish the custom white balance setting.

Note: You can save the images you are using as the basis of a custom white balance on a single (low capacity) memory card so that they can be called up at any time under the same settings. Normally, I recommend creating a custom white balance specifically for each photo shoot. However, if you frequently use the same lighting setups for different shoots, this can be helpful.

This is just a single custom white balance workflow example, but it is typical of the method used by most cameras. Read the manual for your camera to learn the specific method for creating a custom white balance.

Custom Camera Profiles

A custom profile for your digital camera can help ensure the most accurate colors possible in your images. The process is actually very similar to creating a custom white balance setting. The difference is that instead of basing the adjustments to be applied to the image on a single color (typically a white sheet of paper), a custom camera profile is based on a series of color patches (see Figure 5.10). This allows the colors captured by the camera to be adjusted in varying ways for different hues and tonal values. This ensures the most accurate final color possible.

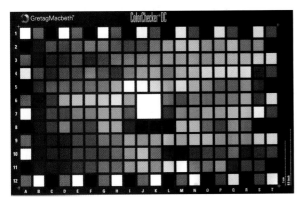

Figure 5.10

Many color samples are considered when building a custom digital camera profile, as this Color-Checker DC target shows. (Courtesy Gretag Macbeth.)

Note: Although the tools available for creating custom digital camera profiles are easy to use and very accurate, I don't recommend using them without a little practice. Before you start an important photo shoot that will utilize a custom profile, create a test profile so that you'll be familiar with the process and confident that you'll be able to create an accurate profile.

However, there is a big catch when it comes to working with digital camera profiles. The fact is that a custom profile isn't the right solution for many photographers or many photographic situations. The problem is a result of the incredible flexibility of a digital camera. Digital cameras are very similar to film scanners when it comes to profiling. Simply record a target and compare the values obtained to the known values for the target, and a profile can then compensate for those differences. The difference is in the lighting. Films scanners use a light source that is very consistent. Digital cameras, on the other hand, operate under a wide variety of different lighting conditions, with the lighting often changing from shot to shot. A custom profile is accurate only when the lighting and camera settings are consistent, making it a less than ideal solution for many photographers. Custom profiles are very accurate if your type of photography allows them, but otherwise you'll have to get by with the other methods discussed earlier in this chapter.

Note: When you consider that a custom digital camera profile uses a target chart that includes gray and white boxes (among other colors), you may be tempted to assume that simply photographing the target and then using the methods discussed in Chapter 6, "Optimization," to make the gray box perfectly neutral will produce the same result as a custom profile. Although it will get you close, a custom profile provides a better solution because it considers a wide range of hues in the calculations, rather than just gray.

Controlled Situations Only

Remember that a custom profile for a digital camera is only accurate if the lighting conditions remain consistent. That means that a custom profile is most helpful when you are in full control of the lighting, as with studio photography. For outdoor photography, camera profiles simply aren't very reliable, because the lighting can change very quickly. Just having a cloud move in front of the sun during a shoot will make your profile less accurate. For photographers who do most of their work outdoors, other options such as using a custom white balance or capturing in RAW mode provide a more practical solution.

Photograph the Target

Regardless of the specific software you use to produce a custom profile for your digital camera, the first step is always the same: photograph the target that is the basis of the profile. This target includes a series of color patches with known color values.

The basic process of photographing the profiling target is as follows:

1. Set the camera to the white balance preset that you think will be most accurate based on the lighting conditions. This will result in a profile that only needs to make minimal adjustments to your image, resulting in an image of higher quality.

2. Photograph the profiling target. Be sure to place the chart in a position where it will be fully illuminated by the lighting, so that the profile will properly compensate for that lighting.

Note: As with creating a custom white balance setting, a custom camera profile eliminates the color cast produced by the lighting. As such, if you are adding lighting to impart a desirable color cast, be sure to turn off that light source when photographing the profiling target. Turn those lights back on after photographing the target.

3. Continue taking pictures of your subject.

Note: You don't need to create the profile immediately after photographing the target. Instead, you can continue to photograph your subject. In fact, if you need to take pictures under different lighting conditions, simply rephotograph the target under those conditions. Then, create a profile for each target image you have photographed, assigning the profile to the series of images captured under the same lighting conditions for each target.

Gretag Macbeth ProfileMaker

When used with the Digital Camera Module, ProfileMaker from Gretag Macbeth (www.gretagmacbeth.com) can be used to build highly accurate custom digital camera profiles. It is available for both Windows and Macintosh, and it sells for about $800. This includes the ProfileMaker software, the ColorChecker DC target chart, and certified readings for that chart. You can get the version without certified readings for about $700, but you will need to use a spectrophotometer to read the target values yourself. Needless to say, I recommend getting the version with certified readings for convenience (and financial savings if you don't have a spectrophotometer for another purpose). The following instructions assume you will be using the certified readings.

If you captured the target in RAW mode, you'll need to convert it to an image file before creating the custom camera profile using the following steps:

1. Convert your RAW capture of the target using the same settings that you will use to convert the final images.

2. Save the converted image in a standard file format. You can save the image in 16-bit per channel mode if you will be converting the actual photos from the shoot the same way.

After the image of the target has been saved, you can create the actual profile by following these steps:

1. Launch ProfileMaker.

2. Select the Camera option.

3. Select the appropriate target from the Reference dropdown. This will be the target that you photographed at the beginning of the photo shoot for the purpose of building a custom profile (see Figure 5.11). For the most accurate profiles, I recommend using the Gretag Macbeth ColorChecker DC chart, which is listed as ColorChecker DC with gray bars.txt.

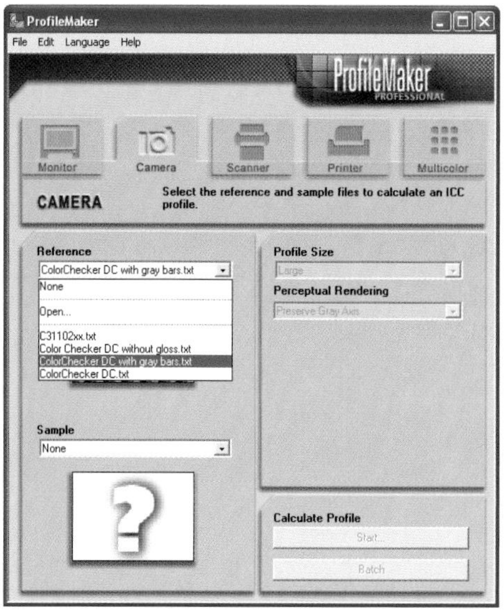

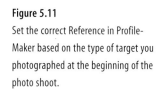

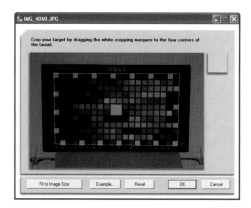

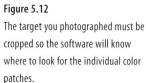

Figure 5.11

Set the correct Reference in Profile-Maker based on the type of target you photographed at the beginning of the photo shoot.

4. Select Open from the Sample dropdown, which will cause the Open dialog box to be displayed.

5. Navigate to the location where you saved the image, select the saved image of the target you photographed at the beginning of your shoot, and then click Open.

6. The target image you selected will open in a dialog box for cropping (see Figure 5.12). Drag each corner of the crop box to the outer edge of the color patches in the target.

Figure 5.12

The target you photographed must be cropped so the software will know where to look for the individual color patches.

7. The Profile Size option can be left to Default for most profiles. If the lighting conditions are likely to require an extreme adjustment to compensate for, you can select the Large option to produce a more accurate profile.

8. Select the desired Perceptual Rendering option. The Preserve Gray Axis is recommended for most situations. This will ensure neutral middle tones. The Paper Gray Axis option will allow all tonal values to be adjusted based on the paper color, which can produce a color cast in the middle tones.

9. Click Start to create the profile, providing a name for it in the Save dialog box. I recommend using a name that references both the camera used and the specific

lighting conditions. If you are a studio photographer, this profile may be useful in the future when using the same lighting conditions. For many photographers, a custom profile may not be useful for future photography, due to variations in the specific lighting conditions.

Note: ProfileMaker also offers a Batch saving mode, which allows you to configure several profiles that need to be built, and then actually build all of them in batch. Considering that it takes very little time to produce the profile, I recommend simply saving the profile directly.

Assigning Custom Profiles

Once you have created a custom digital camera profile for the camera under specific lighting conditions, you can then assign that profile to the images to produce the most accurate color possible.

To assign your custom digital camera profile to an image, use the following steps:

1. Open the image. If the Missing Profile dialog box is displayed, select the option to Assign Profile (see Figure 5.13). Select the appropriate custom profile for your digital camera from the dropdown list. I also recommend that you check the box to convert the image to your working space after assigning the profile. Click OK, and the profile will be assigned to the image. You can then skip the rest of the steps here.

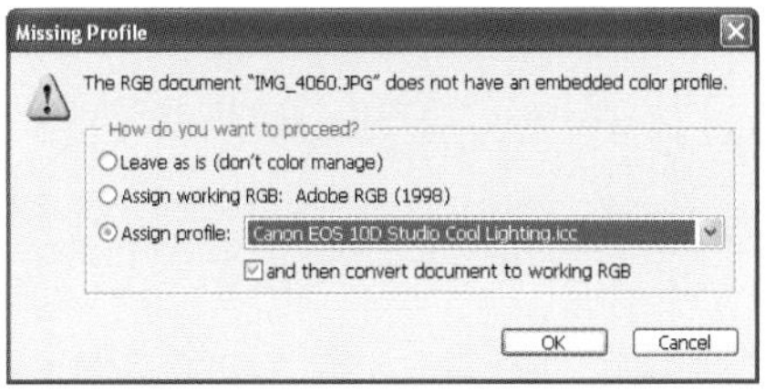

Figure 5.13

If the Missing Profile dialog box is displayed when you open a digital capture for which you have a custom profile, you can assign the appropriate profile immediately.

2. If the Missing Profile dialog box was not displayed, select Image > Mode > Assign Profile from the menu (see Figure 5.14). Note that if the Embedded Profile Mismatch dialog box is displayed, you should select the option to Use The Embedded Profile.

Figure 5.14

The Assign Profile dialog box allows you to select the custom profile that should be used to interpret the colors in your image.

3. Select the Profile option.

4. From the dropdown list of profiles, select the custom digital camera profile you created for the camera under the same lighting conditions used for the images to which you are assigning the profile.

5. Click OK. The colors in the image will now be interpreted based on your custom digital camera profile.

Automating Profile Assignments in Photoshop

Chances are you have captured a series of images that will need to be based on a single digital camera profile. While you will likely need to create a different camera profile for each photo shoot, it can still be a significant workflow benefit to automate the process of assigning a profile to a series of images. You can automate the process by creating an action in Photoshop:

1. Open an image that has been captured but doesn't yet have the custom camera profile assigned to it. Be sure not to assign a profile or convert the image to your working space. If the Missing Profile dialog box is displayed, select the Leave As Is option.

2. Select the Actions palette. If it isn't visible, you can select Window > Actions from the menu.

3. Select the folder on the Actions palette that you would like to use to save your action. You can also create a new folder by clicking the Create New Set button at the bottom of the Actions palette, typing a name in the New Set dialog box, and clicking OK.

4. Click the Create New Action button at the bottom of the Actions palette.

5. Type a name for the action. If you are going to assign a function key to use as a shortcut (which I do not recommend in this situation, because the profile will probably be useful only for a relatively small number of images), you should include that keystroke in the name for the action. For example, you might name the action AssignCameraProfile - F12.

6. If you want to assign a shortcut key to the action (which, again, I recommend against in this case), select it from the Function Key dropdown, and check the boxes for Shift and/or Control (Command on Macintosh) if you would like to include those modifier keys as part of the shortcut.

7. Click Record, and Photoshop will record the steps you take from this point forward until you stop recording.

8. Select Image > Mode > Assign Profile from the menu. Select the Profile option, and then select the custom profile for your scanner from the dropdown list and click OK.

9. Click the Stop button at the bottom of the Actions palette to stop recording the action.

10. Because you probably will be using a different profile for each photo shoot, the specific profile used to record the action won't be the profile you'll use each time. You'll, therefore, probably want to rerecord the action to use the new profile, so that you can run the updated action on the batch of images for which it was created.

Running a Recorded Batch Assignment Action

In the future, you can assign a profile to the image by running the action you have recorded from the Actions palette after opening the image. Even better, you can use the batch processing option to run the action on a folder full of images:

1. Select File > Automate > Batch from the menu.

2. Select the action set that contains the saved action from the Set dropdown.

3. Choose the action from the Action dropdown.

4. Set the source to Folder, click the Choose button, and select the folder that contains the images to which you want to assign the profile. Alternatively, you can choose the File Browser option to apply the profile to the files currently selected in the File Browser.

5. Check the Suppress Color Profile Warnings checkbox so that these alerts won't interrupt the batch processing.

6. Choose a destination option. You can select the Save And Close option if you want to save the files with the same name after assigning the profile. I recommend selecting the Folder option to save the resulting images to a new location, just in case you accidentally use the wrong profile.

7. Check the Override Action 'Save As' Commands checkbox so the batch processing won't be interrupted by the save options dialog box.

8. Click OK and the action will run on the files specified, assigning the profile and saving the image files.

RAW Capture and Conversion

Using a custom white balance setting or even a custom digital camera profile is a great way to ensure very accurate color in your digital photography. Capturing those images in RAW format provides similar benefits, but with a high degree of flexibility. Instead of using a custom adjustment for your images that is relatively fixed, the process of converting your RAW captures to image files allows you to fine-tune your images in terms of both tone and color (see Figure 5.15).

Figure 5.15 Capturing in RAW format allows you to fine-tune the image with great precision, so you can better control the output and produce exactly the image you envisioned at the time of capture.

One of the most significant benefits of RAW capture is the fact that the white balance setting doesn't change the value of the image data. Rather, the white balance setting becomes a default setting for the conversion of your image. You can change the setting during conversion, making the image appear as it would if you had actually captured it using the revised settings, with no penalty in image quality.

Another benefit of RAW capture is that it allows you to preserve high-bit data for your images. This is especially helpful in situations with tricky exposure conditions or when it is critical that you maintain smooth gradations. The more adjustments required to make the final image look perfect, the more benefit a high-bit image will provide. It also provides extended tonal range in the data, providing more latitude for tonal adjustments in the RAW conversion. With the broad support for high-bit files now offered by Adobe Photoshop CS, making the move to RAW capture with a minimal learning curve is easy.

Note: Because you have the ability to fine-tune the white balance during RAW conversion, you can feel totally confident using the Auto White Balance preset when capturing in RAW. In most cases, today's digital cameras do an excellent job of determining an accurate white balance setting. In the event that the automatic setting results in less than accurate color, simply fine-tune during RAW conversion.

RAW capture provides the most flexibility and control for the photographer, allowing you to adjust the appearance of the image with minimal loss of detail. It does require a bit more work, because the images must actually be adjusted in the conversion process, but the payoff is the most accurate color under any lighting conditions and maximum control over the image for the photographer.

Cameras that support a RAW capture mode will also include software for converting those RAW files to a standard image format. These tools vary in the quality of their conversions, the adjustment options available, and the user-friendliness of their interface, but most of them do a very good job.

My preference is to take advantage of the convenience and speed of the Camera Raw plug-in, which is a built-in feature for Photoshop CS. Let's take a look at how you would convert an image with Adobe Camera Raw to achieve the most accurate color and quality in your images.

Adobe Camera Raw

Because Camera Raw is built into Photoshop CS, converting your RAW captures is a simple matter of opening them and setting the conversion options (see Figure 5.16). The File Browser allows you to view thumbnails for your RAW captures, and then open the selected images for conversion.

Figure 5.16

Adobe Camera Raw provides an efficient interface that allows you to quickly adjust all of the options for your RAW conversions.

The following controls are available for you when converting your images with Camera Raw:

The Hand and Zoom tools are available in the top-left corner of the Camera Raw dialog box, and they provide the same functionality as they do in Photoshop. Double-clicking the Hand tool will size the image to fit the window, while double-clicking the Zoom tool will zoom the image to 100 percent scale, so that one pixel in the image is represented by one pixel on the monitor. Both of these zoom settings are helpful for evaluating the color of your image while making adjustments. You can also drag a rectangle selection with the Zoom tool and the selected area will be zoomed to fill the window.

The Histogram provides critical information about the tonal values while adjusting your images (see Figure 5.17). The most important issue is the clipping of highlights or shadows. While making your adjustments, be sure that the histogram chart is not "cut off" at the left (shadows) or right (highlights) ends. If the high dynamic range of the scene you photograph causes a situation where something must be clipped, then I recommend allowing clipping on the shadows rather than highlights. We expect shadow details to be lost to darkness, but blown-out highlights just look wrong.

Figure 5.17

The histogram display in Camera Raw allows you to monitor the effect your adjustments are having on the image, particularly when it comes to the clipping of highlights or shadows.

The histogram in Camera Raw shows you all of the color channels overlaid on top of each other, each in their respective color. White areas are those where all of the color channels overlap. Colored areas show data for that specific color channel only. This allows you to clearly see which color channels are clipping first, before the area of the image shifts to pure black or pure white.

The White Balance controls are the most critical adjustments in Camera Raw from a color management standpoint (see Figure 5.18). They allow you to fine-tune the color appearance of the image by allowing you to adjust the color temperature setting. This is in effect making the image appearance change as though the camera had been set to a different white balance setting at the time of capture. You can select a specific white balance preset from the dropdown list, which is useful if you photographed the image at an incorrect white balance setting.

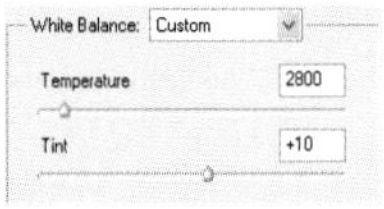

Figure 5.18
The White Balance controls in Camera Raw are the most critical from a color management standpoint.

The Temperature and Tint sliders provide the real strength in this section. The Temperature slider allows you to adjust the white balance of the image by specifying a specific Kelvin color temperature of the lighting under which the image was photographed. Chances are you don't know what the exact color temperature was, but you can use the preview to determine what the best setting is. In addition to being able to neutralize any color cast caused by the lighting conditions, you can also adjust the controls to create a desirable cast in the image. The Tint slider allows you to further refine the adjustment and will cause the colors in the image to shift between green and magenta. I recommend that you start by setting the preset to that which you think is most accurate for the lighting conditions at the time the picture was taken, and then fine-tune the Temperature and Tint sliders to produce the most accurate color.

Note: When photographers who have some knowledge of color temperature use the Temperature slider in Camera Raw, they often think that the scale is backward. This is because a higher Temperature setting results in a "warmer" image, even though a higher temperature equates to what we would call a "cooler" color value. The reason for this apparently incorrect adjustment is that the Temperature slider is changing the temperature under which the photo is assumed to have been taken. Therefore, the colors are compensated in the opposite direction. So, if you set a higher Temperature value, which represents a "cooler" white, the image must be "warmed" up to compensate. A higher Temperature setting causes an image shifted toward red/yellow, and a lower setting causes a shift toward blue/green.

The Tonal and Color adjustments allow you to fine-tune the brightness, contrast, and saturation of the overall image.

- The Exposure control allows you to adjust the overall brightness of the image using an EV (exposure value) scale. For example, a value of –0.5 is the equivalent of an image that is one-half stop darker, while a value of +0.5 is the equivalent of an image that is one-half stop brighter. By holding the Alt key (Option on Macintosh) you'll get a highlight clipping preview (see Figure 5.19). The preview image will go black. As you increase the Exposure value, you'll start to see primary colors and white. The primary colors indicate a loss of detail on that particular channel, while white means those pixels will be clipped to pure white.
- The Shadows slider is similar to adjusting the black point in Levels. You can view a clipping preview of black by holding Alt (Option on Macintosh),

showing which areas are losing detail as you increase the Shadows value (see Figure 5.20).

- The Brightness slider is similar to using the middle-tone slider in Levels. It will adjust the overall brightness of the image without clipping highlights or shadows.

- The Contrast slider allows you to adjust the contrast of the middle tones in your image. I recommend leaving it at a neutral value and adjusting contrast in Photoshop.

- Likewise, I recommend that you leave the Saturation slider at its neutral value, making your saturation adjustments via an adjustment layer in Photoshop.

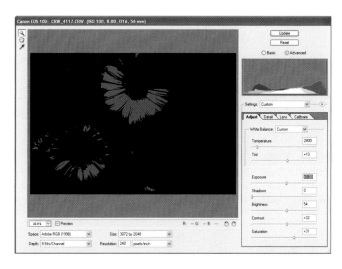

Figure 5.19

The clipping preview for the Exposure control in Camera Raw allows you to see when you are shifting pixels to pure white.

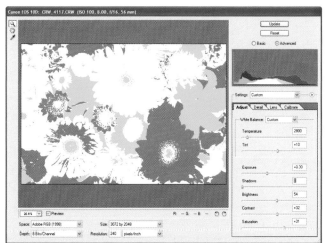

Figure 5.20

The clipping preview for the Shadows control in Camera Raw allows you to see when you are shifting pixels to pure black.

The Detail settings provide sharpening and noise reduction options for your conversion. In my experience, the default value of 25 for Sharpness is too aggressive and can create problems in your image. I prefer to use Photoshop's Unsharp Mask filter for sharpening because it offers much more control, and I strongly recommend leaving the Sharpness setting to 0 for all RAW conversions. The Luminance Smoothing and Color Noise Reduction controls allow you to resolve noise problems in the image, which is a problem for digital captures at high ISO settings or with long exposures. Luminance Smoothing affects noise exhibited as tonal variations. Color Noise Reduction helps to resolve noise exhibited as color variations at the pixel level, and it can also be used to help minimize moiré patterns.

The Output settings affect the configuration of the image file once it is converted by Camera Raw (see Figure 5.21). These settings are primarily for your own convenience. The Space option allows you to convert the image to a specific color space. I recommend setting this to the same color space that you are using for your RGB Working Space, for which I recommend using Adobe RGB (1998) as outlined in Chapter 2. The Depth option allows you to change the bit-depth of the final image. Particularly if you are using Photoshop CS, which offers broad support for 16-bit per channel images, I recommend using the 16-bit option. Size allows you to interpolate the image to a larger output size during the RAW conversion. Although this theoretically produces better quality than waiting to interpolate in Photoshop, I have seen some situations where it actually results in lower quality. I recommend testing this option if you plan to take advantage of interpolation in the conversion. Finally, the Resolution setting allows you to specify the output resolution that the image will be set to after conversion. Note that this will not affect the number of pixels in the image, but only the resolution the file is set to as a convenience.

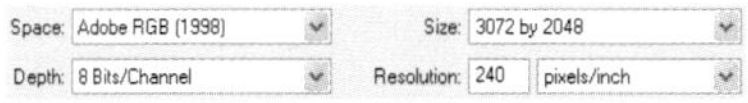

| Space: | Adobe RGB (1998) | ∨ | Size: | 3072 by 2048 | ∨ |
| Depth: | 8 Bits/Channel | ∨ | Resolution: | 240 | pixels/inch | ∨ |

Figure 5.21 The Output settings in Camera Raw allow you to set attributes of the final file.

The Lens settings (which are only available if you have checked the Advanced radio button) allow you to correct problems in the image caused by the camera lens. These settings include sliders to resolve certain forms of chromatic aberration (color fringing, especially along high-contrast edges in the image) and vignetting. If an image exhibits strong color fringing, adjust the R/C (red/cyan) or B/Y (blue/yellow) sliders to offset the colors. For vignetting, you can fine-tune the size and degree of lightening around the edges of your image, allowing you to eliminate vignetting in the image. Of course, you can also darken the corners to create a vignette effect where there isn't one.

The Calibrate settings (also only available if you have checked the Advanced radio button) allow you to effectively fine-tune the camera profiles that Camera Raw uses to interpret the color in your digital captures (see Figure 5.22). If you feel that the profile Camera Raw is using for your camera model is incorrect, you can use these settings to make adjustments to resolve this issue. The Shadow Tint control allows you to make adjustments to the color in shadow areas of your images. Because of lighting variations, the darker areas of your image will tend to have a slight color shift, and this setting allows you to modify that shift. Controls are also provided to adjust the hue and saturation of each of the primary colors (red, green, and blue) used to create your image. The hue adjustments allow you to change the actual color of those primaries, shifting red slightly more toward magenta, for example. The saturation adjustment allows you to modify the purity of each primary color.

Figure 5.22
If you feel that Camera Raw isn't doing an accurate job of interpreting the colors in your images, you can adjust the Calibrate settings to effectively fine-tune the profile Camera Raw is using for that particular model of camera.

Note: If you make changes to the settings on the Calibrate tab in Camera Raw, save the settings, and choose the Set Camera Default option from the side menu. The settings will be used whenever you convert images captured with the same camera model. It is important that you carefully test the settings to be sure they are producing the most accurate color possible.

When you have made the appropriate adjustments to your RAW image, clicking OK will cause the image to be converted and opened. You can also save the settings so they can be applied to future images. You can also set the saved settings as the default for the specific camera used for all future conversions. Doing so will cause the saved settings to be used as the defaults whenever you open an image captured with the same camera model using Camera Raw.

Camera Raw Batch Processing

To convert a group of RAW captures photographed under the same lighting conditions, you can batch process them through the File Browser. You'll want to establish your conversion settings by opening one of the images, making adjustments in the Camera Raw dialog box, and converting that image. Then select the files you want to convert with the same settings in the File Browser. Select Automate > Apply Camera Raw Settings from the menu in the File Browser, and select the Previous Conversion option in the dialog box that appears. This will apply the conversion settings from the first image. If you now hold the Shift key while choosing File > Open from the menu in the File Browser, all of the selected images will be opened and converted. By holding the Shift key when choosing the Open option, the Camera Raw dialog box will not be displayed.

PhaseOne Capture One DSLR

While I prefer the built-in convenience and speed of Adobe Camera Raw, Capture One DSLR from PhaseOne (www.phaseone.com) offers an excellent workflow-oriented solution for your RAW conversions, and it produces converted images of excellent quality (see Figure 5.23). In fact, in most cases I find that Capture One DSLR produces sharper images that have more detail and less noise than those converted by Adobe Camera Raw. Capture One DSLR is available for both Windows and Macintosh for under $600 (a feature-limited version is also available for Windows for under $100), and it currently supports most Canon and Nikon digital SLR cameras.

Figure 5.23
Capture One DSLR provides a workflow-oriented solution for RAW conversions that produces results of excellent quality.

Capture One DSLR revolves around a file browser that allows you to select the images to be converted. It then provides the following controls that allow you to fine-tune the image conversion:

The **Capture tab** provides information about the original capture data, including a histogram display and capture settings (see Figure 5.24).

The **Gray Balance tab** allows you to adjust the color balance of the image, including white balance (see Figure 5.25). Several controls are provided that allow you to make these adjustments, including a white balance temperature adjustment, a color wheel control that allows you to set a specific neutral point to determine color balance, as well as hue and saturation controls to fine-tune the color appearance. I recommend starting with the white balance adjustment, and then fine-tune with the visual reference of the color wheel.

The **Exposure tab** includes adjustments for Levels and Curves that provide excellent control over tonal adjustments to your image for conversion (see Figure 5.26). They behave in much the same manner as the controls by the same names in Photoshop.

The **Focus tab** includes excellent control for applying some sharpening to the image (see Figure 5.27). Unlike the limited control offered by Adobe Camera Raw, the control provided in Capture One DSLR allows you to exercise great control over the sharpening settings. Therefore, I do recommend that you take advantage of these controls to produce the best converted image possible. A small amount of sharpening in the conversion will help to compensate for the loss of sharpness that occurs in the process of converting analog wavelengths of light into digital signals.

The Develop tab is the final step in the process of converting your RAW captures. It allows you to configure final output settings, and then add an image to the queue for conversion (see Figure 5.28). Because Capture One DSLR uses background processing of your RAW captures, you can configure a series of images for conversion without any break in your workflow.

Figure 5.24

The Capture tab in Capture One DSLR provides information about the original capture.

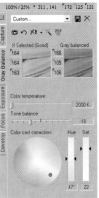

Figure 5.25

The Gray Balance tab provides controls for adjusting the white balance, color balance, and saturation of the image.

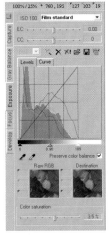

Figure 5.26

The Exposure tab provides adjustments for brightness and contrast with Levels and Curves controls.

Figure 5.27

Capture One DSLR provides excellent control over sharpening applied to the image.

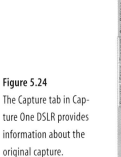

Figure 5.28

The Develop tab in Capture One DSLR allows you to set the final output settings, and then process the adjusted RAW images in batch.

Accurate Conversions

Regardless of the method you use to convert your RAW captures, the key consideration is the accuracy of colors in the converted image. Pay careful attention to the preview image while adjusting the white balance settings in the conversion software to use to produce the most accurate image possible, and then fine-tune the results in your photo-editing software.

Working Space Issues

When you bring your digital captures into Photoshop, you may need to deal with a profile mismatch, or even a missing profile. How you deal with those images depends on whether they are tagged with a profile or not.

Tagged Images

When you take a picture with a digital camera, in most cases the image file will be tagged with a specific profile that tells Photoshop how the colors need to be interpreted. This is certainly the preferred approach. If you set a specific working space in your camera, such as Adobe RGB (1998), then the image should be tagged with that profile. If have used a profile that differs from your RGB working space, you will probably want to convert the image to the working space.

If you configured your Color Settings to alert you when there is a profile mismatch (which I recommend doing, as discussed in Chapter 2), the Embedded Profile Mismatch dialog box will be displayed when you open the image (see Figure 5.29). With digital captures, my recommendation is to select the Convert Document's Colors To Working Space option, so that the image will be converted to your current working space.

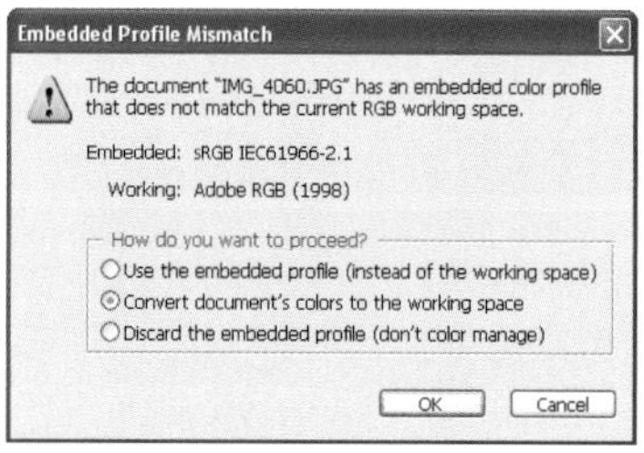

Figure 5.29
If your digital captures are tagged with a profile that doesn't match your RGB Working Space, you can use the Embedded Profile Mismatch dialog box to convert the image to your working space.

Untagged Images

In some cases, your digital camera may not tag the image with a profile. When this is the case, Photoshop doesn't know how to interpret the colors in the image, so you need to tell it. This is done by assigning a profile to the image that defines how the colors should be interpreted.

If you have configured your Color Settings to alert you when an image doesn't have an embedded profile (which I recommend doing, as discussed in Chapter 2), the Missing Profile dialog box will be displayed (see Figure 5.30). However, chances are you don't know exactly what profile should be used to interpret the colors in the image. Therefore, I recommend that you select the Leave As Is option and click OK. The image will be opened, initially interpreting the colors based on your current RGB Working Space.

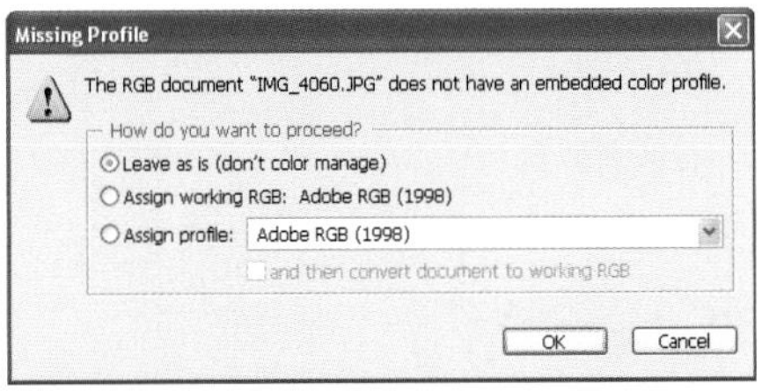

Figure 5.30

If your digital captures aren't tagged with a profile, the Missing Profile dialog box will be displayed if your Color Settings are set appropriately. Select the Leave As Is option.

To assign a specific profile that will determine what the color values in the image really mean, select Image > Mode > Assign Profile (see Figure 5.31). Be sure the Preview checkbox is checked, and select the Profile option. Click the dropdown list, and select an appropriate profile. Based on the way most digital cameras record color, I recommend that you first try the Adobe RGB (1998) and sRGB color space profiles. If they don't seem to provide the most accurate colors, check to see if there are profiles on the list for your camera model, which may have been included with your camera software. Naturally, if you have built a custom profile, as covered earlier in this chapter, that may be an ideal candidate as well. If none of these provide the most accurate color to your eye, you may want to cycle through all available profiles to see if you can find a good match.

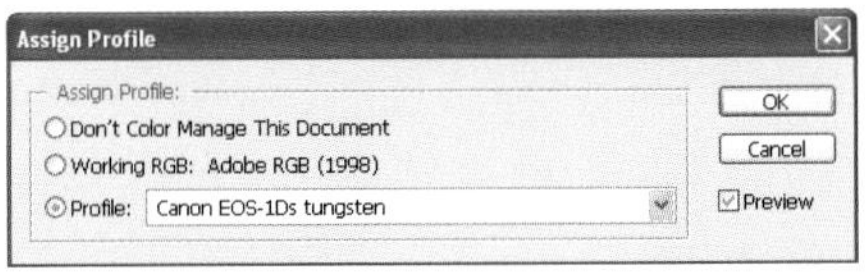

Figure 5.31

The Assign Profile dialog box allows you to select which profile will be used to interpret the colors in your digital captures.

Note: When assigning a profile to your image, you'll find that cycling through them is much easier if you use the arrow keys on your keyboard. Click the dropdown list of profiles, and scroll to the top and select the first profile on the list. Then use the down-arrow key on the keyboard to cycle through the profiles one at a time. You can use the up-arrow to move back up the list.

Optimization

Color correction is not the same as color management, but one without the other is far less valuable. Color management revolves around producing an accurate depiction of your image data, so you'll want to be sure that the image data actually contains the colors you are seeking. This chapter will help you ensure the best color in your images.

Chapter Contents
Evaluating Images
Making Color Adjustments
Color-Adjusting Black-and-White Images
Saving the File

Evaluating Images

If you skipped earlier chapters in order to learn about the best Photoshop techniques to optimize your image, you may want to go read some of those chapters before reading this one. Working with your images demands that you see an accurate depiction of the image on your monitor. For that, make sure you have calibrated and profiled your monitor, as detailed in Chapter 3, "Display." Also, before you take a renewed look at your images, you should consider the color settings you are using in Photoshop, which are covered in Chapter 2, "Photoshop Setup."

Part of getting the best results in your color-managed workflow is looking at your images with a critical eye. For photographers, the most important consideration is the final print. Careful evaluation of the image on your monitor before you print it will help ensure that the print is everything you intend it to be. When the image looks perfect on your monitor, you can be confident it is ready for printing (see Figure 6.1).

Figure 6.1

When photographer Alice Cahill is working on her images in Photoshop, getting the color just right is critical. With this image, maintaining the proper mood requires that the color be adjusted to maintain warm tones that aren't too vibrant. The result is an image that offers a glimpse of a different time with colors that add to the emotion being presented. (Photograph by Alice Cahill, www.alicecahill.com.)

Although many factors influence the quality of an image, the focus for this book is accurate color. Therefore, I'll take a look at some of the issues to watch out for, as well as ways to solve many of the most common color problems.

Memory Colors

The "best" color in your images can be very subjective. Fortunately, as the photographer and artist, you have a certain amount of creative license with your images. You get to decide what the image should look like. This is based in large part on your recollection of what the scene before the lens looked like when you pressed the shutter release button. However, it is also based on how you want to interpret the image. Many times, "memory colors" get in the way of this freedom.

You could be a lot sloppier with your color corrections if it weren't for memory colors. These colors are the ones with which most people, through the normal course of their life experience, are familiar. For example, most people know what a banana looks like. We know the green of an unripe banana, the yellow of a well-ripened banana, and the brown of an overripe banana. If you don't get the color pretty close to accurate, the viewer may notice (see Figure 6.2).

Figure 6.2 If you don't adjust an image properly that contains "memory colors," the viewer may recognize that something isn't quite right with the image. (© CORBIS)

Often, when colors aren't quite right, the viewer might not know what is wrong with the image. They'll just know that the color isn't quite right. This is not the sort of reaction we want viewers to have when looking at our images.

Most images contain some form of memory color, and you need to be careful to maintain those colors accurately. While evaluating your image both before and during the optimization process, be sure to consider whether the viewer will "believe" the colors in your image.

Saturation Testing

One of the methods I like to use when evaluating an image is to boost the saturation to its maximum value temporarily. Doing so will maximize the purity of the colors in your image, so that all colors are effectively saturated to the pure additive and subtractive primary colors (red/green/blue and cyan/magenta/yellow, respectively). This will naturally destroy the detail in your image and make it look a bit odd, but it is an excellent evaluation tool. You are able to see what colors are lurking in areas you didn't expect, and determine the prominent color in each area of your image. This helps you make a decision about what adjustments may be necessary to achieve the most accurate colors.

To use this method, create a new Hue/Saturation adjustment layer by clicking the New Adjustment Layer button at the bottom of the Layers palette and selecting Hue/Saturation from the popup menu. (Adjustment layers can also be made by selecting Layer > New Adjustment Layer from the menu and then selecting the type of adjustment layer you want to create. However, this will cause a dialog box to display, allowing you to change attributes of the adjustment layer that should normally be left to their defaults. Therefore, I find it much more convenient to create adjustment layers from the Layer palette.)

The new adjustment layer will appear on the Layers palette, and the dialog box for the adjustment layer (in this case Hue/Saturation) will be displayed.

Note: Adjustment layers affect all image layers below them. If you have multiple image layers, be sure the new adjustment layer is placed above all of them, unless you don't want the adjustment layer to apply to certain images. When you create a new adjustment layer, it is placed above the currently active layer. Therefore, to position an adjustment layer at the top of the stack of layers on the Layers palette, click the top-most layer before clicking the New Adjustment Layer button.

Increase the Saturation setting to its maximum value of +100, leaving the Hue and Lightness sliders at their default value of 0. Now take a close look at your image and consider what colors are present (see Figure 6.3). Are they the colors you expected? The colors will obviously look different when they are shifted to maximum saturation, but are the hues correct? For example, does the sky go slightly pink rather than becoming a pure blue or cyan? Make a mental note of colors you didn't expect, or areas of the image that don't seem to have the right color. These can be corrected with the methods presented through the rest of this chapter.

Once you have evaluated your image at full saturation, you can click the Cancel button to close the dialog box and remove the adjustment layer from the Layers palette. However, you might want to keep it there for future evaluation. Particularly when working on an image that seems to present some color challenges, I'll keep this adjustment layer, but turn off the visibility of it by clicking the "eyeball" icon to the left of the adjustment layer thumbnail on the Layers palette. I can then continue working on the image without seeing the extreme saturation, but I can reevaluate the color with this technique at any time by turning the visibility of that adjustment layer back on. For example, if I had a sky that went slightly pink with the first full-saturation review, I could turn on the Hue/Saturation adjustment layer after making some corrections to see if the offending color is really gone.

Figure 6.3
Increasing the saturation of your image to the maximum value will provide you with a clear indication of what colors are present in the image, and where. This is a great way to see what areas contain colors they shouldn't.

The Magenta Problem

If there is going to be a color problem in your image, it will most likely be magenta. This is caused by a couple of factors.

For one thing, magenta is composed of light at the very small wavelength end of the visible spectrum. It is, therefore, a color that our eyes have a very difficult time seeing well. Without a neutral image to compare, many people would not notice if an image had a slight magenta cast (which is not to say you should ignore a magenta cast).

The other issue is that magenta is a common result of atmospheric scattering of light from haze or other particulate matter in the air. You may have seen an expansive landscape photograph that appears to have completely accurate color, but the distant haze has a bit of a magenta tint.

Combined, these factors cause magenta to be a common issue in the digital darkroom, so it is worthwhile to keep it in mind, particularly with landscape photography, or with any image that includes a partly cloudy sky. Using the saturation testing method can help locate an unwanted magenta cast so you can correct it.

Making Color Adjustments

There are many methods that can be used to produce the perfect image in Photoshop CS. This book isn't intended to show you every possible method for optimizing your images in Photoshop. However, it is all about getting accurate color, and a major factor in getting the best color results in your image is being able to properly adjust the image in Photoshop. In this section, I will present a number of ways to adjust your image to ensure the accurate colors you are trying to achieve. For more techniques for making the most of your images, take a look at *The Hidden Power of Photoshop CS* by Richard Lynch (Sybex, 2004).

Note: Knowing the relationships between colors will help you better understand the color adjustments you apply to your images. Be sure you understand the color concepts presented in Chapter 1, "Foundations," before proceeding with the adjustments presented in this chapter.

Color Balance

The Color Balance control is the basic adjustment for correcting inaccurate color in your images. It allows you to shift the color value of all pixels in the image toward or away from any of the primary colors. The Color Balance dialog box provides sliders for each axis representing complementary primary colors so you can shift the values of all pixels in your image between those colors: red versus cyan, green versus magenta, and blue versus yellow (see Figure 6.4).

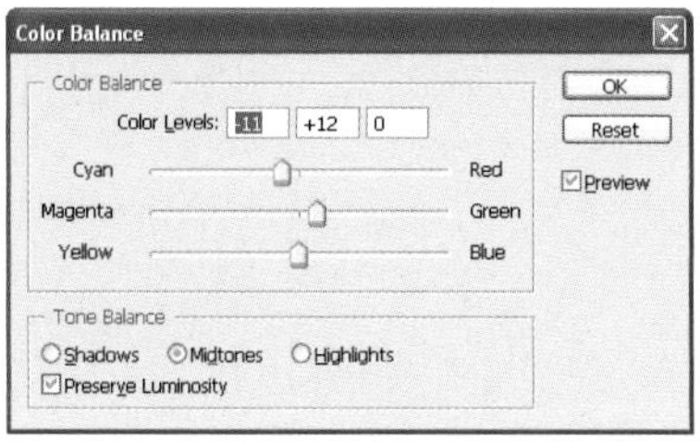

Figure 6.4 The Color Balance dialog box allows you to adjust the colors in the image by shifting them along each axis representing the primary colors.

The Tone Balance section allows you to determine which pixel ranges will be affected by the color balance adjustments. The Midtones option is the default, and it will affect most of the pixels in your image, excluding only the brightest and darkest values. You can select the Shadows or Highlights option to fine-tune the color in the darkest or lightest areas of the image, respectively. For most images, simply adjusting the Midtones will provide adequate control. I also recommend that you keep the Preserve Luminosity checkbox checked. This will cause the values for each color channel to be adjusted slightly to maintain the same perceived brightness for the pixels after making the adjustment.

When taking pictures, particularly of macro subjects, you may find that at times you have a difficult time determining if you have your focus set properly. Making minor changes in the focus setting on your lens doesn't seem to produce any difference. In that situation, it is very helpful to throw the image completely out of focus and then bring it back into focus. The perspective between the out-of-focus and in-focus image makes it easier to evaluate the sharpness of the image through the viewfinder.

Similarly, with color balance adjustments, deciding when you have achieved proper color can be challenging. As with focus evaluation, using extremes to provide perspective can be very helpful. When you are having a difficult time deciding what adjustments are required, try sliding the adjustments to extremes to get a better idea of what direction you want to take the color in the image (see Figure 6.5). In fact, making extreme adjustments to the color balance sliders can be a helpful way to learn to recognize color issues in your image and to learn how shifting the color balance on each axis will affect various colors.

Figure 6.5 Extreme adjustments with the Color Balance control can help you get a better idea of where the balance should be adjusted. The left image is shifted too far toward green, the middle image is shifted too far toward magenta, and the right image represents an accurate color balance.

With three sliders in the Color Balance dialog box, you may wonder where to start. Many photographers simply start at the top and work their way down. My recommendation is to start with the slider that represents the biggest color problem in your image. If there is a strong color cast in the image, use the slider that includes that color cast. For example, if you have a magenta cast in the image, you would want to start with the Magenta/Green slider. Solve your biggest problem first, and then move on to the other sliders.

> **Note:** Once you have eliminated the unwanted color cast in the image, you may be tempted to click OK on the Color Balance dialog box and move on to the other adjustments. However, I recommend that you adjust all three sliders. Besides eliminating an undesirable color cast in the image, you may actually want to introduce a desirable color cast. In fact, I recommend that you adjust all three sliders at least twice. Use the first adjustment of each slider to correct the color as accurately as possible, and then go through each again to fine-tune the color and get it perfect.

Many photographers—especially those who have worked in a color wet darkroom—think that color balance adjustments should be made by adjusting only two of the three sliders. Although it is certainly possible to achieve any adjustment with two sliders rather than all three, most people find it much easier to work with all three sliders. They can fine-tune the color based on the colors they're seeing, without figuring out how to adjust two sliders to achieve the same adjustment that you would obtain by adjusting the third. I recommend making the color balance adjustments easier on yourself by feeling free to adjust all three sliders as you see fit when optimizing the image.

Color Balance with Levels

The Levels adjustment layer is perceived as strictly a tool for tonal adjustments on your image. However, it can also be used to affect color balance adjustments if you select the individual color channels in your image.

To adjust color balance in Levels, select each color channel in turn from the Channel dropdown list. Then adjust the midtone slider to shift the color balance (see Figure 6.6). For example, if you select the Green channel, the midtone slider will shift the color balance between green (by sliding left) and magenta (by sliding right). Of course, because only the primary colors defined by the color mode of the image are displayed, you need to remember which colors are opposite each other on the color wheel.

Figure 6.6
The Levels adjustment can be used to shift color balance by sliding the midtone slider for each of the individual color channels.

While most of your color balance adjustment in levels would be achieved by using the midtone sliders, you can also use the black and white sliders to adjust the color in the highlights and shadows of your image so they don't have any color cast. This is much less important than the midtone sliders, because it can be difficult to see a color cast in those extreme tonal values.

Although you can adjust the black and white point sliders on each of the color channels while looking closely at the shadow or highlight areas of the image, it is often much easier to simply use the black and white eyedropper tools within the Levels dialog box. First, select one of the eyedroppers, and then click the pixel in the image that should have the color value represented by that eyedropper. For example, with the black eyedropper, when you click a pixel in the image, the image will be adjusted so that pixel becomes black. This is achieved by an automatic adjustment of the black points in each of the color channels in the image. You can also modify the value to which the pixel you click on will be shifted. Simply double-click the appropriate eyedropper to display the Color Picker, and select the desired color. For color adjustments, you will obviously want to choose a color that has equal values for red, green, and blue. However, you may want to set a shade of black that is lighter than pure black.

You can find the lightest or darkest pixels in your image by holding the Alt key (Option key on Macintosh) and moving the black or white slider on the histogram inward (see Figure 6.7). This will provide the clipping preview, showing which areas are losing detail. The first pixels to appear are the brightest or darkest in your image (depending on whether you are moving the white or black slider), and show you the area you would want to click on with the white or black eyedropper to set a perfectly neutral highlight or shadow in the image.

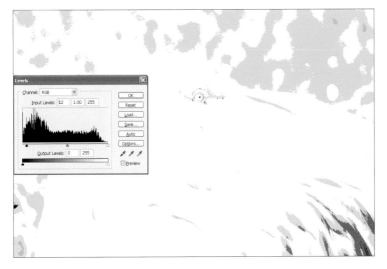

Figure 6.7
You can use the clipping preview in Levels to determine where the brightest (white point slider) and darkest (black point slider) pixels are in the image.

You can also adjust the color balance of the image to produce a perfectly neutral gray automatically by using the middle tone (gray) eyedropper. This will cause the color balance in the image to be adjusted automatically to make the pixel you click on perfectly neutral, with matching values for all three color channels. This can be an effective way to quickly set the color balance in your image if you can find a pixel that should be perfectly neutral (see Figure 6.8). However, this often turns into a game of clicking all over the areas of the image you think should be neutral to find the best place to click. I prefer to use other methods to ensure that gray objects really show up as gray, as discussed later in this chapter.

Figure 6.8 The gray eyedropper in Levels can be used to quickly establish an accurate color balance by clicking an object in the image that should really be neutral. The image on the left doesn't have an accurate color balance. After clicking on a pixel that should be gray with the gray eyedropper in Levels, the image is adjusted to produce the version on the right.

Color Balance with Curves

For maximum control of your color balance adjustments, master the Curves control. Instead of adjusting color balance for highlights, midtones, and shadows, the Curves control allows you to adjust color balance at any tonal value within the image. Like the Levels control, Curves is often considered a tool for tonal adjustments. But like Levels, you can adjust color in the image by adjusting the curve for each of the individual color channels.

For a basic color balance adjustment in Curves, you can simply click on a point around the middle of the curve on a particular channel, which will create an anchor point. Drag this anchor point up or down to adjust the color balance in the image. This is effectively the same adjustment as manipulating one of the sliders in the Color Balance dialog box.

Note: The Curves dialog box includes the same black, gray, and white eyedroppers found in the Levels dialog box, and they produce the same result, so you can also put them to use in the Curves dialog box if you prefer.

It is important to keep in mind that less is more when it comes to making adjustments with Curves. It doesn't take a very significant movement to make a big change in the image. Once you have adjusted an anchor point with the mouse, it will be selected and you can fine-tune the position of that anchor point with the arrow keys on your keyboard.

Of course, if you were only going to use a single anchor point for each channel in Curves, there wouldn't be much point using it instead of Color Balance. Using more anchor points allows you to exercise tremendous control over the color in your images. Instead, you can create an anchor point at any tonal value for each color channel, so you can fine-tune the color balance for pixels at all brightness levels in the image independently.

When you determine an area of the image that needs a color balance adjustment, first select the channel from the Channel dropdown that requires adjustment. You can then click and drag your mouse over the area of the image that needs adjustment, and a "bouncing ball" will show what area on the curve represents the values under your mouse (see Figure 6.9). Even better, you can hold the Ctrl key (Command key on Macintosh) while you drag the mouse over the image, and when you release the mouse button an anchor point will be placed on the curve in the position represented by the pixel under your mouse. You can then click and drag that anchor point (or use the arrow keys on the keyboard) to shift the color balance in that area of the image (see Figure 6.10).

Figure 6.9

When you click and drag over your image with the Curves dialog box active, a "ball" will show you where on the curve the pixel under the mouse falls.

Figure 6.10

The Curves adjustment allows you to fine-tune the color balance in specific tonal ranges within the image.

Adjusting one point on a curve will cause the rest of the curve to shift slightly, which means you may adjust colors in areas of the image you don't want to adjust. In this situation, you can create another anchor point on the curve and bring it close to the other anchor point to help "normalize" the rest of the curve (see Figure 6.11).

Figure 6.11
Adjusting an anchor point on the curve may cause shifts on the rest of the curve that you don't want. You can create an additional anchor point to "normalize" the curve in that area.

Neutral by the Numbers

With many images, you can achieve accurate color balance simply by making sure than the pixels that should be neutral really are. Neutral is defined as having no color cast. When we're talking about color numbers in an RGB image, neutral means all three color values for the gray pixels are the same.

As discussed earlier in this chapter, you can use the midtone (gray) eyedropper in the Levels or Curves dialog box to adjust the image to make a particular pixel value neutral. However, this often doesn't provide the maximum amount of control, and can make it difficult to select just the right pixel to achieve the best color balance. Instead, I recommend using Color Samplers so that you can take full control over the adjustment while monitoring the pixel values for the areas you think should be perfectly neutral.

Targeting a Neutral Value

The key to adjusting your image to produce a truly neutral area is to be able to monitor the value of pixels that should be neutral. The Info palette allows you to check the value of any pixel in your image simply by holding your mouse over that pixel. However, when making adjustments, you want to be able to monitor pixel values without the need to hold your mouse over those pixels. This is the job of the Color Sampler tool.

The Color Sampler tool is found on the Tool palette under the Eyedropper tool (see Figure 6.12). Click and hold your mouse on the Eyedropper tool to access the fly-out menu, and then choose the Color Sampler tool. You can also press Shift+I to cycle through the Eyedropper, Color Sampler, and Measure tools. Then, make sure the Info palette is visible and select Window > Info if it isn't.

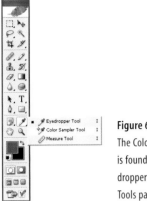

Figure 6.12

The Color Sampler tool is found under the Eyedropper tool on the Tools palette.

With the Color Sampler tool active, you can set the Sample Size option on the Options bar. The Point Sample option will cause the Color Sampler to measure only a single pixel. I don't recommend using this option because it is possible to select a pixel that is randomly different from surrounding pixels, such as film grain, digital noise, or a dust spot. Instead, I recommend using either 3 By 3 Average (which will average a total of nine pixels including the pixel you click) or 5 By 5 Average (which will average a total of fifteen pixels). My preference is the 3 By 3 option, but either will work well for most images (see Figure 6.13).

Figure 6.13 I recommend using the 3 By 3 Average setting on the Options bar for the Color Sampler tool.

To place a sampler, simply click on an area of the image that you think should be neutral. This will place a Color Sampler target icon on the image, and it will also place a new section in the Info palette that shows you the values of the pixels under the Color Sampler points. You can have up to four Color Samplers on the Info palette. While you can certainly find a neutral value with a single Color Sampler, it is often helpful to place more than one so that you can monitor several areas of your image and make a decision about which one should *really* be neutral.

When you have an adjustment dialog box open, two values are shown for each number for the Color Samplers on the Info palette. This shows you the "before" and "after" values for the pixels. The numbers on the left are the values before the adjustment, and the numbers on the right are the values based on the adjustment you are making. This allows you to monitor the values of the pixels while making your adjustment. When all three values on the right for a given Color Sampler are equal, you have achieved a neutral value for those pixels.

To get the values equal, you'll need to adjust the color balance of your image. You can use a Color Balance adjustment, but in order to be able to adjust each channel independently, you'll need to uncheck the Preserve Luminosity checkbox. You can also use the Levels adjustment by adjusting the midtone slider for each color channel, or you can use the Curves adjustment by adjusting an anchor point around the middle of the curve. I recommend using a separate adjustment layer for this specific adjustment, rather than using an adjustment layer that you will use to fine-tune other aspects of the image.

Note: Besides making adjustments with a Color Balance, Levels, or Curves adjustment layer to achieve a neutral value for a particular Color Sampler, you can also use the middle tone (gray) eyedropper in the Levels or Curves dialog box. Simply click on the middle tone eyedropper, then click directly on the center of a Color Sampler on the image, and the image will be adjusted to make that area neutral.

If you created more than one Color Sampler, you can adjust the image to neutralize each of them in turn, making an evaluation of the overall image to decide which of them represents an area that should be truly neutral (see Figure 6.14).

Figure 6.14 While making adjustments to the color balance of the image, you can monitor the Color Sampler values on the Info palette (left). The numbers on the left are the "before" values for the sampler, and the numbers on the right are the "after" values. When all three after values are equal, the pixel under the Color Sampler is neutral (right). (Photograph by Jon Canfield, www.joncanfield.com.)

Once you are finished making your adjustments, you may want to remove the Color Samplers. I actually recommend simply hiding them so they aren't visible; that way you can refer to them again if needed for future adjustments. To hide the Color Samplers, you can select View > Extras from the menu, or press Ctrl+H (Command+H on Macintosh). If you want to delete a Color Sampler, first select the Color Sampler tool from the Tool palette. Then hold the Alt key (Option key on Macintosh) and move the mouse over the Color Sampler you want to delete. The mouse pointer will turn into a scissors icon, and when you click the Color Sampler will be deleted.

When Gray Isn't

Just because something *is* gray doesn't mean it actually *should* be gray in your image. For example, I've often heard the suggestion to place an 18 percent gray card in a corner of the image so you can use it as the basis of your color adjustments and then crop it out. The problem is that in many cases a gray object shouldn't actually appear gray in the final image.

Nature photographers are notorious for taking a midday break for a nap. Of course, the truth behind this notion is that they want to take advantage of the warm glow of early morning and late afternoon light. They choose these times to photograph to intentionally capture images with a desirable color cast. If you were to place a gray card in the scene, and then make that card appear gray when adjusting the image, you would neutralize a desired color cast in the image.

Of course, most photographers don't place a gray card in the scene anyway. If you used a Color Sampler to achieve a perfectly neutral gray in the image, you would have to select something in the scene that was naturally neutral. Depending on the lighting conditions, it is very possible that you wouldn't want to actually make this area of the image neutral, as it would flatten the color in the overall image.

However, in such a situation you could still use a Color Sampler as the basis of your adjustment, finding a neutral value to target, but then shifting the balance to produce the desired color cast in the image.

Targeting and Fine-Tuning

When it turns out that the area of the image you think should be gray actually shouldn't be perfectly neutral, you can still use that area as the basis of your adjustments. In this case, use the same method I outlined in the "Targeting a Neutral Value" section earlier. This will give you a neutral starting point for the image. Then, you can fine-tune the color balance to achieve the desired color cast in the image. For example, you might shift the color balance toward yellow and slightly toward red to warm up the scene, or slightly toward blue and cyan to cool off the scene.

Selective Color

At times you may find that even with the most careful adjustment to the color balance of your image, you're not able to get certain colors to look "just right." In those situations, the Selective Color control offers a solution.

Selective Color is designed for CMYK output, allowing you to adjust the purity of the primary colors in your image. It allows you to adjust the color balance of a single color within the image. For example, you may have an image where you have achieved a perfect color balance adjustment for the overall image, but where the blues in the sky aren't quite blue. In this case, you could use the Selective Color adjustment to adjust the color balance of the blues, making them more pure.

Because the Selective Color control is geared toward CMYK output, the adjustments represent the percentages of each of those inks for the final output (see Figure 6.15). This requires you to make some translations about what adjustments are necessary for a particular color, but it can be used to great effect.

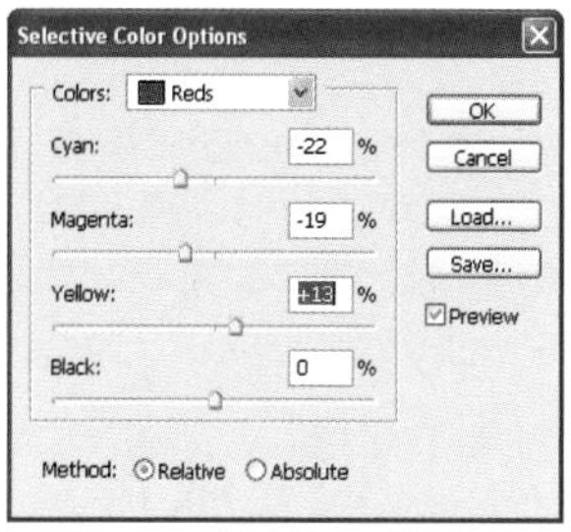

Selective Color Options

Colors: Reds

Cyan: -22 %
Magenta: -19 %
Yellow: -18 %
Black: 0 %

Method: ⊙ Relative ○ Absolute

OK
Cancel
Load...
Save...
☑ Preview

Figure 6.15
The Selective Color control allows you to effectively change the color balance of a specific range of colors within the image.

Using the sky example, you could select Blue (or Cyan) from the Colors dropdown in the Selective Color adjustment. Then adjust the sliders for Cyan, Magenta, Yellow, and Black. The first three allow you to shift the color balance of the image by adding or subtracting each. The Cyan slider adjusts the balance between red and cyan, the Magenta slider adjusts the balance between green and magenta, and the Yellow slider adjusts the balance between blue and yellow. The Black slider allows you to increase or decrease the amount of black ink used in the production of the color you have selected, which effectively provides a tonal adjustment for those areas. For the blue sky, you may want to increase cyan and reduce yellow. It may also be helpful to reduce magenta (commonly found in the sky due to atmospheric scattering of the light), and possibly reduce the amount of black.

Selective Color doesn't replace the color balance adjustments presented earlier in this chapter, but it certainly offers a way to fine-tune certain colors in your image when color balance doesn't seem to provide the degree of control needed.

Hue/Saturation

The Hue/Saturation control packs a surprising amount of power. Most photographers only use it to slightly boost the saturation in their images, providing more "snap" to the colors. This is certainly something most of us want to apply to many of our images. In this section, I'll address this basic adjustment, as well as some of the other great uses for the Hue/Saturation adjustment layer.

A basic increase in saturation purifies the colors, bringing them closer to the fully saturated primary colors. To achieve this result, simply increase the Saturation slider value in the Hue/Saturation adjustment layer. Be careful not to increase the saturation too much. Doing so can cause two problems. For one thing, too much saturation will cause the colors in your image to look fake. Also, purifying the colors in your image makes the values of highly saturated pixels become closer to each other, causing a loss of detail in those saturated colors.

Note: For some images you may actually want to slightly reduce saturation to produce a more subtle, muted appearance. This is particularly effective for "watercolor" type images.

Desaturating a Color Cast

When a particular color is causing a problem in your image that a color balance adjustment won't resolve, you can desaturate that color to minimize its influence or even eliminate it altogether. As I have mentioned several times throughout this chapter, a common offender is magenta, but any color can cause an undesirable influence on the image.

If you aren't able to get accurate colors throughout the image with a color balance adjustment, you may want to reduce the saturation of the problem color. To do so, simply select the appropriate color channel from the Edit dropdown in the Hue/Saturation dialog box. Then reduce the saturation for that color (see Figure 6.16). In some cases, you may be able to reduce the saturation for that color completely, but be careful not to eliminate the selected color so much that you remove it from areas that should contain it. To get a better idea of what areas of the image will be affected, you can increase the saturation for the selected color to the maximum value first, which will provide a clear visual indication of where those colors exist in the image. By doing so, you'll know exactly from what areas of the image you are removing color.

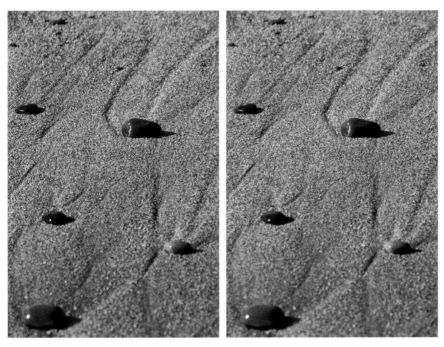

Figure 6.16 By selecting a specific color from the Edit dropdown in the Hue/Saturation dialog box, you can eliminate a color cast caused by that color. The image on the left includes a color cast that has been eliminated in the image on the right by reducing the saturation of magenta.

Fine-Tuning Saturation Adjustments

The ability to adjust the saturation of individual colors in the Hue/Saturation provides significant control over the colors in your image. In addition to being able to desaturate a specific color to eliminate a color cast, you can increase the saturation of specific colors to emphasize them in the image.

In addition to this control over individual colors, the Hue/Saturation dialog box allows you to designate a specific range of colors you want to adjust. To select a specific range of colors to adjust, first select the color channel from the Edit dropdown list. You can then select a specific range of colors using two methods.

The first method is to use the eyedropper buttons within the Hue/Saturation dialog box. The first eyedropper allows you to click on a color in the image to specify that color as the "center" of the range of colors that will be affected by your adjustments. You can then use the "plus" and "minus" eyedroppers to add or subtract colors from the range of colors to be adjusted.

The second method is to manually adjust the range of colors using the controls between the two color gradients at the bottom of the Hue/Saturation dialog box (see Figure 6.17). Again, start by selecting a specific color from the Edit dropdown list, isolating a specific range of colors. The two vertical bars between the color gradients define the range of colors that will be fully affected by the adjustment you make. The angled bars outside the vertical bars represent the extent of the "feathering" of the colors. The adjustments you make will taper off from the colors at the vertical bars through the angled bars, helping to provide a gradual change between colors so the adjustment is not obvious. To change the range of colors, simply click and drag the vertical bars and angled bars to change the range. I recommend setting the Saturation control to the minimum value; that range of colors in the image will be shifted to gray while you are changing the range, so you can better see what areas of the image you will be adjusting (see Figure 6.18). Then change the Saturation setting as desired for that range of colors.

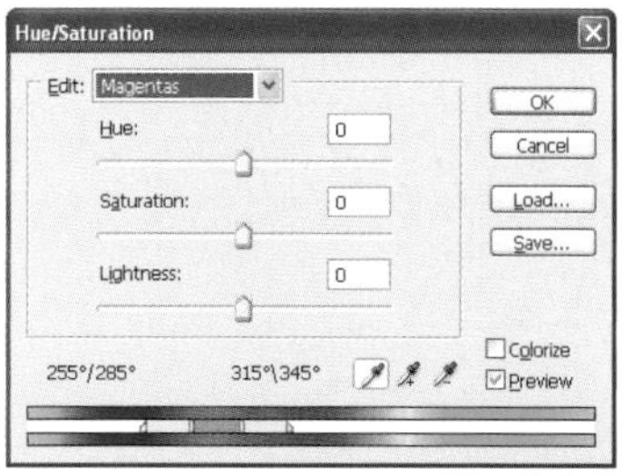

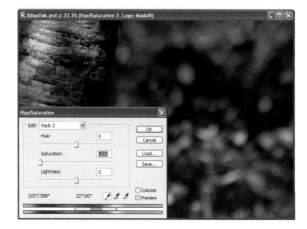

Figure 6.17
To change the range of colors you are adjusting with Hue/Saturation, adjust the bars between the two color gradients.

Figure 6.18
While adjusting the range of colors to be adjusted with Hue/Saturation, reduce the saturation completely so you can better see what areas of the image will be adjusted.

Targeted Adjustments

Many of the adjustments discussed so far in this chapter allow you to change only certain color ranges in your images. However, often you need to adjust a specific *geographic* area within your image, rather than a specific *color range*. In those situations, you want to target your adjustments to a particular area of your image.

Fortunately, adjustment layers provide tremendous flexibility over the areas of the image they affect through the use of a layer mask. This mask defines which areas will and will not be affected by the adjustment layer. You can define the area to be adjusted by creating a selection first or by painting on the adjustment layer mask.

If you have a well-defined area that you want to adjust, creating a selection that defines that area first is probably the best approach. Using any of the many selection tools available to you, create a selection of the area you want to adjust. I recommend that you don't apply any feathering to this selection, and I'll show you how to produce the same effect with much greater control later in this section.

Once you have an active selection, simply create a new adjustment layer for the type of adjustment you want to make to the selected area. The adjustment layer will automatically be masked based on the selection (see Figure 6.19). Make the necessary adjustments, and then click OK. If you made a relatively strong adjustment to the image, the boundary of the original selection may be obvious, with a harsh transition because the original selection was not feathered.

Figure 6.19 If you have a selection active (as seen in the image) when you create an adjustment layer, the adjustment layer will automatically be masked based on that selection (as shown on the Layers palette), so that the adjustment layer only applies to the selected area. (Photograph by Jon Canfield, www.joncanfield.com.)

I don't recommend feathering the original selection because you don't have any quality information about how many pixels you should use to feather that selection. Instead, after you have made your adjustment, apply a Gaussian Blur to the adjustment layer, which will actually affect the layer mask that controls the area of the image the adjustment layer applies to. I recommend zooming it to a 100 percent view and viewing an area of the image that shows a transition between the adjusted and nonadjusted area (see Figure 6.20). Select Filter > Blur > Gaussian Blur from the menu. Be sure the Preview checkbox is checked, and then adjust the Radius slider to change how much the transition edge should be blurred (see Figure 6.21). This produces the same net effect as feathering the selection in the first place, but it allows you to make a decision about how much feathering should be applied based on a visual review of the image.

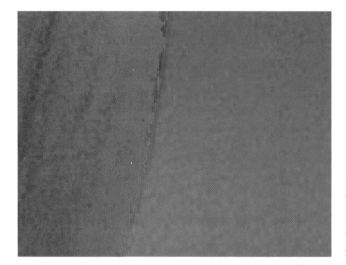

Figure 6.20
When you create an adjustment layer masked from a nonfeathered selection, the transition zone from the adjusted to the nonadjusted area will be very abrupt.

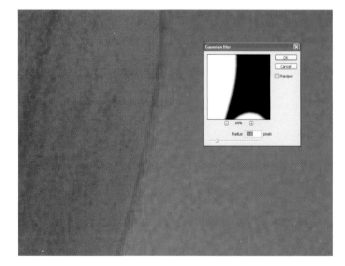

Figure 6.21
By applying a Gaussian Blur to the adjustment layer mask, you can create a smooth transition between the adjusted and nonadjusted areas.

The other method of defining what area the adjustment layer should apply to is to paint pixels directly onto the layer mask for the adjustment layer. This is most effective when the areas you want to adjust aren't clearly defined in the image. First, create an adjustment layer to apply the desired change to the image. Focus your attention on the area you want to affect, make the appropriate adjustments, and click OK.

Then select the Brush tool with a soft-edged brush, and set the foreground color to black. Be sure the adjustment layer is active on the Layers palette (click on it if it isn't), and then paint on the image in the areas where you don't want the adjustment layer to apply. If you accidentally block the adjustment from some areas, change the foreground color to white and paint back over those areas.

After defining the area the adjustment layer should apply to, you can always double-click on the adjustment layer thumbnail on the Layers palette to further refine the designated areas of the image.

Besides painting with black or white, you can also paint with any shade of gray. Black will block the adjustment, and white will allow the adjustment to have its full effect on the image. A shade of gray will block the effect to the degree that the shade is close to black. For example, 50 percent gray will cause the adjustment layer to have half the effect in those areas, and 75 percent gray will cause the adjustment to have 25 percent of the effect.

In fact, besides painting with black, white, or shades of gray, any method you can use to apply pixels to an image can be used to apply pixels to an adjustment layer. You can use any of the painting tools, the Gradient tool, the Fill option, or any other method to add or remove pixels to the adjustment layer, altering what areas of the image are affected.

When you have created an adjustment layer that affects only certain areas of the image, you may want to apply other changes to the areas defined by the layer mask for that adjustment layer. To do so, Ctrl+click (Command+click on Macintosh) on the layer mask thumbnail for the adjustment layer (the black-and-white thumbnail to the right of the adjustment layer thumbnail on the Layers palette). This will turn the layer mask into a selection. Then create a new adjustment layer, and it will automatically be masked based on that selection, so that the new adjustment layer will apply to the same areas as the original adjustment layer.

Color-Adjusting Black-and-White Images

Many photographers who have worked in a wet darkroom with black-and-white images want to be able to reproduce the same results in the digital darkroom. This is most certainly possible, but many printers make it a challenge to get truly neutral prints of the highest quality.

Black-and-white images fit into a color-managed workflow right along with your color images. For the most part, they don't represent any special challenges (see Figure 6.22). The one exception is in printing, which I'll address in Chapter 7, "Output."

When working with black-and-white images in the digital darkroom, I recommend keeping the images in RGB rather than grayscale mode. Although this introduces the possibility of unwanted color in your images, using RGB mode will give you more flexibility with your images, with more information that can allow for greater detail and quality in the final print.

In fact, you can convert your color images to black-and-white with excellent results. Regardless of whether the original is black-and-white or color, I recommend scanning or converting the image to RGB for the optimization process.

Figure 6.22
Black-and-white images, such as this digital infrared photograph by Dewitt Jones, fit into a color-managed workflow right along with your color images. With the right workflow, you can produce stunning prints with no color cast. (Photograph by Dewitt Jones, www.dewittjones.com.)

Convert with Channel Mixer

The method you use to convert your color images to black-and-white can have a signif-icant impact on the quality and detail in the image. I recommend against using the Desaturate option on the Image > Adjustments menu, or simply converting your image to grayscale by selecting Image > Mode > Grayscale. Instead, I recommend using the channel mixer so that you can blend detail from the individual channels to produce an image with optimal density and detail in the areas that are important to you.

The following steps can be used to convert an image with the Channel Mixer adjustment:

Note: Using the Channel Mixer on an adjustment layer allows you to create a black-and-white version of your image without discarding any color data. In the future, you can print a color version of the image by turning off the visibility of the Channel Mixer adjustment layer.

1. Select the Channels palette. If it isn't visible, select Window > Channels from the menu.

2. Click on each of the individual color channels one at a time. This will show you a grayscale representation of the information on that channel. Decide which chan-nel represents the best black-and-white image to begin with (see Figure 6.23).

Figure 6.23
To use the Channel Mixer to produce a black-and-white image, first select the channel that represents the best black-and-white image with which to begin. These images show, from left to right, the red ⓡ, green ⓖ, and blue ⓑ channels. (Image courtesy San Luis Obispo County Historical Society.)

3. Click on the RGB channel at the top of the Channels palette and return to the Layers palette.

4. Create a new adjustment layer for Channel Mixer.

5. Check the Monochrome box in the Channel Mixer dialog box.

6. Set the value for each of the color channels to zero percent. This will create an image that is completely black.

7. Gradually increase the slider value for the color channel that you decided was the best starting point for a black-and-white version of the image in Step 2. Stop when you feel the detail in the image is optimized based on that channel.

8. Increase the values of the other channels to bring detail into the image in other areas.

9. Fine-tune the sliders for each of the channels to produce the image you are happiest with in terms of density, detail, and overall appearance (see Figure 6.24).

10. To maintain accurate density in the image, it is best to end up with values for the channels that add up to 100 percent. Don't treat this as an absolute rule, but understand that targeting values that add up to 100 percent will ensure accurate density in the image. This may mean that you need to have one or more channels at a negative value to offset increases in other channels.

11. Click OK to apply the conversion.

12. You can then use other adjustment layers to fine-tune the overall image, such as Levels or Curves to adjust the brightness and contrast.

Figure 6.24 Adjust the level of each channel in the Channel Mixer to produce the best black-and-white image. (Image courtesy San Luis Obispo County Historical Society)

Note: You can produce a very nice effect for your image by slightly reducing the Opacity setting for the Channel Mixer adjustment layer on the Layers palette. Using an Opacity setting of around 85 to 90 percent will produce an image that looks black-and-white at first glance, but on closer inspection has a subtle wash of color.

Colorize for Print

Many desktop photo inkjet printers have a difficult time producing neutral black-and-white images. In fact, with some printers it seems nearly impossible to produce a neutral print.

It is possible to produce a perfectly neutral print by setting the printer property option to use only black ink. However, this will greatly limit the tonal range the printer is able to produce. Without the other ink colors, the only way to produce different tonal values with black ink is to create ink droplets of varying sizes. Without being able to produce small enough ink droplets, using only black ink will result in an image with rough gradations and jagged curves. The quality with most printers would not be considered photographic quality when using only black ink.

That means you'll have to use all of the inks in your printer to produce a black-and-white print, taking the risk that the image will have a color cast to it. The worst situation is where the color cast is unpredictable, resulting in a slightly different color cast each time the image is printed.

To compensate for a printer that isn't able to produce a neutral print, you can add a desired color cast to the image. You won't get a neutral print, but at least the color cast will be something you selected. To apply the color cast to the image, you can use the Colorize option of the Hue/Saturation adjustment as follows:

Note: Besides using this method to apply a desirable color cast to a black-and-white image, you can also use it to create a "colorized" version of a color image, such as a sepia tone image.

1. Create a new adjustment layer for Hue/Saturation.

2. Check the Colorize box.

3. Adjust the Hue slider to choose the color you would like to use for the colorization. For example, a value of around 50 will produce a sepia tone color, and a value of around 195 will produce a cool-blue color (see Figure 6.25).

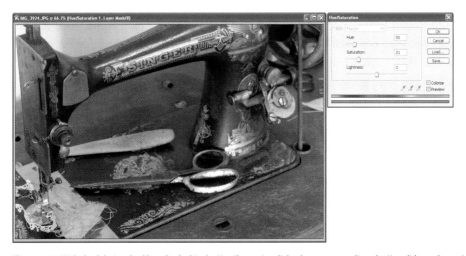

Figure 6.25 With the Colorize checkbox checked in the Hue/Saturation dialog box, you can adjust the Hue slider to determine the color to be applied to the image.

4. Adjust the Saturation slider as desired. I usually find the default value of 25 to be too strong. I prefer to reduce it to around 5 to 15, depending on the image.

5. Click OK to close the Hue/Saturation dialog box and apply the adjustment.

Note: If you use an adjustment layer to apply this Hue/Saturation adjustment, you can turn off the visibility of this adjustment layer to turn off the color cast and print a noncolorized version of the image.

Saving the File

Once you have optimized the color in your image, you should save the resulting "master" image file so you can easily make prints or other output from the image in the future. This requires you to consider the file format you will use, as well as the issue of an embedded profile in that image that defines how the color values should be interpreted.

To flatten the image, select Layer > Flatten image from the menu, or select Flatten Image from the side menu on the Layers palette. This will cause all layers to be merged into a single background layer. If there are any hidden layers in the image when you select the Flatten Image option, a dialog box will be presented asking if you want to discard those hidden layers.

Note: You can also flatten the image in the process of saving it by choosing the Discard Layers And Save A Copy option from the TIFF Options dialog box. However, I recommend flattening the image first so you don't accidentally save the image with layers intact.

If you are sending a file to someone else to use, resize the image so that it is just large enough for the intended usage. This will help ensure that the image isn't used at a larger size than you intend. To size the image, select Image > Image Size from the menu, make sure the Resample checkbox is checked and set the output resolution and dimensions needed for the particular usage.

To save a copy of the image, select File > Save As, and set the Format option to TIFF. Select a folder for the Save In option, and enter a filename (be sure it isn't the same name as the layered TIFF if you have saved your master image with layers in the TIFF format). When you click OK, the TIFF Options dialog box will be displayed.

The first section of the TIFF Options dialog box allows you to set options for Image Compression, as discussed in the previous section. For files that you will be sending out to others, I don't recommend using any compression. This will result in a larger file, but it ensures maximum compatibility. Many applications are not able to open TIFF files saved with compression.

If you haven't already flattened the image, you can do so while saving the TIFF file by selecting the Discard Layers And Save A Copy option. This will result in a flattened image with no layers.

Photoshop PSD

As mentioned in the discussion of the Layered TIFF option, there really isn't anything the Photoshop PSD (Photoshop Document) format can do that you can't do with TIFF. For the most part, that means the Photoshop PSD format is effectively obsolete. In fact, the TIFF file format offers features that Photoshop PSD does not. For one thing, TIFF has broader compatibility, so using TIFF rather than Photoshop PSD makes sense if you send a file out to others.

The TIFF format also offers more compression options. Photoshop PSD files do get slightly compressed when you save a file, but the reduction in file size is minimal.

This certainly makes the TIFF file format look better than the Photoshop PSD file format, and that is exactly my point. So why would you ever use the Photoshop

PSD format? The main reason why many choose to use the Photoshop PSD file format for their master image files is that it makes it easy to distinguish between your layered and flattened images. The Photoshop PSD file would be the image with layers intact, and the TIFF would be the flattened version. This can certainly provide an organizational benefit, but my preference is to use the TIFF format because of the wide range of options it provides.

JPEG

The JPEG format, with its "lossy" compression that causes a loss of quality and detail in your image, is most certainly not a format you would want to use for your master image files. The JPEG format also doesn't support layers.

However, the JPEG format is an excellent choice when a small file size is more important than image quality. That doesn't mean that a JPEG image will have poor quality. Quite the contrary, when you use a high-quality (low compression) setting, the image quality can be excellent.

The JPEG format is an excellent choice for images that need to be displayed on a website, in a digital slideshow, or shared via e-mail. Naturally, you should first save your image with layers intact and lossless compression (or no compression at all). You can then flatten the image and size it to an appropriate size for the intended usage. As I'll discuss in Chapter 7, you may want to convert the image to the sRGB color space as well.

When you are ready to save your image as a JPEG, select File > Save As from the menu. Select a folder for the Save In option, and enter a filename. When you click OK, the JPEG Options dialog box will be displayed (see Figure 6.27). The most important setting is the Image Options, which allows you to select a Quality level. A low-quality setting results in higher image compression, while a high-quality setting results in minimal compression. For web, digital slideshow, or e-mail use, a moderate quality setting of 7 or 8 represents a good compromise between file size and image quality.

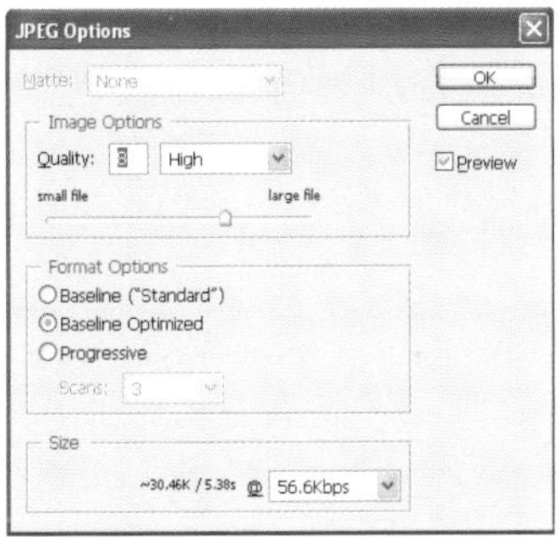

Figure 6.27
The JPEG Options dialog box allows you to set a specific quality/compression setting for the image.

The Format Options section allows you to select a method for how the image is encoded. These are primarily useful for web use, where the image will be displayed gradually while it is being downloaded. The Baseline "Standard" and Baseline Optimized options will result in an image that is displayed line by line, with Baseline Optimized resulting in a slightly smaller file size. The Progressive option will cause the image to be displayed in several passes, gradually improving in quality as it is displayed.

Embedded Profiles

When you save an image file, each pixel is described with numbers representing the color value. For your master image file, this would typically be RGB values, describing how much red, green, and blue light would be required to produce the color of each pixel. However, those values are device-dependent. Without an embedded profile to designate what the color numbers really mean, the actual color of the pixel will be determined by the color behavior of the device displaying it. A profile translates the device-dependent color values to a device-independent color space (typically LAB) so that the colors can be identified based on the way they are actually perceived by the human visual system.

It is, therefore, important that each image you save be embedded with a profile. For your master image file, that would be your working space, so that the colors are described based on the actual working space you used to optimize the image. If the image has a profile that doesn't match your current working space, a number sign (#) will be displayed in the title bar. If this is the case, and you don't have a reason for keeping the embedded profile for the image, you can convert the image to the current working space by selecting Image > Mode > Convert To Profile, selecting the profile you are using as your working space, and clicking OK.

If the image doesn't have an embedded profile, an asterisk (*) will be shown in the title bar. I recommend assigning a profile to the image, so that the colors will be properly interpreted in the future. If you have optimized an image without an embedded profile, the color values will be interpreted based on the current working space. Therefore, I recommend assigning your working space as the profile for an image with a missing profile if you have optimized it without an embedded profile. Note that if the image is from a source where a custom profile is available, as discussed in earlier chapters, you will probably want to assign that custom profile to the image. To assign a profile to the image, select Image > Mode > Assign Profile. Select the profile you are using as your working space (or another appropriate profile), and click OK. When you save the image, the profile you assigned will be embedded.

When you save an image in Photoshop, the Save As dialog box includes a checkbox that allows you to embed a profile in the image. Be sure the ICC Profile checkbox is checked, and that the profile listed after the checkbox is the profile you want to be embedded in the image (see Figure 6.28). If not, cancel, and select Image > Mode > Convert To Profile to embed a different profile in the image.

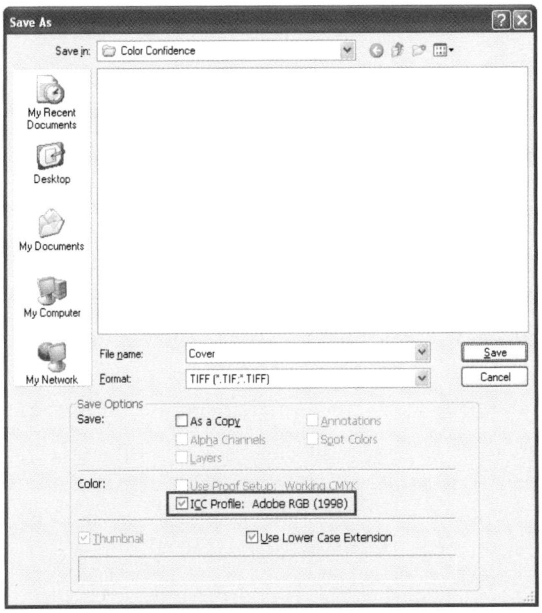

Figure 6.28

The Save As dialog box in Photoshop includes a checkbox allowing you to determine if a profile should be embedded in the image file, and showing you which profile will be used.

In Chapter 7, I'll address the issue of embedding profiles based on particular output methods.

All of the previous chapters in this book are really about getting to this chapter. The end result of all of our preparations with color management is the quality of the final output. Whether that output is a print, a web page, a digital projection, or any other method, your goal is to have the final display look the way you want it to look.

Chapter Contents
Choosing a Printer
Printer Profiles
Preparing Images
Evaluating Prints
CMYK Output
Web, E-mail, and Digital Slideshows

Choosing a Printer

When photographers think of output, the first thing that comes to mind is a print. The defining moment for photographers working in the digital darkroom is when the ink meets paper. To get the best results, be sure you use a printer that includes features that will make your workflow efficient and will produce the quality you demand (see Figure 7.1).

Figure 7.1

John Shaw captures stunning images of our natural world and shares those images through remarkable prints. When producing those prints, he needs to be assured of the most accurate color possible, which requires a high-quality printer and highly accurate printer profiles. (Photograph by John Shaw, www.johnshawphoto.com.)

Fortunately, there is no shortage of excellent printers capable of producing exceptional photo-quality output (see Figure 7.2). Most photographers will want to use a photo inkjet printer because of the excellent quality and flexibility offered. Dye-sublimation printers have some advantages, but I don't consider them to be the best solution for most photographers because they tend to be more expensive and don't support a wide range of print media (papers). You should consider using a photo inkjet printer to produce prints of your images.

Figure 7.2

There is no shortage of excellent photo inkjet printers available. The Epson Stylus Photo R800 uses pigment-based inks that provide long print life while maintaining an excellent color gamut, aided in part by the unique use of red and blue inks in addition to the typical CMYK mix. (Photograph Courtesy Epson America, Inc.)

When choosing a photo inkjet printer, consider the following issues:

Output size   Most photo inkjet printers fall into two categories of maximum output size: 8.5"×11" and 13"×19". There are also other printers that offer larger output options, including wide-format printers with widths up to 44". When deciding on the right printer for you, consider how large you'll likely need to be able to print both now and in the future.

Ink type   The basic choice here is between dye-based inks and pigment-based inks. Pigment-based inks will last longer, but they have a narrower color gamut than dye-based inks. Still, the latest pigment-based inks, such as the UltraChrome inkset from Epson, provide vibrant colors that come close to matching dye-based inks. I recommend using pigment-based inks if you are producing prints for sale or that will otherwise be on long-term display. If you don't need your images to last terribly long, and color vibrancy is more important, then dye-based inks may be an excellent choice.

> **Note:** Just because pigment-based inks last longer than dye-based inks doesn't mean that dye-based inks will necessarily fade quickly. Many dye-based inks, when used in conjunction with appropriate papers, are able to produce prints that will last many decades. For details on print longevity estimates for a variety of printers, visit the Wilhelm Imaging Research website at www.wilhelm-research.com.

Number of inks   Inkjet printers produce various tonal values for each color by adjusting how large the droplets are (if possible) and by adjusting the spacing between the droplets. The smaller and farther apart the droplets are, the lighter the color will appear. To maintain the finest detail, many printers utilize "light" ink colors so that the droplets don't need to be spaced as far apart as would otherwise be necessary. These diluted inks (usually light cyan and light magenta, with some printers using a light black as well) provide for higher quality in the final print, while maintaining the ability to produce a wide range of color and tonal values. As a general rule, printers with six or more ink colors will produce the best results.

> **Note:** Epson has a new UltraChrome inkset that uses red and blue inks instead of light cyan and light magenta. This is possible because the ink droplets are so small that the diluted inks are no longer necessary to produce excellent quality. The red and blue inks also help to expand the color gamut of the printer by offering additional hues that would otherwise be difficult to produce. Unfortunately, these new inks are not compatible with previous printers that use the original UltraChrome inks.

Ink droplet size   The smaller the ink droplets, the wider the range of tonal values and finer detail the printer is able to produce. Anything below 6 picoliters is very good, with the best printers now offering droplet sizes of 2 picoliters or smaller.

Resolution   You can pretty much ignore this specification. Any recent model photo inkjet printer will be able to produce output at 1,440 dpi or higher. I conducted extensive testing of the output quality for several printers capable of output resolutions higher than 1,440 dpi (sometimes considerably higher), examining the results with a loupe. This testing convinced me that anything above about 1,440 dpi does not provide any benefit in perceived quality. In fact, if your printer offers a higher quality setting, I recommend using the 1,440 dpi setting, which will still provide excellent quality indistinguishable from the higher settings, faster print times, and less ink usage. Keep in mind that this resolution specification is not the same as image resolution. The printer resolution should be thought of only as an output quality setting.

Media support   The variety of print media that a printer is able to print to successfully isn't usually included in the specifications provided by the manufacturer. With some ink formulations, the type of paper you can print to with good results can be limited. I recommend checking reviews in magazines or on the Web to determine the range of papers and other print media supported by the printer.

Software capabilities   It is very difficult to get information from a manufacturer about the flexibility and ease-of-use of the dialog boxes you will use to configure the printer settings. Again, refer to reviews in magazines or on the Web for information on whether the printer settings allow you to adjust the output to get the most accurate colors, and to see how easy it is to operate.

Printer Profiles

In many ways, printer profiles perform much the same work as monitor profiles. As you'll recall from Chapter 3, "Display," monitor profiles provide a way to translate the color values in the image to values that will produce the intended colors on the monitor (provided all colors are within the color gamut of the monitor). Printer profiles likewise contain information on how the color values in the image file should be translated to produce accurate output on the printer. A profile, therefore, allows you to take color information in an image file and produce a print with matching appearance (see Figure 7.3).

Figure 7.3
Printer profiles allow you to produce prints that are accurate relative to the data in the image file, allowing you to match the appearance of the image displayed on a calibrated monitor. (Photograph by Peter Burian.)

Don't Forget Limitations

As I delve into the issue of final output for your images, remember that even the best color-managed workflow has limitations. For example, producing a print that perfectly matches what you see on your monitor is impossible because the mediums are so different. One is glowing with light and the other depends upon reflected light, and both have their own unique color characteristics. Color management isn't so much a way to produce a perfect match, but rather a way to produce a *predictable* match. With practice, you'll learn to interpret what you see on your monitor compared to the final output. This chapter will help you learn to use the available tools and methods for getting as close a match as possible.

Most monitors have a very similar color gamut, and out-of-the-box most monitors will produce a pretty accurate picture. That isn't to say each monitor will have a perfect match. If so, we wouldn't need to worry about calibrating and profiling our monitors. But in most cases that profile is solving a relatively small variation from one monitor to another—enough to see the difference between two monitors, but often not so much that a given monitor looks "wrong" before profiling.

Of course, with printers things are a bit more complicated. As with monitors, there are many brands and models of printers. There are also many varieties of ink in use, both from the printer manufacturers and third-party providers. In addition, most printers can be used with a wide variety of papers. This is where the real variations occur. The different surface properties of papers have a surprising effect on the color appearance of the inks, because inks of different colors are absorbed in slightly different manners. If you print on several different paper types with the same output settings, you'll likely see a significant difference between each print.

Printer profiles contain data that describes, in effect, the color properties of a specific printer, ink, and paper combination. Because of the differences in output on different papers, a specific profile is required for each combination to ensure the most accurate color. The profiles allow the color values in your image to be translated into a device-independent color space, and then translated in turn into color values that will ensure accurate colors from the printer.

There are several categories of profiles, relating to whether they are designed for a specific printer (meaning the specific one sitting on your desk) or for a particular model of printer (meaning any printer on anyone's desk that is the same model):

- Canned
- Generic
- Commercial
- Custom

The category of profile you use has a direct impact on the accuracy of that profile. I'll discuss them in order from the method I recommend the most to the one I recommend the least.

Building Custom Printer Profiles

A custom profile is created to produce the most accurate results possible with very specific output conditions. That means it is created for a specific printer, using specific inks, with a specific paper. By "specific printer" I don't mean a single model from a particular manufacturer. This means a single specific printer, as in the actual one sitting on your desk. Although most printers are quite stable, and tend to produce consistent output, some degree of variation can exist between printers of the same model. Creating a profile for a specific printer will take into account any characteristics unique to that printer and ensure the most accurate prints.

> **Note:** Remember that a custom profile is specific to the printer, ink, and paper for which you build the profile. If the ink or paper formulation changes, you'll need to rebuild the profile. Keep in mind that sometimes manufacturers don't let you know when they've changed formulations. If you suddenly aren't getting the accurate output to which you have grown accustomed, you may want to rebuild your profile.

Building a custom printer profile is a relatively simple process, wherein you use tools to measure and describe the color behavior of the printer, so that behavior can be taken into account during printing to ensure the most accurate colors. The basic process of building a profile includes the following steps:

1. Print a target that contains known color values. This could be an industry-standard target, such as the IT-8, or a simple series of colored boxes. The more color samples included in this target image, the higher the probability of producing an accurate target, since a broader range of color behavior can then be measured.

2. Allow the print to dry completely. While most current inksets are dry to the touch immediately upon printing, they won't fully cure for about 24 hours after printing. The colors in a print can shift considerably as the inks dry, so to get the most accurate profile, measure the samples based on their "final" appearance.

3. Measure the target values from the print. The most accurate profiles are built from measurements using a calibrated spectrophotometer, because they provide the most accurate reading of the color values in the sample. Flatbed scanners or other measurement devices can also be employed. These solutions don't provide the most accurate profiles, but they are popular because they are much less expensive.

4. Generate the actual profile data file based on the measurements read from the target print. This profile will describe the color behavior of a specific printer, ink, and paper combination, allowing you to produce prints with accurate color whenever that combination is used.

5. If necessary—and with the proper software tools, such as a profile editor—you can modify the profile to improve the accuracy of the final prints. This step is only recommended for advanced users.

A variety of hardware and software tools are available for building custom printer profiles. The following sections describe some of them.

Gretag Macbeth Eye-One Photo

The Eye-One Photo package (about $1,500, Windows and Macintosh) from Gretag Macbeth (www.gretagmacbeth.com) is the best, reasonably priced package for building custom printer profiles. It may be beyond the budget of many photographers; however, for those who can justify the expense, it produces highly accurate profiles. The process of creating a profile with Eye-One Photo is as follows:

1. Launch the Eye-One Match software.

2. Select the Printer option from the screen asking what type of device you want to profile, and then click Next.

3. Select the printer you want to profile from the Choose Your Printer dropdown list.

4. Select the "i1 RGB" test chart from the chart dropdown list (see Figure 7.4).

Figure 7.4 Select the printer for which you are building a profile and the appropriate chart to print, and then click the Print Chart button.

5. Select the Measure The Chart option, and click the button to Print Chart.

6. Select your printer from the Print dialog box, and click the Preferences to bring up the Printing Preferences dialog box. Set the printer properties to the options that will result in no adjustment to the printed output, such as a "No Color Adjustment" setting. When you have properly configured the printer properties, click OK and then click Print in the Print dialog box.

7. Allow the print to thoroughly dry. I recommend allowing a minimum of 30 minutes for the print to dry, but allowing it to sit overnight so it will completely cure is even better. Click Next in the Eye-One Match window.

8. Place the spectrophotometer (sensor) on the calibration holder, and click the Calibrate button. When calibration is completed, click Next.

9. Select Strip mode for reading the patches. Place the guide over the first row of color patches on the target chart, and place the spectrophotometer in the guide

just outside the "A" patch. Press and hold the button on the spectrophotometer, and wait until you hear a beep. Then drag it down the guide from patch "A" to patch "R," releasing the button after you pass the final patch (see Figure 7.5).

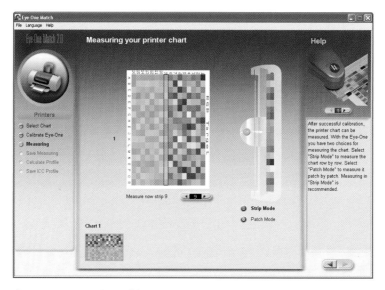

Figure 7.5 Measure each row of the patches on the print target to read the values for profiling.

10. Repeat Step 9 for each row of patches. When you are finished reading all of the patches, click Next.

11. You can save the measurement data if you like, but there isn't really a good reason to do so (see Figure 7.6). If you need to rebuild the profile, you should rescan new patches. Click Next to proceed, and Eye-One Match will start generating the profile (see Figure 7.7).

Figure 7.6 You can save the measurement data after reading the patches, but I don't recommend doing so.

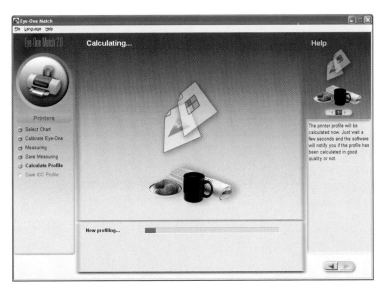

Figure 7.7 Once you have read all of the patches, the data will be calculated to produce the profile.

12. Enter a name for the profile that will identify the printer, ink, and paper combination for which you are building the profile. Click Save As to open the Save As dialog box to actually save the profile (see Figure 7.8).

13. After you have saved the profile, click Next to return to the main Eye-One Match window.

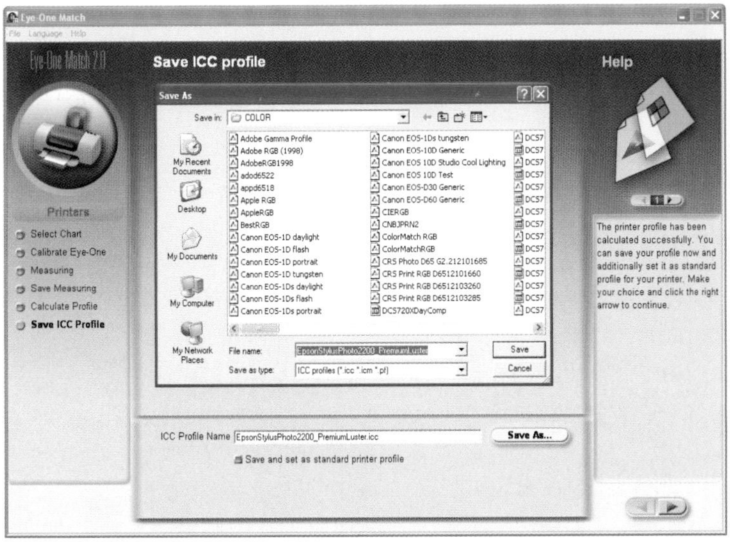

Figure 7.8 Save the profile with a name that will reflect the printer, ink, and paper combination for which you are building the profile.

MonacoEZcolor

MonacoEZcolor (about $300, Windows and Macintosh) from Monaco Systems (www.monacosys.com) is a simple and inexpensive way to build a custom printer profile. Rather than using a dedicated spectrophotometer to read the target color patches, it uses your flatbed scanner. Instead of relying on the wide variations in scanned color from flatbed scanners, it effectively profiles your scanner in the process of reading the target color patches by having you include a scanner calibration target in the scan. The result is a profile of very good accuracy. Follow these steps to build a custom printer profile with MonacoEZcolor:

1. Launch MonacoEZcolor.

2. Click the Create Printer Profile button (see Figure 7.9).

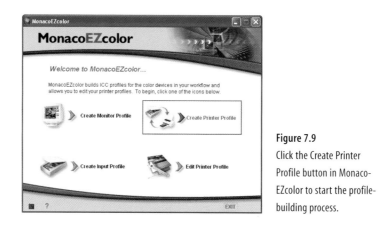

Figure 7.9
Click the Create Printer Profile button in Monaco-EZcolor to start the profile-building process.

3. Read the reminders on the Before You Begin page, and click Next.

4. Set the printer type to RGB Printer, and click Next.

5. Click the Print button to print the target chart directly from MonacoEZcolor (see Figure 7.10).

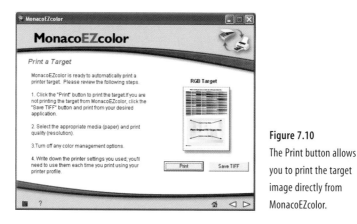

Figure 7.10
The Print button allows you to print the target image directly from MonacoEZcolor.

6. Select your printer from the Print dialog box, and click Preferences to bring up the Printing Preferences dialog box. Set the printer properties to the options that will result in no adjustment to the printed output, such as a "No Color Adjustment" setting. When you have properly configured the printer properties, click OK and then click Print in the Print dialog box.

7. Allow the print to thoroughly dry. I recommend allowing a minimum of 30 minutes for the print to dry, but allowing it to sit overnight so it will completely cure is even better. Click Next in the MonacoEZcolor window.

8. Attach the included scanner IT-8 target to the print target. You can tape it down, but be careful not to get any tape on the color patches.

9. Place the printer and scanner target document face down on the glass of your flatbed scanner and close the cover.

10. Click the TWAIN Acquire button to scan the target document from your flatbed scanner directly into MonacoEZcolor (see Figure 7.11). If you aren't able to import the target document directly, use your scanner to scan the target document, save it, and then click the Load An Image button to retrieve that scanned image. Scan the target document at 200 dpi, making sure not to use any adjustments in the scanner software.

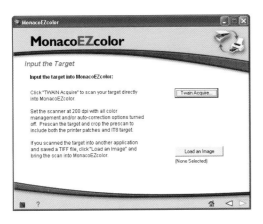

Figure 7.11
Clicking the TWAIN Acquire button allows you to scan the print target with the IT-8 target directly into MonacoEZcolor. If you aren't able to directly import with your scanner, you can scan the image, save the file, and then load that image for profiling.

11. Verify the scan by reviewing the thumbnail of your scan against the samples provided (see Figure 7.12). If it isn't a good scan, click the Back button and rescan. When you have a good scan, click Next.

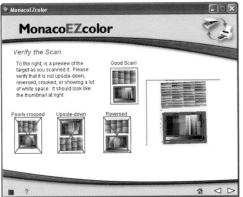

Figure 7.12
Verify that you have obtained a good scan of the image by comparing it to the thumbnails showing good and bad scans.

12. Click the Select Reference button, and choose the reference data file that corresponds with the information in the bottom-left corner of your IT-8 target (see Figure 7.13). After selecting the appropriate reference data file, click Next.

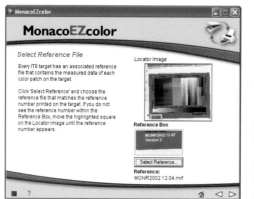

Figure 7.13

The reference data enables MonacoEZcolor to profile your scanner based on known values for the IT-8 target. Select the appropriate reference data file based on the information shown on the IT-8 target.

13. Set the crop marks in the corners of the IT-8 target using the boxes provided (see Figure 7.14). When the image is cropped properly, click Next.

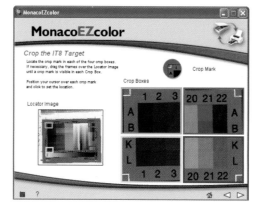

Figure 7.14

Use the tools provided to set the crop marks for each corner of the scanned IT-8 target. You'll repeat this process for the print target image.

14. Set the crop marks in the corners of the printer target using the boxes provided. When the image is cropped properly, click Next.

15. Click the Name button to provide a name for the printer profile (see Figure 7.15). Use a name that describes the printer, ink, and paper combination used for this profile. Click Next.

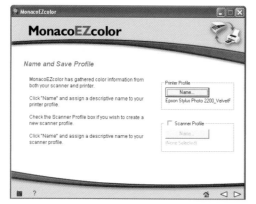

Figure 7.15

Save the profile with a name that references the printer, ink, and paper combination for which you are building the profile.

16. The profile will be generated and saved. When the process is finished, click Next to return to the main MonacoEZcolor window.

Color Vision PrintFIX

The PrintFIX package (about $300, Windows and Macintosh) from Color Vision (www.colorvision.com) is an affordable solution for creating custom printer profiles. It includes a customized print scanner that serves as a patch reader, allowing you to create profiles for as many ink and paper combinations as you need. It is limited in terms of the number of printers it actually supports, so be sure to check the Color Vision website to see if your printer is supported. New printers are being added to the list regularly.

Because the scanner used to read the target patches isn't profiled, the results are not as accurate as they could be. In general, I find that the PrintFIX package produces profiles that aren't much more accurate than the generic profiles included with the printer. However, it is still an excellent choice for photographers who will print with a wide variety of third-party papers. Creating a profile with this package is simple:

1. From within Photoshop, select File > Automate > PrintFIX from the menu.

2. Select Load Calibration Chart from the left dropdown list, and select the printer you are profiling from the right dropdown list (see Figure 7.16). Then click OK to load the target chart into Photoshop.

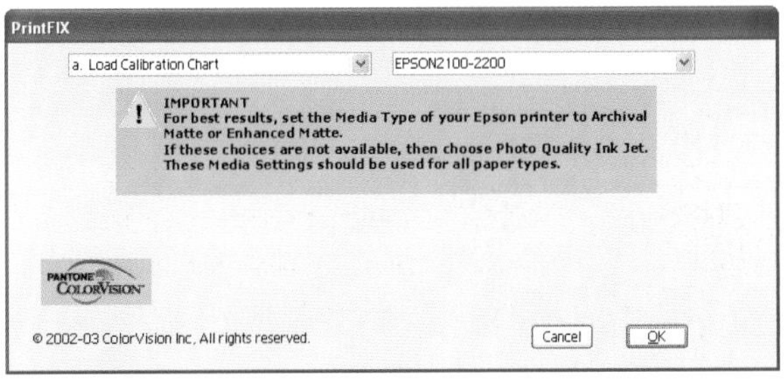

Figure 7.16
Set the appropriate options to load the calibration chart for the printer model for which you are building a profile.

3. Select File > Print With Preview, and set the Print Space Profile to Same as Source. Click Print, select your printer from the Print dialog box, and click Preferences to bring up the Printing Preferences dialog box. Set the printer properties to the options that will result in no adjustment to the printed output, such as a "No Color Adjustment" setting. Regardless of the type of paper for which you are actually building a profile, set the paper type to Enhanced Matte or Archival Matte. When you have properly configured the printer properties, click OK and then click Print in the Print dialog box.

4. Allow the print to thoroughly dry. I recommend allowing a minimum of 30 minutes for the print to dry, but allowing it to sit overnight so it will completely cure is even better.

5. Cut out the print target along the dashed line, and place it in the sleeve included in the package with the color patches visible through the clear plastic cover.

6. In Photoshop, select File > Import > PrintFIX.

7. Click the Calibrate button to bring up the Calibration Page dialog box. Insert the calibration page into the patch reader with the black and white stripes facing down, and click the Calibrate button in the Calibration Page dialog box.

8. When calibration is complete, click OK.

9. Configure the PrintFIX scan settings for Color, Resolution of 400 dpi, Scan Size set to PrintFIX, and all other settings at their defaults (see Figure 7.17).

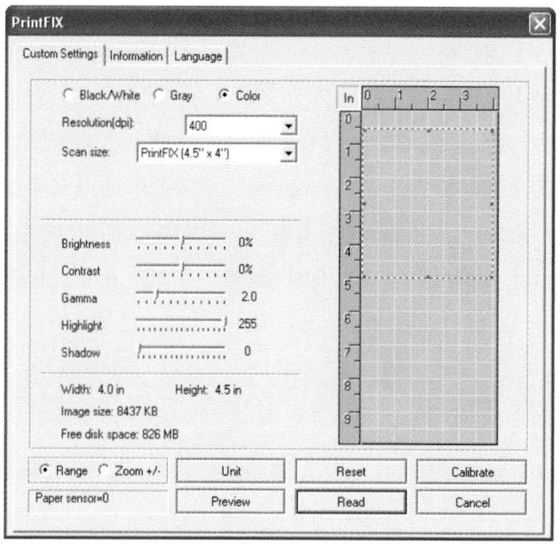

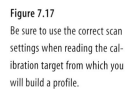

Figure 7.17
Be sure to use the correct scan settings when reading the calibration target from which you will build a profile.

10. Place the calibration target in the sleeve into the patch reader with the color patches facing down.

11. Click the Read button to scan the calibration target. The PrintFIX dialog box will close when the scan is completed.

12. Select File > Automate > PrintFIX from the menu in Photoshop.

13. Select Build Profile from the dropdown list on the left (see Figure 7.18). Do not adjust the sliders in this dialog box unless the calibration target includes instructions on what settings to use. Click OK to build the profile.

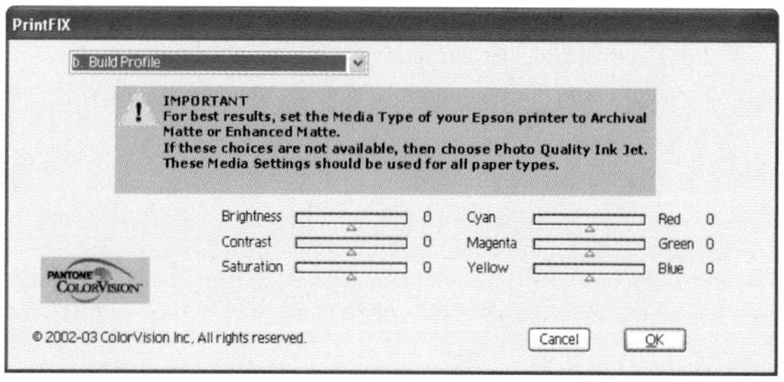

Figure 7.18
Select the Build Profile option to build a profile from the scanned calibration target.

14. When prompted, enter a name for the profile that will identify the printer, ink, and paper combination for which you are building the profile (see Figure 7.19).

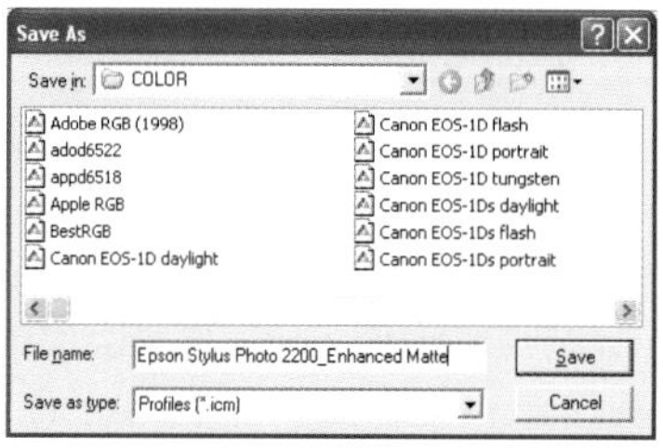

Figure 7.19
Save the profile with a name that will identify the printer, ink, and paper combination for which you are building a profile.

15. Close and restart Photoshop so it will update the list of available profiles so that you can use the profile you have built.

Commercial Services

If you don't want to build your own custom profiles, services are available that will build them for you. One of the most popular is the ProfileCity service (www.profilecity.com) from Integrated Color Solutions. For about $100 you can have a single profile built for a specific printer, ink, and paper combination. The process is very simple. Download their target image, print it using printer settings that will result in no color adjustment to the output, and send the print to Integrated Color Solutions. They will scan the target color patches you produced and then e-mail you a custom profile. Copy the profile to the appropriate location on your hard drive, and you're ready to use that custom profile to get accurate prints.

> **Note:** You may be thinking, "If purchasing a custom profile is so easy and cheap, why not try it first?" Primarily because you're depending on someone else (the service provider) to create the profile. If a patch is read incorrectly, or if there are other slight errors, the profile may be a bit off. Also, you won't have the ability to regenerate profiles for new papers or to deal with changes in ink formulations. This is a good solution, but it is not my preferred solution.

Using "Canned" Printer Profiles

The profiles that are included with a particular printer are referred to as "canned" profiles. They are developed by the printer manufacturers to be as accurate as possible across all of the printers for a given model, using the inks the printer is designed to use, and with a variety of papers from the printer manufacturer. The effectiveness of these profiles depends in large part on the methods used to produce the profiles and on the consistency in output from one printer to another of the same model.

When you install the printer drivers from the CD included with a printer, the canned profiles are installed on your system, making them available for use. However, there are other sources for additional or updated profiles for your printer. Updated drivers found on manufacturer websites often include new profiles. Also, special plug-ins may include printer profiles that are more accurate than those included with the printer drivers. A good example of this is the Print Image Matching (PIM) plug-in from Epson. Individual PIM plug-in updates are available for download for most Epson printers at Epson's website (www.epson.com). These profiles have proven to be much more accurate than those included with the drivers for the individual printers.

Canned profiles aren't created for your specific printer and, therefore, don't take into account any unique characteristics that may cause your output to differ from the output of another printer of the same model.

With any type of printer profile, you need to be concerned about changes to the ink or paper formulations you are using. If the manufacturer makes a slight change to either, the impact on the colors produced by the printer can be significant. Unfortunately, it is virtually unheard of for a printer or paper manufacturer to announce when they have updated inks or paper. With canned profiles, you are at the mercy of the printer manufacturer. If your results suddenly seem less than accurate, check their website for an updated download of new profiles or drivers that will include those profiles.

Note: In some cases, the canned profiles may be "hidden" within the printer driver. In those cases, you'll only be able to specify a single profile that is generic to the printer, and then designate the specific paper within the printer properties. I'll address this situation later in this chapter.

Using Generic Profiles

Generic profiles are very similar to canned profiles. In fact, many canned profiles would be considered generic profiles if they weren't included with the original printer software. Generic profiles are profiles designed for a specific model of printer with specific inks printed on a particular type of paper.

The most common source of generic profiles is from third-party paper manufacturers. These include LexJet Direct (www.lexjet.com), Legion Paper (www.legionpaper .com), Pictorico (www.pictorico.com), Red River Paper (www.redrivercatalog.com), and others. They provide generic profiles as a service to their customers, to help ensure the most accurate color when using these papers with a variety of printers for which they were not specifically formulated.

Third-party papers provide some excellent alternatives, including papers with unique surface types to produce a completely unique interpretation of your images. If you use third-party papers, I encourage you to explore the accuracy of their generic profiles if you don't have the necessary tools to create your own custom profiles.

> #### Closest Match
>
> If you are using third-party papers, or even papers from your printer manufacturer for which you don't have a canned profile, and you haven't purchased tools for creating custom profiles, you may feel that you don't have any options for producing accurate output.
>
> The key factor that determines how colors appear in a print is the surface of the paper due to different absorption properties. Therefore, if you use a profile that is designed for a paper with a similar surface type, you may be able to get very good results. This certainly doesn't replace a custom profile, but in some cases different paper types are so similar that you can get great results using a profile with one that was designed for the other. This isn't a perfect solution in most cases, but it may be worth a try when you don't have any alternatives.
>
> For most printers, the printer properties dialog box allows you to make adjustments to the output, helping you compensate for output that is less than perfect. However, this option (discussed later in this chapter) is usually not available if you are using a custom profile.

Choosing a Rendering Intent

While we're talking about output profiles, let's take a look at the rendering intents used to process your image data based on the profile. A rendering intent provides "rules" about how color values will be changed when converting an image from one profile to another. For example, when you print an image, a rendering intent determines how the color values will be processed when converting the image from the working space (or other embedded profile) to the print profile.

Four rendering intents are available in Photoshop CS for you to choose from:

Perceptual focuses on maintaining the color relationships between colors. It functions by compressing the entire color gamut of the source profile so that it fits within the color gamut of the destination profile. This can result in a loss of overall saturation in your image. However, colors will maintain the same relationships within the image, which can be very important. The Perceptual rendering intent is my preferred option when working with photographic images with many out-of-gamut colors.

Relative Colorimetric keeps all colors the same if they are within the color gamut of the destination profile, only changing out-of-gamut colors to the closest reproducible hue. It also maps white in your source profile to white in the destination profile (paper white), so that pure white areas will simply appear as the color of the paper. The Relative Colorimetric rendering intent is a better choice than Perceptual for images with few out-of-gamut colors because it maintains the appearance of more colors in the image.

Absolute Colorimetric is very similar to Relative Colorimetric in that it maintains the appearance of colors within the color gamut of the destination profile, shifting out-of-gamut colors to the closest reproducible hue. It differs from Relative Colorimetric in that white in the source profile is not mapped to the white of the destination profile. That means ink may be added to white areas to produce the color of white in the source profile. This can be helpful when you are trying to simulate with one printer what the image will look like on a different printer, but this is not a rendering intent I recommend using for normal printing.

Saturation is not an appropriate rendering intent for anyone reading this book. This rendering intent attempts to maintain the saturation of colors with no regard for the actual color of those colors. In other words, if a highly saturated color is out-of-gamut for the destination profile, this rendering intent will shift the color to a different hue (color) in order to maintain the high saturation of that color. This results in a vivid image with inaccurate colors. It is appropriate for business graphics such as charts and graphs, where you don't really care what the color precisely looks like as long as it is vivid; however, for photographic images, it is a poor choice.

Preparing Images

At this point, your image should be perfect. You've already optimized it based on the appearance of the image on a calibrated and profiled monitor. You've saved the image with all the adjustment layers intact so you can go back and fine-tune the image if you decide your adjustments weren't perfect or if you simply want to present a slightly different interpretation. You should be confident that the master image file you've saved contains accurate information based on how you want the image to appear. Now it's time to prepare that image file to produce the best results for your specific output conditions.

Note: In this chapter, I'll provide information on preparing your image for CMYK output. However, you should still keep your master image in RGB mode. Saving a CMYK image involves assigning a specific CMYK profile, which will restrict the range of colors in the image for a single output process. Saving in RGB maintains the maximum amount of color, with an image file that can be repurposed for a variety of output conditions.

Soft Proofing

Soft proofing is a wonderful feature in Photoshop that allows you to preview what your image will look like when output with a specific profile. In other words, it allows you to see on your monitor what the final print will look like (within reason) when you print it using a specific printer, ink, and paper combination. More importantly, it allows you to adjust the image to get the very best results for your particular print process.

Soft proofing is especially helpful when you are preparing an image to be printed by someone else, so that you can ensure the most accurate results possible. When you are printing an image on your own printer, soft proofing may not be necessary, as you will become accustomed to the slight variations between your print and monitor display, particularly when using different paper types. However, it can still be used very effectively in this situation to produce the best prints possible.

Note: If you don't have a profile specifically designed for your printer, ink, and paper combination, you won't be able to use soft proofing to get an accurate preview of your image. For example, if your printer software only includes a generic printer profile, with output options set in the printer properties dialog box, soft proofing isn't possible.

In order to preview your image with soft proofing, you need to configure it so it knows how to simulate the particular output method you are using. To configure soft proofing, use the following steps:

1. Open the image you want to soft proof before printing.

Note: If you configure the Proof Setup options without having an image open, the settings will become the default for all images.

2. Select View > Proof Setup > Custom from the menu to display the Proof Setup dialog box (see Figure 7.20).

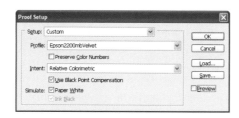

Figure 7.20

The Proof Setup dialog box allows you to configure soft proofing for a specific profile.

3.   Uncheck the Preview option.

> **Note:** It may sound odd that I recommend turning off the Preview checkbox, when normally we want to see the effect of our settings in Photoshop. This is simply so you can configure the dialog box without seeing what may appear to be problematic changes in your image.

4.   Select the appropriate profile from the Profile dropdown list. This may be a custom profile you have created, a profile provided by a printing lab, or a profile from your printer manufacturer or third-party. Be sure to select the correct profile for the specific printer, ink, and paper combination you will be using to print the image.

5.   Make sure the Preserve Color Numbers checkbox is *not* checked. Having the box checked would be the same as assigning the output profile to the image and changing the interpretation of the color numbers, and it could result in unpredictable and inaccurate results. Instead, you want the color appearance to be maintained as accurately as possible, much like converting an image to a different profile.

6.   Select the appropriate rendering intent from the Intent dropdown list. If you are using soft proofing, you should also be using the gamut warning option (View > Gamut Warning) and adjusting the image to ensure all colors are within the color gamut of the output profile you are using. Therefore, all colors should be in gamut, and I recommend using the Relative Colorimetric rendering intent.

7.   Make sure the Use Black Point Compensation checkbox is checked. This will ensure that any black pixels in your image are mapped to the black in the destination profile, maintaining deep blacks in the print.

8.   Check the Paper White checkbox to simulate the appearance of the paper to which you are printing. This will automatically turn on the Ink Black checkbox as well, so that black will be simulated on your monitor based on how it will actually appear in print. That usually means that black will be toned down so that it won't be as dark on your display, since your monitor is able to produce a darker black than a printer can.

9.   If you frequently will be using the output method you are configuring, I strongly recommend saving the setup for future use. Click the Save button, enter a name for the setup, and click OK. The name should reflect the specific printer, ink, and paper combination for which you are configuring this setup.

10. Move your mouse over the OK button in the Proof Setup dialog box, but don't click it. Instead, close your eyes. (Yes, I know that sounds weird, but it can be a bit disconcerting to see the change actually take place in your image.) With your eyes closed, click the OK button, and then open your eyes. This way you'll simply see the simulation of the final output without having to see the shift in appearance (see Figure 7.21).

Figure 7.21 By using soft proofing, you can get a much better idea of what the image will look like in the final print. The image on the left is seen without soft proofing. The image on the right is seen with soft proofing configured for Epson's Velvet Fine Art paper, which produces blacks that are not as deep as the blacks other papers are capable of producing. (Photograph by John Shaw, www.johnshawphoto.com.)

I recommend saving the Proof Setup so you can easily access it again whenever preparing an image for the same output process. To save the setup, click the Save button in the Proof Setup dialog box. Select a location and filename for the saved settings. You can then access this proof setup later by selecting it from the bottom of the View > Proof Setup menu, or by clicking the Load button in the Proof Setup dialog box and locating the saved settings.

When you click OK in the Proof Setup dialog box, the Proof Colors preview option will be turned on, so that you see a soft proof of your image. You can turn off the Proof Colors option at any time, returning to the "normal" image with no output preview, by selecting View > Proof Colors from the menu or pressing Ctrl+Y (Command+Y on Macintosh). You can confirm that Proof Colors is active by selecting View from the menu and confirming that a checkmark is displayed in front of Proof Colors (see Figure 7.22).

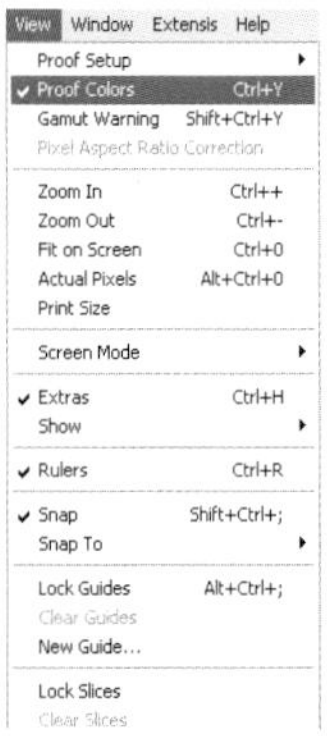

Figure 7.22
You can verify that you are viewing a soft proof of your image by confirming there is a checkmark in front of Proof Colors in the View menu.

Interpreting the Image

When Proof Colors is turned on, the monitor display will be adjusted to simulate what the image will look like in the final print. Although Proof Colors does a remarkable job, a certain amount of interpretation is still required to get a sense of what the final image will look like. The image will still look different on your monitor. In large part, this is because your monitor is emitting light rather than reflecting it, and your monitor's surface (which can be anything from a semi-matte to glossy appearance) may not have the same reflective properties as the paper on which you'll be printing.

The issues related to differing appearance don't make soft proofing any less valuable. You just need to keep in mind that a certain amount of interpretation is necessary. With practice, you'll get a better sense of how the monitor display differs from the final print, so you'll have a better understanding of the information being presented to you. Think of soft proofing as giving you a better tool to *predict* what the output will look like, rather than a precise simulation of that output.

Gamut Warning

The Gamut Warning option in Photoshop allows you to flag the areas of your image that are outside the color gamut of your output process. In other words, it lets you see which colors in the image can't be reproduced accurately and, therefore, allows you to adjust the image to ensure that you get the best results possible within the limitations of your specific output process. It functions by overlaying a designated color on the areas of your image that contain out-of-gamut colors. Where that color is shown, the output method you have configured for soft proofing isn't able to reproduce the underlying colors accurately.

> **Note:** The Gamut Warning option should only be used in conjunction with an appropriate Proof Setup. If you haven't configured the soft proofing options to match your output conditions, the Gamut Warning display operates based on your CMYK working space. Depending on the output method you're actually using, this could render the Gamut Warning completely useless. On the other hand, with a proper Proof Setup, the Gamut Warning is invaluable.

Configuring Gamut Warning

The Gamut Warning comes with default options, so technically you don't actually have to configure it first in order to use it. However, I recommend that you change the default settings so you can better see which areas of your image are out of gamut. In fact, you may want to change the settings based on the contents of the image to make it easier to see which areas are out of gamut.

To configure the Gamut Warning options, select Edit > Preferences > Transparency & Gamut from the menu. The Preferences dialog box will be displayed with the Transparency and Gamut options shown (see Figure 7.23). The Gamut Warning section contains only two options: Color and Opacity.

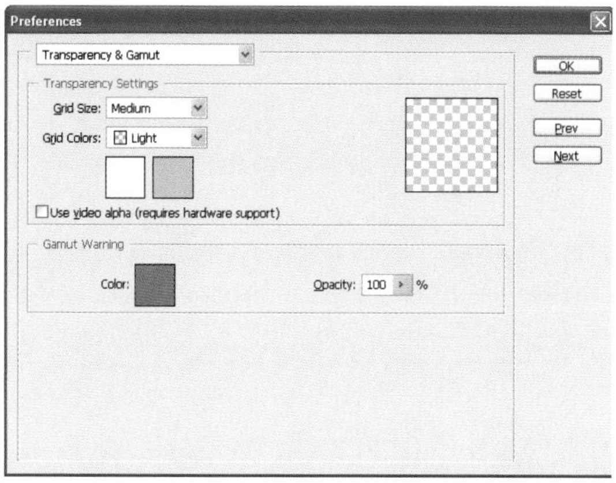

Figure 7.23
Before using the Gamut Warning display, configure the settings in the Preferences dialog box.

The Color setting determines which color will be used to show you the out-of-gamut color areas within the image. The default is gray, but this can easily get lost in any neutral areas of your image. I recommend using a highly saturated color that doesn't appear within the image. For example, I usually use a fully saturated magenta. To change the color, simply click on the Color box to bring up the Color Picker (see Figure 7.24), select a new color, and click OK.

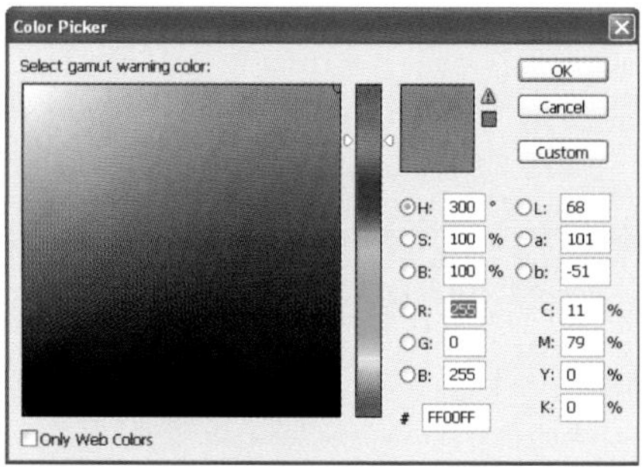

Figure 7.24
Clicking on the Color box for the Gamut Warning Color will display the Color Picker dialog box, allowing you to select a new color.

The Opacity setting determines whether the Gamut Warning color display will allow your underlying image to show through, and to what extent. I prefer to leave the Opacity at 100 percent, so that the Gamut Warning display completely blocks the image in those areas. If you prefer to see some detail under the Gamut Warning display so you have a better understanding of what is in those areas, you can use a lower Opacity setting. I don't recommend reducing it below 50 percent under any circumstances, as that can make the Gamut Warning display difficult to see.

The Preferences you establish for Gamut Warning are not actually applied until you click OK in the Preferences dialog box, so you aren't able to preview the effect of different settings while you make adjustments.

Activating Gamut Warning

With the Gamut Warning preferences established with appropriate settings for the image you are working on, you can turn on the gamut warning (see Figure 7.25) by selecting View > Gamut Warning from the menu, or by pressing Shift+Ctrl+Y (Shift+Command+Y on Macintosh) on the keyboard. You can confirm that the gamut warning is active (if it isn't obvious from the display of your image) by clicking the View menu and confirming that there is a checkmark in front of the Gamut Warning option (see Figure 7.26).

Figure 7.25 When you activate the Gamut Warning display, the color you selected in Preferences will be shown over areas of the image that are out of gamut for the current Proof Setup. In this example, the Gamut Warning color was set to a highly saturated green so it would show up better against the colors in this image. (Photograph by John Shaw, www.johnshawphoto.com.)

Figure 7.26
You can verify that you are viewing the image with Gamut Warning turned on by confirming that there is a checkmark in front of Gamut Warning in the View menu. Be sure that Proof Colors is also turned on when you are using the Gamut Warning display.

Note: In addition to using the Gamut Warning display, you can also observe which colors are out of gamut for the current CMYK working space or Proof Colors setup using the Info palette. With the Info palette visible, simply move your cursor over the image with the mouse. The CMYK values will be displayed for the pixel under your cursor. If an exclamation point (!) is shown after one or more numbers, the pixel under your mouse is out of gamut. However, this is not nearly as helpful as the Gamut Warning option.

Adjusting Images

Once you have established your Proof Colors and Gamut Warning settings and are viewing your image with both options turned on, you may very well want to adjust the image to ensure the best final appearance of the image for the specific output conditions and to make sure that all colors are within the color gamut of that output process.

I strongly recommend using new adjustment layers for these adjustments, so you can fine-tune later as needed, and so you can easily switch between different versions of your image for different specific output methods. In fact, I encourage you to use a layer set to contain the adjustments being used to a single "package."

Follow these steps to adjust the image using adjustment layers packaged into a layer set:

1. Make sure that you have enabled soft proofing (View > Proof Colors) and the gamut warning display (View > Gamut Warning) so that you see a simulation of the output based on the profile to be used, with out-of-gamut colors clearly indicated.

2. Create a new layer set to contain the adjustments you will apply to the image to ensure all colors are within gamut and as accurate as possible. To create a new layer set, click the New Layer Set button (it has a folder icon on it) at the bottom of the Layers palette. If you hold the Alt key (Option key on Macintosh) while clicking on the New Layer Set button, you will be prompted to enter a name for the layer set. Otherwise, you can double-click the name of the layer set on the Layers palette to change the name. I recommend using a name for the layer set that references the printer, ink, and paper combination you will be using to print the adjusted image (see Figure 7.27).

Figure 7.27
Creating a new layer set for your print-targeting adjustments allows you to keep the Layers palette organized and to keep these adjustments separate from your normal adjustments. (Photograph by John Shaw, www.johnshawphoto.com.)

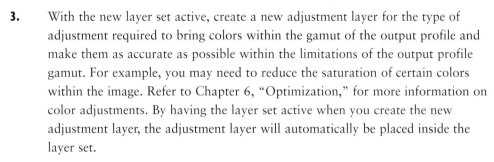

Note: If you will be printing an image using a variety of printer, ink, and paper combinations, you may want to create separate adjustments for each combination, with each in a separate layer set. With the ability to nest layer sets in Photoshop CS, you could create a layer set called "Output Adjustments," for example, putting an additional layer set for each output process within that set.

3. With the new layer set active, create a new adjustment layer for the type of adjustment required to bring colors within the gamut of the output profile and make them as accurate as possible within the limitations of the output profile gamut. For example, you may need to reduce the saturation of certain colors within the image. Refer to Chapter 6, "Optimization," for more information on color adjustments. By having the layer set active when you create the new adjustment layer, the adjustment layer will automatically be placed inside the layer set.

4. Create additional adjustment layers within the layer set, and fine-tune the image until the Gamut Warning display indicates that all colors are within the color gamut of the output profile being used (see Figure 7.28).

Figure 7.28 Create new adjustment layers within the layer set you created, adjusting the image until it looks good with no out-of-gamut colors. (Photograph by John Shaw, www.johnshawphoto.com.)

5. Once you have adjusted the image with adjustment layers in the layer set, you can collapse the layer set to keep your Layers palette tidy. Simply click on the triangle to the left of the layer set to collapse the set, so that you only see the folder and not the adjustment layers within the folder. You can expand the layer set at any time by clicking the triangle again.

6. After the layer set is created and it contains all the adjustment layers to optimize the image for a specific output process, all you need to do when printing is make sure the layer set is visible (see Figure 7.29). For general adjustments to your master image, you would want to keep the visibility of this layer set turned off. To turn off the visibility of the layer set, simply click on the eyeball icon to the left of the layer set. Turning off the visibility of the layer set will automatically turn off the visibility of all adjustment layers within that set, hiding the adjustments they cause in the image.

Figure 7.29
By using the Proof Colors and Gamut Warning options, you can produce excellent prints that take full advantage of the capabilities of your printer. (Photograph by John Shaw, www.johnshawphoto.com.)

Print Preparation

With adjustments made to ensure the most accurate output possible, you're ready to perform the final steps in preparing the image for print. This includes sizing and sharpening the image for output, along with some other adjustments along the way. I'll address each of the steps individually.

Save the Master Image

At the end of Chapter 6, I said that after optimizing the image you should save the master file for all future output. Now we're saving that master file yet again, with the additional updates discussed earlier in this chapter that were created based on the Proof Colors and Gamut Warning displays. You can never save too often, and at this point you have a new master image to save.

Many of the other steps of print preparation are destructive to your image. "Destructive" may sound like a harsh word, especially considering that the whole process is geared toward producing the best print possible. By destructive, I mean that pixel values are changed, and in fact some pixel values will be thrown away. It is, therefore, important that you save the image at this point, with all the adjustments intact, so that you have an updated "master" image file.

Duplicate the Image

Once you've saved the image, you're ready to start making the necessary adjustments so you can send the image data to the printer and finally get that gorgeous image hanging on the wall. However, the conservative approach is best. If you perform the destructive tasks that follow on your master image file, and then you accidentally save the final result, you may end up with a master image that is virtually useless.

For example, let's assume that you've perfected an image and you are ready to make a big print. But first your significant other, friend, parent, or other person who is proud of your accomplishments asks if they can have a wallet-sized print of the image so they can show it off to all their friends. So, you resize the image, flatten it, sharpen it (don't worry, I'll address all of those steps in detail shortly), and make a print. Then, when you go to close the image, Photoshop asks if you want to save the revised image file. You've gotten so accustomed to always saying "Yes" when you close a word processing document you haven't saved since changing that you instinctively click Yes. When you open the image at a later date to produce that large print, you are disheartened to discover you have saved that little 3"×2" wallet print, losing the large image with which you started. With any luck, you have at least saved the original image so you can start over again.

To avoid any sort of problems, you should immediately duplicate your image when you start the print preparation process. To do make a duplicate, select Image > Duplicate from the menu. You will be prompted to provide a name for the image, with the default of the existing file name with "copy" appended. I usually replace "copy" with "print," so I'll know why I produced this version of the image file if I accidentally save it (see Figure 7.30). Because it is a duplicate, I won't have to worry about closing the file and saving changes, because the name will be different from the original master image file.

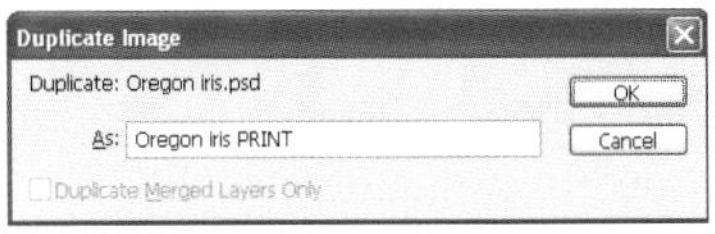

Figure 7.30 Duplicating your master image to produce a working copy is an excellent way to ensure you don't accidentally save a less-than-optimal image in place of your master file.

By working on a duplicate image (the "working copy"), you don't have to worry at all about the changes you make in the print process, because your master image file will be safe and untouched. In fact, as soon as you have duplicated the image, you can close the original image to free up memory so you won't have to worry about accidentally making changes to the wrong version.

Flatten the Image

The many layers (especially the adjustment layers) you have likely created in order to optimize your image are very good things, because they allow you to return to the image later to fine-tune your adjustments. However, for the purpose of printing, they consume more memory than is needed, and they could cause problems with the sharpening that will be applied to the image. This is because the Unsharp Mask filter we are going to use can apply only to a single layer. If you used multiple image layers in your document, such as by using the Clone Stamp or Healing Brush tools on a separate layer, you will need to sharpen each of these layers individually.

Instead, you can flatten the image so it doesn't contain any layers, allowing you to sharpen the image as a whole and consuming less memory. First, be sure that all the layers that should be included in the image you are printing are currently visible and all layers you don't want included are invisible. For example, if you created several layer sets with adjustments to optimize the image for various output methods, turn on the visibility of the layer set for the current output process and turn off the visibility of any other such layer sets.

To flatten the image, select Layer > Flatten Image from the menu, or select Flatten Image from the side menu on the Layers palette. This will merge all visible layers into a single background image layer. If there are any invisible layers, you will be asked if hidden layers should be discarded. Click Yes, and the image will be flattened.

Resize for Output

The first step after creating a working copy of your image is to size it to the dimensions you want to use for printing. To do so, select Image > Image Size from the menu to bring up the Image Size dialog box. The basic settings you need to adjust are in the Document Size section. In order to be able to actually change the number of pixels in the image, you'll need to check the Resample Image checkbox. If you aren't already familiar with resizing your images, you can use the following approach:

1. Select Image > Image Size from the menu to open the Image Size dialog (see Figure 7.31).

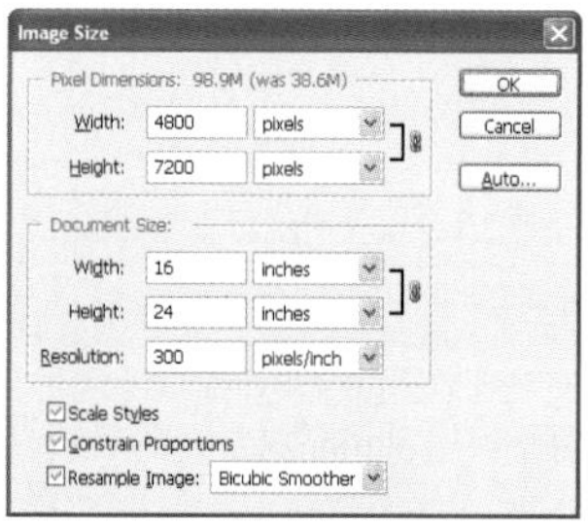

Figure 7.31

The Image Size dialog box allows you to resize your image for print.

2. Uncheck the Resample Image checkbox, and then set the Resolution to the desired output resolution. For most output, a setting of 300 pixels/inch will produce excellent results. By setting the output resolution while the Resample Image checkbox is unchecked, the Width and Height settings in the Document Size section will automatically update to indicate how big the image can be printed at the Resolution entered with no interpolation. In other words, it shows you how big your image is initially. This can be very helpful in understanding how much you are changing the overall image size and, therefore, how much the quality is likely to suffer in the process.

3. Now check the Resample Image checkbox so you can actually change the size of the image.

4. Check the Constrain Proportions checkbox also, so you aren't able to stretch the image in one direction or the other.

5. If desired, you can change the interpolation method using the dropdown list provided. Bicubic is an excellent general choice. However, Photoshop CS adds two new options: Bicubic Smoother is best for increasing the size of the image, and Bicubic Sharper is better for reducing the size of the image.

6. Change the Width or Height as needed to produce an image of the size you intend to print. In general, this means sizing the image so it is slightly smaller than the paper on which you will be printing.

7. The document size will be shown in megabytes at the top of the Image Size dialog box, after the Pixel Dimensions caption. An indication of the size of the image file before resizing (based on the current values) will appear in parentheses after this value. This gives you one more indication of the degree to which you are resizing the image.

8. Click OK and the image will be resized based on the settings you have entered.

Once you are familiar with resizing, you won't need to go through this process. Simply make sure the Resample Image and Constrain Proportions checkbox is checked, confirm the interpolation option in the dropdown list after the Resample Image checkbox, and set the Width, Height, and Resolution settings in the Document Size section of the dialog box before clicking OK.

Crop for Resize

I normally recommend that you crop your images based on an aesthetic decision, not based on the size of the frame you'll be using for the image. Of course, this often means that your images must be custom framed, which can get to be expensive. If you need an image to fit a specific frame size, you can use the crop tool to automatically size the image to specific dimensions, cropping to fit that aspect ratio in the process.

To use the Crop tool to resize your image, first select the tool from the Tools palette (or press **C** on your keyboard). The Options bar will then reflect the options available for the Crop tool, including Width, Height, and Resolution settings. Set the Width and Height as desired, using "in" to reflect inches, such as "10 in" for Width and "8 in" for Height. Then set the Resolution to the output resolution you'll be using, such as 300, with the dropdown set to "pixels/inch."

Drag the cursor across your image, starting from one corner and releasing the mouse when you reach the opposite corner. Notice that as you draw the cropping rectangle, the aspect ratio will remain fixed. Adjust the outer edges of the crop box to encompass the area of the image you want to keep. When the cropping rectangle is sized and positioned the way you want it, press Enter (Return on Macintosh) or double-click inside the cropping rectangle. The image will then be cropped and resized in one step, resulting in an image of the exact dimensions you entered. If necessary, the image will be interpolated based on your settings in the Preferences dialog box.

Note that the Width, Height, and Resolution settings will be remembered until you change them. Therefore, it is a good idea to click the Clear button on the Options bar to clear out these settings. That way you won't have to worry about the Crop tool behaving unexpectedly in the future.

Set Target Black and White Values

Many printers are unable to produce discreet shades of black throughout the complete tonal range available in your digital image files. In some cases, printers may not be able to produce a full range of bright white values either. When this happens, detail will be lost in an image. For example, consider the range of very dark tones that have a value of 0 through 10, with 0 representing pure black and 10 representing a very dark gray that is nearly black. Let's assume your printer is only able to produce a discreet value down to a shade of black represented by a value of 8 in our example. That means that any values between 0 and 8 will all be printed as the same tonal value, which is the darkest black the printer is able to produce. That means that dark shadow areas containing detail in the ranges from 0 to 8 will not contain any detail in the print.

By targeting specific black and white values, we can fully utilize the available tonal range for a given printer. Using the example outlined here, if we were to make the darkest pixel in the image equal to a value of 8, those pixels would print as black, and everything lighter would print as a discreet tone, so that no detail is lost.

This can be achieved by using the Output sliders in the Levels adjustment (it can also be done with Curves, but I consider Levels to be easier for this type of adjustment). But first, you need to figure out what values to use. To figure that out, use the following process:

> **Note:** If you don't want to build your own target image to determine the appropriate black and white point values for your printer, you can download a target from my website, www.timgrey.com

1.   Create a new document by selecting File > New from the menu. Set the Width to 10 inches, the Height to 8 inches, and the Resolution to the value you generally use for the printer you are testing. Set the Color Mode to RGB and the Background Contents to White.

2.   Select the Rectangular Marquee tool from the Tools palette.

3.   On the Options bar, set the Style to Fixed Size, the Width to "0.5 in" and the Height to "2 in."

4.   Click near the top-left corner of the document to place the Marquee selection with the designated dimensions. Point inside the selection, and click and drag to place it all the way against the left edge of the document.

5.   Click the foreground color on the Tools palette to bring up the Color Picker. Set all three values for R, G, and B to 0, and click OK.

6.   Press Alt+Delete to fill the Marquee selection with the foreground color.

7.   With the Rectangular Marquee tool still active, point inside the selection and click and drag the selection to the right, so that the left edge of the selection matches up with the right edge of the black box you created in Step 6. You can allow the selection to overlap with the black box if necessary to ensure they are touching each other.

8. Repeat Steps 5 through 7, incrementing the values for all three R, G, and B fields each time by a single value until you have created boxes for values 0 through 19.

9. Repeat Steps 5 through 8 on a new row in the document, but this time increment each value by 2, so that if you can't see any distinction between the increments of 1, you'll still be able to determine what values to use.

10. If desired, repeat Steps 5 through 8 again for the white values, creating boxes with R, G, and B values ranging from 250 to 255. With most printers, this won't be necessary because they are able to produce discrete tones all the way up to R, G, and B values of 254, before leaving only the paper to show with no ink at values of 255.

11. Use the text tool to label all of the boxes so you'll know what values they correspond to in the test print.

12. Print this target image using the same settings you will use to print your photographic images (see Figure 7.32).

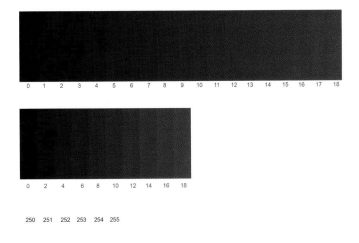

Figure 7.32 You can use a test image to determine the darkest black and brightest white your printer is able to produce, so you can target your images to fully utilize the range available with the printer.

13. Evaluate the print under bright lighting conditions, preferably with a 5000 K illumination source. Determine the darkest value that doesn't blend in with the lighter value adjacent to it. This will tell you the value of the darkest discrete black your printer is able to produce. If you also created blocks to test the white value, determine which value represents the brightest discrete tone. Make a note of the black and white values, which will be used to adjust the image for the specific output conditions under which you tested the target image. Note that the paper properties will affect the ability of the printer to produce discrete values,

so you'll need to perform this test for each printer, ink, and paper combination you intend to use.

Once you have determined the darkest black and brightest white your printer is able to produce for the particular printer, ink, and paper combination you are using, you can set the image to use those values as the darkest and lightest points in the image, ensuring that the image will contain only values the printer is able to produce. This allows you to make full use of the tonal range of the printer.

To adjust the image, select Image > Adjustments > Levels from the menu. Note that we don't want to create a new adjustment layer at this point because we've already flattened the image. The only values that need to be adjusted to target the desired black and white points are the two Output Levels text boxes. The left box is the black point, and the right box is the white point. Enter the values you determine through the testing outlined above, and click OK (see Figure 7.33). The contrast of the image will appear to be reduced to some degree, but the final print won't represent this reduced contrast because you are targeting the darkest and lightest tones the printer is able to produce.

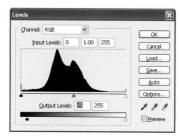

Figure 7.33

Enter the values you determined through testing in the Output Levels boxes in the Levels dialog box. For example, when printing to Premium Luster Photo Paper on the Epson Stylus Photo 2200, I typically target a black point of 15, with no adjustment for the white point.

Sharpen for Output

The process of converting an analog scene into a digital image, whether through scanning a piece of film or taking a picture with a digital camera, results in a loss of sharpness. When you print an image, the spreading of ink on paper (known as "dot gain") also results in a loss of perceived sharpness. Therefore, it is important to sharpen the image just before printing to ensure the best results.

Sharpening an image involves increasing the contrast in areas of the image that already contain contrast. In other words, you are increasing the contrast along the edges of objects in your image. This creates the appearance of greater sharpness, because it exaggerates edges and brings out detail in fine textures.

The best way to sharpen your image is with the Unsharp Mask filter, accessed by selecting Filter > Sharpen > Unsharp Mask from the menu (see Figure 7.34). Despite its name, it is indeed used to sharpen an image.

Figure 7.34

The right settings for Unsharp Mask will ensure that you are optimizing the detail in the image without causing quality problems. (Photograph by John Shaw, www.johnshawphoto.com.)

The Unsharp Mask dialog box contains the following settings:

Amount controls the intensity of the sharpening applied, effectively determining how much you are increasing the contrast along the edges within the image.

Radius is the most important setting, as it determines how large a "halo" will be created when contrast is enhanced along the edges in your image.

Threshold determines how much contrast must exist in order for an area to be considered an edge. At a very low, setting virtually all pixels within the image will be considered edges and, therefore, sharpened. At a very high setting, virtually no pixels will be considered edges, which could result in virtually no sharpening being applied to the image. This setting can be used to help minimize the exaggeration of fine detail, noise, or grain in an image.

Now that you understand what these settings are used for, you need to consider what settings would be best for the image with which you are working. The main issue to consider here is whether the image contains a great deal of fine detail or mostly contains smooth areas. With fine texture, the contrast edges within the image will be very small. Therefore, you want the halos created when sharpening to be very small. Otherwise, the halos might end up being larger than the texture you are trying to enhance. Conversely, with images containing mostly smooth areas, you'll need to use larger halos that aren't as intense.

The Amount and Radius settings relate to each other in an inverse fashion: the higher the Amount the smaller the Radius, and vice versa. Refer to Table 7.1 for the basic range of values you will want to consider when sharpening your image.

▶ **Table 7.1** Unsharp Mask Settings

Unsharp Mask Setting	High-Detail Image	Average Image	Low-Detail Image
Amount	200% to 300%	100% to 150%	75% to 125%
Radius	0.5 to 0.8	1.0 to 1.5	2.0 to 3.0
Threshold	0 to 4	4 to 8	8 to 12

When evaluating the sharpening settings you are using for an image, you always want to look at the actual pixels. That would typically mean zooming the image to 100 percent before selecting Unsharp Mask from the menu. However, with large images, having the preview turned on can slow things down considerably. Therefore, my preference is to size the actual image so that I can see it in its entirety. I then uncheck the Preview checkbox in the Unsharp Mask dialog box and use the preview in the dialog box for evaluating conditions. You can click anywhere on the image to focus the preview on that area. Also, you can click and hold the mouse on the preview image within the dialog box to see that area without sharpening applied, and you can then release the mouse to see that area with sharpening applied.

Rather than using generic values for sharpening an image, I use a method that allows me to determine the best settings for a specific image. I start with the Amount set to the maximum value of 500 percent and the Threshold set to 0. I then adjust the Radius setting, which is the most important setting in the dialog box. Watching the preview, which will show an exaggerated view of the sharpening effect due to the Amount and Threshold settings used, I can determine how big a halo is most appropriate for the current image. Once I have settled on the best Radius setting, I reduce the Amount setting to produce the desired level of sharpening. Finally, I adjust the threshold as needed to ensure that areas with relatively smooth texture aren't sharpened. For example, with a portrait you would use a slightly higher threshold setting so that the pores on the face are not exaggerated to produce a result that is less than pleasing.

Once you have established the ideal Unsharp Mask settings, click OK to apply the sharpening to your image.

Note: If you expect to make a number of prints of this image in the future, you might want to save it with a new name at this point. I recommend adding the print size (such as Print_8x10) to the end of the existing filename so you'll be able to easily identify the image. Because there are no layers in this image, I recommend saving it in TIFF format even if you use Photoshop PSD for your master image file. If you save a file in this way, all you'll need to do is open this file and print it, without any of the other preparation steps.

Convert to Profile?

Some photographers also convert the image to the output profile as the final step before printing. Personally, I prefer not to use this method. However, if you are using a custom profile, you most certainly can. It won't make any difference in the final output if you use the correct settings, so it is really a matter of preference.

If you prefer to convert the image to the output profile, as the final step after sharpening, you can select Image > Mode > Convert To Profile from the menu. The Source Space will reflect the current profile for your image, which would most likely be the current working space. For Destination Space, select the appropriate profile for your printer, ink, and paper combination from the Profile dropdown list. The Conversion Options section should reflect the same settings you would otherwise use for the final printed output. I recommend leaving the Engine set to Adobe (ACE). (ACE is an acronym for Adobe Color Engine.) Rendering intent would be either Relative Colorimetric or Perceptual. If you used the procedures outlined earlier in this chapter to adjust the image based on Proof Colors and Gamut Warning, then I recommend using Relative Colorimetric. I always recommend checking the Use Black Point Compensation and Use Dither checkboxes. The dithering option is available only for 8-bit-per-channel images, and it helps to simulate colors that are out of gamut for the output profile. If you still have layers in the image (at this point you probably won't if you've followed my recommended workflow), you can check the Flatten Image box to flatten if preferred at this point.

If you do convert your image to the output profile, the final print settings will also change slightly. I'll address that issue later in this chapter.

Print Setup

With a perfected image that is optimized for your specific printer, ink, and paper combination, you're ready to send the image to the printer and get that image hung on the wall! Of course, getting the best print isn't as easy as selecting File > Print from the menu. However, once you understand the optimal settings to be used, you'll be able to quickly configure the settings for printing each time you're ready to produce another print.

Print with Preview

In order to designate which profile should be used to interpret the color numbers in the image file, you'll need to use the Print With Preview dialog box in Photoshop, which can be accessed by choosing File > Print With Preview from the menu, or by pressing Ctrl+Alt+P on the keyboard (Command+Option+P on Macintosh).

To be able to set the profile for printing, you must have the Show More Options checkbox checked. Make sure that Color Management (rather than Output) is selected from the dropdown list below the Show More Options checkbox. Changing this dropdown doesn't change the way the print will be produced, but rather simply determines which settings will be displayed in the dialog box.

The Source Space should be set to Document, which will reflect the profile embedded in the image you are printing. In most cases, this would be the same as the working space you are using for RGB images. The only time you would use the Proof Setup option here is if you want to simulate the output of a different printer using your own printer.

The Print Space section allows you to specify the profile settings for this print job. The Profile dropdown list should be set to the appropriate profile for the printer, ink, and paper combination you are using (see Figure 7.35). If you have a custom, canned, or generic profile specific to the print setup, select it from the dropdown list. If you don't have a profile specific to the type of paper you are using, you can also use the generic profile for the printer that does not specify a paper type (see Figure 7.36). If your printer doesn't include a generic profile, and you don't have any custom profiles, you'll need to let the printer driver handle all color management tasks. In that case, set the Profile option to Printer Color Management.

Note: If you converted your image to the printer profile you are using, then the Profile should be set to Same As Source.

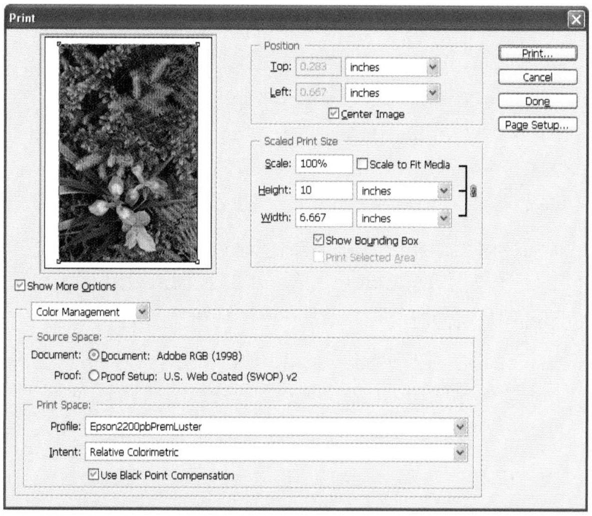

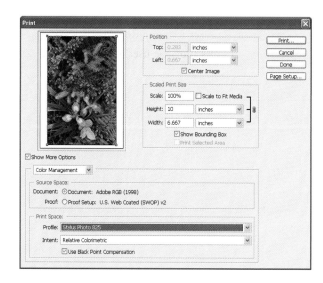

Figure 7.35
The Print With Preview dialog box allows you to specify the profile to be used to interpret the colors in the image for the specific printer, ink, and paper combination you are using. (Photograph by John Shaw, www .johnshawphoto.com.)

Figure 7.36
If you don't have a custom profile for the paper you will be printing to, you can select a generic profile for your printer. (Photograph by John Shaw, www.johnshawphoto.com.)

The Intent should be set to the appropriate rendering intent for this profile. If you used the Proof Colors and Gamut Warning displays to optimize the print for the profile being used, then the Relative Colorimetric rendering intent is the best choice. If there are a significant number of out-of-gamut colors, Perceptual is a good choice because it will help maintain the relationships between colors in the image.

I recommend that you always check the Use Black Point Compensation box so that the black in your image will be mapped to the black in the printer profile.

When you have adjusted all of the options on this dialog box, click Print to proceed to the Print dialog box. Select the appropriate printer from the dropdown list, and then click Properties to adjust the printer properties.

Printer Properties

When you click the Properties button in the Print dialog box, the software for your specific printer will determine the dialog box that is displayed. This means that for each brand of printer there will be a unique dialog box setup, and even for different models of printers within the same manufacturer there can be considerable variation. Therefore, I can't provide you with the exact settings used for your specific printer. However, I can provide the following guidelines so you'll better understand which settings should be used:

Paper type   The type of paper you use can have a dramatic influence on the colors produced by the printer. Therefore, selecting the correct paper type is critical. If your paper type is not listed, select the closest paper in terms of surface type. Note that this setting should be exactly the same as the one used to create a custom profile if you are using one. Also note that with some profiles or custom profile packages, using a setting that doesn't match your specific paper type is best. For example, Color Vision recommends using a matte paper type when using profiles generated with their PrintFIX package.

Output quality   This is the setting that relates to the resolution of the printer as promoted by the printer manufacturers. Use a setting equivalent to 1,440 dpi. In many cases this is simply referred to as "Photo," "Best Photo," or a similar name. Refer to your printer documentation to confirm the appropriate settings.

Inks   Even if you are printing a black-and-white image, be sure the option for which inks to use is set to "Color" or whatever setting will use all of the available inks. As mentioned in the "Colorize for Print" section of Chapter 6, using only the black ink will result in a neutral print of poor quality, so all inks must be used in balance to produce a print of the best quality.

Special output settings   Some printers offer special output settings to optimize the colors or other aspects of your image. These print modes should generally not be used in conjunction with custom profile. However, if you are using a generic profile for your printer, you may want to take advantage of some of these options.

Color management settings   These settings are the critical ones that determine the accuracy of the prints you are producing. Two basic scenarios dictate which settings should be used. The first is when you are using a "custom" profile that is specific to the printer, ink, and paper you are using. The other is when you are using a generic profile for your printer that is not specific to the type of paper being used.

Custom Profiles

A custom profile provides you with the best possible accuracy in your printed output, provided the profile itself is highly accurate. Regardless of the type of printer you are using, I strongly recommend that you build a custom profile for the specific printer, ink, and paper combination you are using.

Note: For purposes of this section, custom profiles include profiles you have built yourself; profiles from third-party profile-making services; canned profiles that are specific to printer, ink, and paper combinations; and generic profiles that are specific to particular models of printers and specific paper types, such as those from third-party sources.

When using a custom profile, you really don't want the printer software to do anything that would alter the output. In the printer properties dialog box, look for an option to disable any adjustment to the image, such as No Color Adjustment (see Figure 7.37).

Figure 7.37

When using a custom printer profile, configure the printer properties so that no color adjustment is applied to the image data by the printer.

Most importantly, the settings used in the printer properties when you are utilizing a custom profile should match the settings that were used when the profile was actually created. However, in general they should be the same settings that would cause no adjustment in the colors produced by the printer on the part of the printer software.

Note: If you obtain a profile from a third party, get information from them as to what printer settings should be used to obtain the most accurate results.

Generic Printer Profiles

If you are using a generic profile for your printer that isn't specific to a particular type of paper, you need to adjust the printer settings for optimal results on that paper. Start by using the appropriate paper and quality settings, as outlined earlier in this section. Then produce a print with the printer's automatic settings to see if the results are accurate. If not, use the color adjustment options within the printer properties to fine-tune the color balance of the output until it matches what you see on your calibrated monitor. This will take some trial-and-error to find the right settings, but once you have established those settings for a specific printer, ink, and paper combination, you'll be able to use those settings any time you print an image with the same setup.

If the printer properties dialog box provides an option to save the settings once you have determined the ones that produce the most accurate results, I recommend doing so. Use a name for the settings that references the type of paper for which it was designed. Then you can simply load those settings in the printer properties dialog box whenever you are printing to that paper type.

No Profile

If your printer does not include any ICC profiles that are accessible to you, and you don't have a custom profile for the printer, ink, and paper combination you are using, you need to use the Printer Color Management option in the Print With Preview dialog box and then configure the printer properties to obtain the best results. In this case, consult your printer documentation for the best settings to use.

Evaluating Prints

It should be clear to you by now that the color management systems available to us revolve around very specific standards. Those standards extend to the conditions under which you evaluate your final prints to decide if they match the image file as you saw it on your monitor (see Figure 7.38).

Figure 7.38
Once you have properly optimized and prepared your image, you can expect to obtain an excellent print with accurate colors and fine detail. (Photograph by John Shaw, www.johnshawphoto.com.)

Environment

Color management revolves around a standard illumination source with a color temperature of 5000 degrees Kelvin. That means, to fairly evaluate the accuracy of a print from the standpoint of a color-managed workflow, you'll need to evaluate the final print under a 5000 K light source (see Figure 7.39).

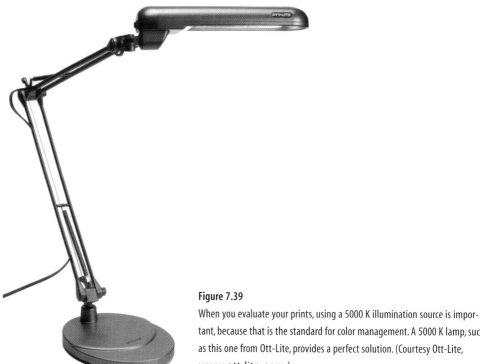

Figure 7.39
When you evaluate your prints, using a 5000 K illumination source is important, because that is the standard for color management. A 5000 K lamp, such as this one from Ott-Lite, provides a perfect solution. (Courtesy Ott-Lite, www.ott-lite.com.)

Of course, in the real world, your images are not likely to be displayed under a 5000 K illumination source. Just because your image looks perfect under a 5000 K light source doesn't mean it will still look perfect under a different light source. Recall from Chapter 1, "Foundations," that any change in the illumination source, the object, or the observer will cause a change in the perceived color. Therefore, it makes sense to evaluate your prints under the type of lighting under which they will be displayed.

In fairness to current color management standards, you should still evaluate your prints under a 5000 K light source to confirm the accuracy of the print. Then, view the print using the type of lighting it will be displayed under and determine if it still looks accurate. The wash of color caused by different light sources will certainly affect the perceived colors in the image (see Figure 7.40). However, the human visual system is quite adept at automatically compensating for these differences. This is sort of like an automatic white balance compensation in the brain. Anything that is white in the image will be compensated for by your brain, so that you "know" the object is really white and you judge the other colors in the image based on that established white point. In order for this to work most effectively, some white must be visible around the image. You can introduce white into the displayed image by letting some of the white paper show around the image area or by matting the image with a white mat board. In other words, if white is visible near the print under the same lighting, variations caused by that lighting probably aren't an issue.

Figure 7.40 The color of the lighting can dramatically alter the appearance of a print. The image on the left shows the appearance under a 5000 K light source, while the image on the right shows the same image under an incandescent light source. (Photograph by Art Morris, www.birdsasart.com.)

If you decide that the lighting conditions do present a problem, you can adjust the image to compensate for the influence of the lighting. However, there is no method to simulate the effects of different lighting conditions when making these adjustments. It, therefore, becomes a matter of trial-and-error to find the adjustment that will provide a good compensation. Keep in mind the color influence the lighting conditions create, and make an adjustment to shift the color balance of the image in the opposite direction. For example, to compensate for the yellow to orange cast caused by incandescent lighting, you would need to shift the color balance toward blue and cyan slightly.

Standard Print Target

When you are testing your color-managed workflow, it may be best to use a special test image for print testing, so that you have a better range of tones and colors to evaluate. This target should ideally include neutral values to confirm they are reproduced as truly neutral, objects that represent "memory colors" with a variety of hues, and people so you can evaluate flesh tones, because they can be a particular challenge to reproduce accurately.

A variety of sample print targets are available. I recommend the PhotoDisc target, which contains a variety of real-world objects, a gray ramp to evaluate neutrality, a color checker chart, and four models representing a variety of flesh tones (see Figure 7.41). Using such an image can help you better evaluate the accuracy of colors in your color-managed workflow.

Note: You can download the PhotoDisc target image from my website, www.timgrey.com.

Figure 7.41
The PhotoDisc target image is an excellent tool for evaluating the accuracy of your printing process.

When Prints Don't Match

Since you're reading this book, chances are you've run into the situation on more than one occasion where the print doesn't match what you see on the monitor. This is the single biggest source of frustration for photographers when it comes to color management. In fact, getting prints to match the monitor is the reason color management exists (and the reason for this book). When a print doesn't come out as expected, the experience can be quite frustrating.

It is often tempting to adjust the image in Photoshop when the printed image doesn't match what you see on the monitor. For example, if the print comes out too magenta, you may be tempted to adjust the color balance in the image toward green to offset that magenta. The problem with this approach is that you are making the image itself intentionally inaccurate in an effort to produce accurate results for a single output condition. What happens when you print that same image with a different printer, ink, and paper combination? You'll have to find new ways to manipulate the image in an effort to produce an accurate print. In effect, you're chasing the print, trying to find just the right way to adjust the image to make it look wrong in just the right way so the print will look the way you want it to look (see Figure 7.42). This is not a good way to work with your images.

Figure 7.42 When the monitor image looks good Ⓐ, but the print doesn't match Ⓑ it may be tempting to adjust the monitor display in the opposite direction Ⓒ to produce an accurate print Ⓓ. However, by chasing the print in this manner, you are producing an inaccurate image Ⓔ, that will print incorrectly when you are using an accurate profile Ⓕ or sending the image to someone else.

When you feel that a print doesn't look accurate, evaluating the print under proper viewing conditions is important. As mentioned earlier, the standard illumination source for current color management systems is 5000 K. In order to fairly assess the accuracy of a print, you should evaluate it under a 5000 K light source. If you examine the print under lighting with a different color temperature, the print will be influenced by that color. If the lighting is dim, the print will appear dark because it depends on reflected light.

When you've decided that the print isn't accurate, the first thing to do is determine where the blame lies. Printer profiles and settings can be a real hornet's nest of issues, but be sure that's where the problem lies before you start looking for the source of the problem in those areas.

When I run into a situation where the print doesn't appear as selected, the first thing I do is open an image that is known to be accurate. I usually use the PhotoDisc target image as my reference, but any image that you are confident contains accurate values is perfectly fine. Open this image and evaluate the appearance on your monitor. If it doesn't look accurate, then you may have a problem with your monitor display. Recalibrate your monitor, and view the test image again to confirm you are getting an accurate display.

If the monitor looks correct, print the image while paying very close attention to the profile and printer settings being used. For example, many printers default to settings for plain paper rather than photographic output, which can cause unpredictable results in your prints. Step through the printer properties dialog box very slowly to confirm that all settings are accurate for the test print. If the image prints incorrectly and you're positive you have used the right settings, do some basic printer testing to confirm that it is functioning properly.

> **Note:** Printers are subject to various problems that affect the accuracy of their output. For example, inkjet printers experience clogged nozzles that prevent certain inks from being completely laid down on the paper. This can result in a significant color cast in the image. If your prints don't match, especially if you are using output settings that have worked well in the past, perform maintenance tasks on your printer such as running the nozzle cleaning utility, cleaning excess ink from the sponges in the printer, and other items that may contribute to inaccurate output.

If the monitor image looks accurate, and you've carefully confirmed all of the printer settings, the profile being used becomes suspect. If you are using a custom profile that you have created yourself, you may want to attempt to create a new profile. If you obtained the profile from a third party, inquire about updated profiles that may be available, or special settings that should be used when using the profile. If all else fails, you can resort to the generic profile for your printer, using the adjustment options available in the printer properties to fine-tune the color balance of the output.

Other Mismatch Issues

Other issues can cause variations in printed output and can cause some colors to appear inaccurate. These issues include "metamerism" and "bronzing."

Metamerism is frequently confused with simple variations in appearance under different lighting. A more accurate description of metamerism would be a situation where two colors appear to match under one lighting condition, but don't match under a different lighting condition. If we expand that to broaden its application, metamerism could be described as having two colors with one relationship under one lighting condition, but a different relationship under another lighting condition. In other words, a change in lighting can cause some colors in the image to have a larger perceptual change than other colors.

Such a problem can be very difficult to correct, particularly because different colors are affected differently. This relates to reviewing your images in the lighting conditions under which they will be displayed, and then making adjustments to the image in an effort to compensate for those variations. This is a trial-and-error process, and it can be very frustrating. Fortunately, most printers don't exhibit significant metamerism issues, so it isn't likely that you will need to deal with it.

Bronzing is another issue that can be a problem with certain printers. This is when certain inks (typically black) have different reflective properties than the other inks, causing variations in their appearance under some lighting conditions. It usually manifests as a slightly bronze appearance, particularly where black ink is prevalent in the print. Unfortunately, if the inks exhibit this behavior, there isn't much you can do about it. Framing the print under glass will often minimize or eliminate the appearance of bronzing.

CMYK Output

While most photographers are primarily interested in producing their own prints in their digital darkroom, many of them need (or desire) to obtain prints from outside services, typically using a CMYK output process such as an offset press.

> **Note:** Even though desktop photo printers use CMYK inks, they should still be considered RGB devices because they are optimized to process RGB data. Therefore, CMYK conversions should not be performed for images that will be printed to such devices, and the best results will be obtained by keeping the image in RGB.

Two basic options are available to you when you need to provide images for CMYK output: send an RGB image or convert the image to CMYK yourself.

RGB with Proof Print

Sending an RGB image with a proof print showing exactly what you want it to look like is the best option for photographers who don't have experience working with CMYK files. It places the responsibility for an accurate CMYK conversion and final print on the print lab. This is why most printers (the people, not the devices) won't want to provide this option. They'd rather let you take responsibility for any inaccuracy in the final print, so that they don't have to print it again for free.

> **Note:** Even when sending an RGB image to the print lab and letting them deal with the CMYK conversion, communication is key to a good relationship and accurate results. Talk to the staff about how the file should be prepared, what type of proof print they prefer, and any other details that will help ensure the best results possible with no misunderstandings.

Because you already have your master image perfected in RGB mode, providing this image is easy. Follow the same process as preparing the image to print on your own desktop printer, which includes:

1. Create a duplicate working copy of the image by selecting Image > Duplicate from the menu.

2. Flatten the image to merge all layers into a single background layer. Be sure that you have turned off the visibility of adjustments designed to optimize the image for a specific output process. Flatten the image by selecting Layer > Flatten Image from the menu or selecting Flatten Image from the side menu on the Layers palette.

3. If recommended by your print lab, convert the image to an appropriate profile. For example, some labs want the image converted to sRGB to fit their workflow, even though you would normally prefer to use Adobe RGB (1998) for your own output.

4. Resize the image to the size needed for the final output by selecting Image > Image Size from the menu and using the appropriate options. You can also use the Crop tool with specific output dimensions set on the Options bar if you need to produce an image with specific dimensions.

5. Target black and white points, if this is recommended by your print lab. The settings you use will depend on the specific process being used to prepare your image, and you should get specific information on these settings from the lab. They will most likely provide recommendations on adjustments to make using the Curves adjustment.

6. Sharpen the image with Unsharp Mask (Filter > Sharpen > Unsharp Mask) based on recommendations from the print lab.

Note: An experienced print lab will be able to quickly provide recommendations on the best settings to use for the steps above. If the person you are dealing with isn't familiar with these details, ask to speak to someone who is. If nobody can help you with this information, consider using a different lab.

7. The print lab is probably able to work with only 8-bit-per-channel images. If your file is in 16-bit mode, convert to 8-bit by selecting Image > Mode > 8 Bits/Channel from the menu.

8. Save the resulting image as a TIFF file with no compression applied to it.

Note: This process also produces an image that is optimized for direct photo printers such as Chromira or Iris, which is used by fine-art printing companies such as Fine Print (www.fineprintimaging.com).

Besides just preparing the image file, producing a proof print so the printer will know exactly what you want that image to look like is important. Check with the lab to find out what size and materials are preferred for this proof print, and then produce the print within your color-managed workflow. This image needs to very closely match what you see on your calibrated monitor so it can be trusted as an accurate reflection of the image data in the file. This print can then be used by the lab to make the necessary adjustments to your file or their printing process to ensure the print they produce will meet or exceed your expectations.

Converting to CMYK

Perhaps you were hoping that producing a CMYK version of your image from the RGB master image file would be as easy as selecting Image > Mode > CMYK Color from the menu. Although that will certainly give you a CMYK file, it won't ensure the most accurate results. Instead, you need to configure your color settings for the best results, prepare the actual image file, and then convert the image to CMYK.

> **Note:** If you don't have much experience working with CMYK images (and I'm assuming you don't or you probably would have skipped this section), doing your own conversions can be a bit overwhelming. If you must do your own conversions, be sure to talk to the lab to determine exactly what the optimal settings are for the specific output conditions to be used. Clear communication with the staff is the key to getting the best results. If you have a question, ask.

Color Settings

The key to getting a good CMYK conversion is the Color Settings dialog box. It includes a variety of options that allow you to fine-tune the CMYK setup to be used for the actual conversion. Using the right settings is critical here.

> **Note:** Your print lab should be able to either provide a specific CMYK profile for the output process to be used for your images, or they (more likely) can provide you with specific settings to use in the Color Settings dialog box to produce the best CMYK conversion for their printing methods.

To get started, select Edit > Color Settings from the menu. Virtually all of the settings in this dialog will remain exactly as we configured them in Chapter 2, "Photoshop Setup." The only adjustments we need to make are to the CMYK Working Space. If your printer has provided a CMYK profile for you to use, you'll simply need to copy it to the appropriate folder on your computer (see Table 7.2) and then select it from the CMYK dropdown list in the Working Spaces section.

> **Note:** After you copy a new profile onto your computer, you'll need to restart Photoshop so it will update its list of available profiles.

▷ **Table 7.2** Profile Locations

Operating System	Standard Location
Macintosh OS 9	System Folder/ColorSync Profiles
Macintosh OS X	Library/ColorSync/Profiles
Windows 9x/Me	c:\windows\system\color
Windows NT	c:\winnt\system32\color
Windows 2000	c:\winnt\system32\spool\drivers\color
Windows XP	c:\windows\system32\spool\drivers\color

In many cases, the print lab may require customized settings, and the Color Settings dialog box certainly allows for this through the Custom CMYK and Ink Colors dialog boxes.

To create custom CMYK settings, you'll need to set the CMYK Working Space to Custom CMYK (see Figure 7.43). This will cause the Custom CMYK dialog box to be displayed (see Figure 7.44). Chances are, most of the settings in this dialog box won't make any sense to you, underscoring the importance of obtaining the correct settings from your printer. The first option is to provide a name for this profile. I strongly recommend that you use a name that will refer to the printer you are using, along with any information about the output conditions that are known to you.

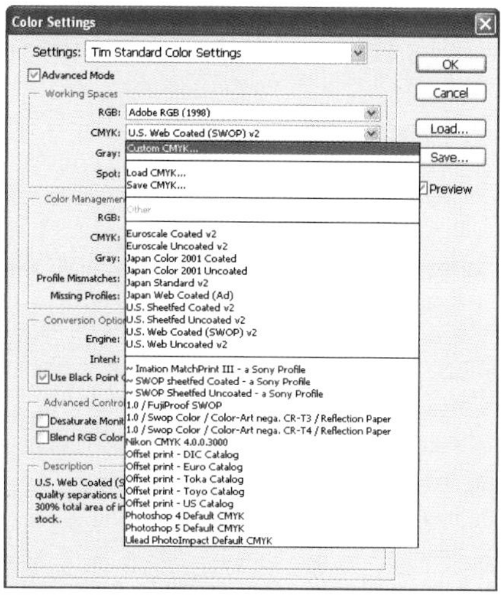

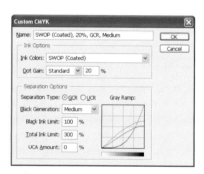

Figure 7.43 To enter custom CMYK settings, first set the Working Space for CMYK to Custom CMYK in the Color Settings dialog box.

Figure 7.44 The Custom CMYK dialog box allows you to set specific parameters for your CMYK configuration, based on information received from your printer.

The next settings on the Custom CMYK dialog box relate to the Ink Options. The Ink Colors dropdown list allows you to select from a list of standard inksets used for offset printing. Your lab may even have you configure custom inks by selecting the Custom option, which will bring up the Ink Colors dialog box.

The Ink Colors dialog box (see Figure 7.45) includes an array of numeric fields that allow you to specify "Yxy" values for the inks to be used by your printer. You can use LAB values by checking the "L*a*b* Coordinates" checkbox. The setting used will depend on the information provided by your print lab. If you need to enter custom ink information, be sure to enter all of the values exactly as they are provided to you by the lab. The Estimate Overprints checkbox allows you to have the color values calculated automatically for the colors produced when two (or three) inks are overprinted on top of each other. Only use this option if the printer hasn't provided specific ink values for all boxes in the Ink Colors dialog box.

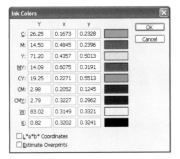

Figure 7.45
The Ink Colors dialog box provides a way to configure the specific ink colors being used by your printer. The values would be entered based on information from your print lab.

When you click OK in the Ink Colors dialog box, you will return to the Custom CMYK dialog box. The next setting to consider is Dot Gain, which specifies how much the inks will spread when they come in contact with the paper. Absorbent papers will have more dot gain, while coated or glossy papers will have less dot gain. Enter the value specified by your lab, or select Standard from the dropdown list to automatically use the value appropriate for the type of ink being used (which also specifies whether coated or uncoated stock is being used for printing).

The Separation Options section of the Custom CMYK dialog box deals with how the individual color channels will be separated in your image. These options specify how the separations are created, how black is used and to what extent, and what the total amount of ink in a given area is limited to (for example, the total ink limit may be 300%, even though with four inks you could theoretically go up to 400%). These options should be set based on specific recommendations from your print lab. Click OK when you have configured the settings for Custom CMYK.

Once you have established the Color Settings based on the recommendations of your lab, I recommend saving those settings so you can access them quickly if you need to convert an image for the same output conditions after having changed the Color Settings. To save the settings, click the Save button in the Color Settings dialog box and provide a name for the settings that indicates the specific printer and press conditions to be used. In the future, you can load these saved settings by clicking the Load button in the Color Settings dialog box and selecting the saved settings, or you can simply select the saved settings from the Settings dropdown list if you saved them in the standard location.

Preparing Files

With the Color Settings established for the specific output conditions under which the image will be printed, you're ready to prepare the image before actually converting it to CMYK. Using the CMYK profile that the print lab has either provided or recommended, configure the Proof Colors setup (View > Proof Setup > Custom). You can then fine-tune the image to ensure that all colors are within gamut and that the image is optimized within the limitations of the output profile. This is the same process as was covered earlier in the "Soft Proofing" section in this chapter.

You will also want to prepare the image with the same workflow presented in the "RGB with Proof Print" section earlier in this chapter. Again, it is important that you obtain recommendations on the best settings from your lab. For example, the optimal Unsharp Mask settings may cause the image to appear extremely over-sharpened on your monitor, but the settings are necessary to compensate for high dot gain under certain printing conditions.

Applying CMYK Conversion

Once you have configured the Color Settings dialog box properly and prepared the image based on recommendations from your lab, converting the image is a simple matter of selecting Image > Mode > CMYK Color. This will cause the image to be converted to CMYK based on the current Color Settings. Save the resulting file in the TIFF format with no compression applied, and you're ready to send it to the print lab.

Note: After converting the image to CMYK, it may not look very good on your monitor. If you used the Proof Colors and Gamut Warning options to optimize the image for the CMYK profile to be used, and set the correct options in the Color Settings dialog box, you should obtain excellent results from the printer regardless of the on-screen appearance. If you used soft proofing to optimize the image, there is no need to further adjust the image at this point, and doing so may actually cause problems in the final print.

Web, E-mail, and Digital Slideshows

Most photographers consider the "real" final result of their effort with an image to be a print. Those photographers working in their own digital darkrooms usually produce that print themselves on a desktop printer, most commonly a photo inkjet printer. However, the digital world opens up a host of other ways to share your images electronically, including putting them on a web page, sending them to friends, family, clients, and others via e-mail, and producing digital slideshows to share your images with a large group at one time.

All of these methods share output methods that are very similar. Whether displayed on a monitor or projected with a digital projector, the images will be produced by emitted light of red, green, and blue. Of course, each device will have its own idea of what red, green, and blue look like, but the similarity allows us to prepare images for these various output methods in the same way.

Preparing images for these display methods is largely a matter of sizing the image appropriately for the intended display, dealing with profile issues in an effort to ensure the most accurate display possible, and saving the file in an appropriate format. The basic process is the same for all three output methods, with the only real difference being the size to which you'll set the image.

Note: As with preparing the image for print, you may want to select Image > Duplicate to create a working copy of the image that will be saved separately, without the risk of accidentally saving the master image at a smaller size.

Resize the Image

I'm sure we've all received an image via e-mail from a friend or family member who was anxious to share their latest photo but didn't know about resizing the image. So, they send the JPEG image produced by their digital camera to you via e-mail. The several-megabyte attachment takes a bit of time to download, and when you view the image (if your image viewer doesn't automatically scale the image), you'll only be able to see a small portion of the image because it requires many more pixels than are available on your monitor. Sizing the image appropriately will produce a smaller file size and optimize the image for the specific display conditions. Therefore, the first step in resizing is to determine the size to which you want to set the image.

For images displayed on a monitor, such as those shared on the Web or via e-mail, the only issue to consider is the pixel dimensions of the monitor display. Most intermediate to advanced computer users are using a monitor resolution of *at least* 1024×768 pixels. Some beginners may still be using a lower resolution of around 800×600. You'll have to decide what resolution setting you think the average visitor to your website is using, or what resolution the recipient of your image via e-mail will use. You may want to assume a lower resolution for friends and family, for example, but a higher resolution for clients reviewing your images for commercial purposes.

Based on the assumed monitor resolution setting for those who will view your images via the Web or e-mail, you can decide how big you want to make the image. In most situations, you don't actually want the image to fill the screen, so it will need to be set to a size slightly smaller than the assumed monitor resolution. In fact, you may not want the image to fill the screen at all, especially for web use. For example, you may want to limit the image to about a quarter of the display resolution, cutting the height and width of the assumed monitor resolution in half. So, if you are assuming most viewers will have their monitors set to 1024×768, you might set the image size to around 500×350 pixels.

Another method for resizing the image is to first set your monitor resolution to the setting you are assuming for the average viewer. Then open the image in Photoshop, and set the zoom setting for the image so it looks as big as you'd like it to be for the viewer. I recommend using the Navigator palette to resize the image, because the slider gives you excellent control over the specific zoom setting for the image. Once you have the zoom set to produce the image size you want, all you need to do is select Image > Image Size from the menu, change the unit of measure from Pixels to Percent, and enter the percentage the image is zoomed to (see Figure 7.46).

With digital projection, you only need to consider the resolution of the projector you will be using. Most entry-level digital projectors currently offer resolution of 800×600 pixels, with the higher-end units offering 1024×768. Some very expensive projectors offer higher resolutions, and over time the more modestly priced projectors will also start to offer higher resolution. Whatever the resolution you will be using, you will need to set the size of your image accordingly. I recommend sizing images for digital projection so they will fit within the dimensions of the projector resolution. If you are using a digital projector that offers 1024×768 resolution, resize the image to fit as closely within those dimensions as possible. That would typically mean that horizontal images get set to a Width of 1024 and vertical images get set to a Height of 768, assuming the other dimension still fits within the overall limit (see Figure 7.47).

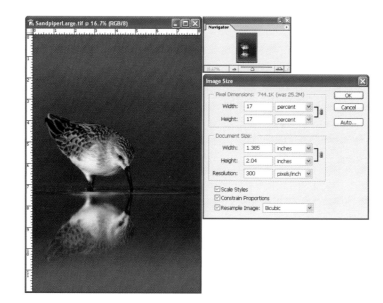

Figure 7.46 When Art Morris sends out his Birds As Art e-mails, he includes samples of his latest bird images, helping photographers learn to improve their own bird photography. For this type of use, resizing the image based on the zoom percentage can be helpful, so you'll have an idea of about how large the image will be for the viewer, assuming they are using a similar display resolution. (Photograph by Art Morris, www.birdsasart.com.)

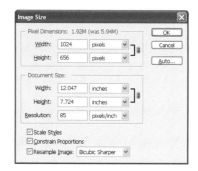

Figure 7.47

When sizing an image for digital projection by setting the pixel dimensions in the Image Size dialog box, make sure it fits within the constraints of your digital projector's resolution.

Note: If you have a large number of images to prepare for a digital slideshow, resizing all of them individually can be a bit of a hassle. Fortunately, Photoshop offers an excellent tool for resizing multiple images. You can record an action that utilizes the Fit Image tool (File > Automate > Fit Image), which allows you to enter the resolution dimensions for your digital projector for Width and Height so the image can be sized to fit within those dimensions, making maximum use of the available area.

To actually resize the image, select Image > Image Size from the menu to display the Image Size dialog box. Be sure the Resample Image box is checked, and set the interpolation option to either Bicubic or Bicubic Sharper. The latter is generally best for reducing the image size, but it can over-sharpen some areas. Also be sure the Constrain Proportions checkbox is checked. Then set either the Width or Height under Pixel Dimensions at the top of the Image Size dialog box based on the settings you determined as being optimal. If you used the zoom setting to find the right size, change the unit of measure in the dropdown list from "pixels" to "percent" and enter the percentage you decided to use.

> **Note:** Only the actual pixel dimensions of the image will determine what size it will appear on a monitor or digital projector, with the output resolution setting being irrelevant. However, some software for producing digital slideshows, such as Microsoft PowerPoint, does take the output resolution into account when you import an image. In that case, setting the resolution to around 85 pixels/inch can help ensure the image will be sized appropriately when you import it into your slideshow software.

When you click OK in the Image Size dialog box, the image will be resized based on the dimensions you entered. However, the image will still be displayed at the zoom setting you were using before resizing the image. This will usually mean that the image will look very small on your monitor. By setting to zoom to 100 percent, you'll see the image at its actual display size, assuming the image will be seen on a monitor or with a digital projector that uses the same resolution your monitor is set to use. You can quickly go to a 100 percent zoom setting by double-clicking on the Zoom tool on the Tools palette or by pressing Ctrl+Alt+0 (⌘+Option+0 on Macintosh).

> **Note:** Because low-resolution images are too small to be closely scrutinized, you can often get away with more aggressive adjustments than might otherwise be possible. For example, you can often increase the contrast and saturation to higher levels than you would for print, and you can sharpen a bit more. The loss of detail or quality with these adjustments is very difficult to see with such a relatively small image, providing some additional margin for error.

Convert to sRGB

Accurate color has the potential to be a real problem with images that will be shared via the Web, e-mail, and digital projection. At this writing, I don't know of a single web browser that supports color management, so any embedded profile is simply ignored. When sending images via e-mail, you don't know what software will be used to view them, but there's a good chance it won't support embedded profiles. With digital projection, software lacking color management support is the primary limitation.

Fortunately, there is a way to deal with this issue of lack of color management support to some degree. Of course, the accuracy of the image will still depend on the accuracy of the monitor or digital projector being used. There is a very good chance that the person viewing your images on their monitor has not calibrated and profiled their display. With digital projectors, you can build a profile (which I'll discuss later in this chapter), but you also have some control over the output because you can adjust the color balance settings on most digital projectors directly.

To help ensure the most accurate color possible even when images are viewed with software that doesn't support color management, we want to configure the color values in the image so they will appear reasonably accurate on most displays. This makes the sRGB color space a perfect match. You may recall from Chapter 2 that the sRGB color space is not ideally suited for printed output because it is aimed at being able to reproduce the colors on a "typical" monitor. That very limitation proves to be a considerable asset when displaying images on a monitor or digital projector. By converting the image to the sRGB color space, the color numbers will be changed so that they reflect accurately when interpreted based on the sRGB profile. This doesn't guarantee accuracy on all monitors, but it gives you the best chance of producing the best results possible.

To convert your image to sRGB, select Image > Mode > Convert to Profile from the menu and set the Destination Space Profile to sRGB (see Figure 7.48). Leave the Engine set to Adobe (ACE). I recommend using Relative Colorimetric as the Intent, to maintain most colors as accurately as possible and, more importantly, to maintain overall saturation. If the image has a significant number of out-of-gamut colors, you can use Perceptual, but the overall saturation will suffer. The Use Black Point Compensation checkbox should be checked so that black pixels will be maintained accurately. I recommend not checking the Use Dither checkbox for this conversion, because any dithering will increase the file size, which is typically of concern for this type of usage. Click OK and the image will be converted to the sRGB profile (see Figure 7.49).

Note: The sRGB profile will actually be named "sRGB IEC61966-2.1" in the Convert To Profile dialog box.

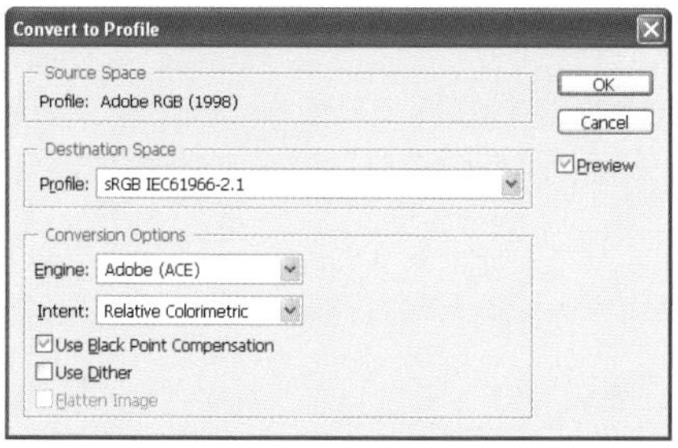

Figure 7.48

If your image will be displayed on a monitor or digital projector, you'll get the best results by converting it to the sRGB color space.

Figure 7.49

The image on the left is a screen capture of a typical display when the image is set to the Adobe RGB (1998) color space, while the image on the right has been converted to the sRGB color space. Using sRGB will help to maintain more saturated and accurate colors on a wide variety of monitors and digital projectors. (Photograph by John Shaw, www.johnshawphoto.com.)

Save the Image

With the image sized and converted to sRGB, you're ready to save the image and put it to use. The best file format for Web, e-mail, and digital slideshow usage is JPEG, because it can retain excellent quality while producing a small file.

Note: If the master image you are using to create this version of the image is in 16-bit mode, you must convert to 8-bit by selecting Image > Mode > 8-Bits/Channel from the menu in order to save it as a JPEG.

To save the image, select File > Save As from the menu. Select the folder you would like to save the image in from the Save In dropdown list, enter a name for the file, and set the Format to JPEG.

Note: Be sure to select JPEG and not JPEG 2000 when saving your images for web, e-mail, and digital slideshow use. Most programs don't support the new JPEG 2000 format yet.

When you click OK, the JPEG Options dialog box will be displayed (see Figure 7.50). The most important setting in this dialog box is Quality. This determines the amount of compression applied to the image. A higher Quality setting results in less compression, and vice versa. For images that will be displayed on the Web or via e-mail, I recommend a Quality setting of 8 for most images. This provides an excellent balance between image quality and file size. For digital projection, the file size isn't as critical an issue, so I recommend using a Quality setting of 10.

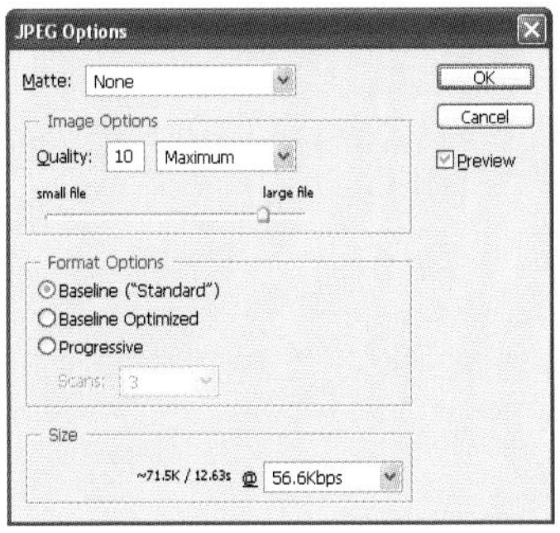

Figure 7.50
The JPEG Options dialog box provides several options for your JPEG images, the most important of which is the Quality setting, which determines the amount of compression to be applied to the image.

Note: You can also select File > Save For Web from the menu to save the image. This option provides the benefit of allowing you to preview the effect of various Quality settings to decide what setting will be optimal for the specific image you are saving.

The Format Options section allows you to specify the way the file will be encoded. Most software currently supports all three options, but the Baseline ("Standard") option ensures the broadest compatibility (and largest file size). The Baseline Optimized uses additional methods to reduce file size. Progressive creates a JPEG image that will load in multiple passes, with the quality improving with each pass. This can be a nice option for web use for viewers with relatively slow connections.

At the bottom of the JPEG Options dialog box is a Size section. This is for information only and doesn't affect any aspects of the image being saved. You can select various connection speeds from the dropdown list, and the estimated file size and download time will be reported based on the selected connection speed.

 Note: The entire process of preparing your image for web, e-mail, and digital projection can be automated by recording an Action in Photoshop that performs the steps of resizing, converting to sRGB, saving the image, and then using the File > Automate > Batch option to run that action on a folder full of images.

Digital Projector Profiling

If you have used a digital projector to share your images, you have no doubt been frustrated that the color is never consistent from one projector to another, and it can be very difficult to properly adjust the projected image to get satisfactory results. Some digital projectors don't even include controls allowing you to adjust the color of the display.

To avoid this frustration, you can create a custom profile for the digital projector, ensuring the most accurate projected colors possible. One of the best solutions for this purpose is the Gretag Macbeth Eye-One Beamer (about $1,500 or upgrade an Eye-One bundle to include Eye-One Beamer for under $600, Windows and Macintosh; www .gretagmacbeth.com) This package allows you to quickly and easily build a custom profile for your digital projector.

 Note: The profile you create with Eye-One Beamer is specific to the computer, display adapter, digital projector, projection screen, and ambient light. You'll need to create a new profile whenever any of these conditions change.

The following process is used to create the projector profile:

1. Set up your digital projector and screen in the room you will be displaying the slideshow in, and dim the lighting to the level you will be using.

2. Turn on the projector and allow it to warm up for about 30 minutes.

3. Disable any monitor profiling software on the computer you will use to run the slideshow.

4. Reset the projector's color settings to the defaults.

5. Launch the Eye-One Match software.

6. Select the Digital Projector option from the screen asking what type of device you want to profile. Select the Advanced mode and click Next.

7. Connect the Eye-One sensor to the Beamer support stand by aligning the arrows and rotating the sensor downward.

8. Place the Beamer support stand in front of the projection screen with the sensor pointed to the center of the screen.

9. Close the "shutter" slider to block incoming light from reaching the sensor, and click the Calibrate button. When calibration is complete, you can open the shutter and click Next.

10. Set the Whitepoint to 6500 K and the Gamma to 2.2, so that you are calibrating the projector to the same standards used for your monitor.

11. Point the sensor as close as you can to the center of the screen. Click Start to begin the position-alignment process. After taking basic measurements, a multicolored screen will be used to measure the point on the screen to which the sensor is currently pointed. Rotate the Beamer support stand and loosen the knob to rotate the sensor vertically, tightening the knob when you have the sensor pointed at the center of the screen. Then click Stop in the Positioning dialog box.

12. The projector will measure the area the sensor is able to read by displaying a series of circles. When this process is complete, you will be returned to the main Eye-One Match window. Click Next to start the profiling process.

13. A series of colors will be displayed on the screen, which will be read by the sensor. When this process is complete, you will be prompted to enter a name for the projector. Use a name that will reflect the computer, projector, and environmental conditions (location) for this profile. Click Next to save the profile and have it set as the default display profile.

Note: If you are using Microsoft PowerPoint to present your images, use the Eye-One ColorPoint module, which adds features to PowerPoint that enable you to produce a slideshow that will accurately reflect the colors you see on your monitor.

Workflow

All of the previous chapters addressed a single aspect of color management, providing the details you need to implement a specific component of the complete color-managed workflow. This chapter is about putting it all together and assembling each of the components into a single workflow for your images from start to finish.

Chapter Contents
Predictable Output
The Pre-Workflow Checklist
Process-Specific Workflows

Predictable Output

I was tempted to call this section "Perfect Output," but that would be misleading. As I've repeated several times throughout this book, color management can't provide "perfect" results. First, there are limitations in what is possible with present technology, especially considering our relatively limited understanding of how the human visual system functions. Furthermore, keep in mind that each output method has its own unique look. An image will always look different on a monitor display, compared to inkjet output, compared to digital projection, and compared to any other output method used. The very nature of each medium causes variations in how the image will appear, even if the color is a "perfect" match.

Although color management tools may attempt to achieve a perfect match between all possible output methods, this simply isn't possible. However, that doesn't take away from the value of color management. While it may not yield a perfect match, when properly implemented, a color-managed workflow can help you achieve *predictable output*. In other words, while the final print still looks different from the monitor display, simply because the monitor is emitting light while the print is reflecting light, you can still predict what the print will look like based on your monitor display. In the best case, the accuracy between the two is very evident. Under less-than-ideal circumstances, the match may not be as evident, but if you can anticipate what the final print will look like based on your monitor display, color management is working for you (see Figure 8.1).

Figure 8.1

A color-managed workflow allows you to predict the appearance of output, even when it won't perfectly match your monitor display. For example, when an image contains subtle shadow detail, some of that detail may be lost in the print due to dot gain, even when you are able to see the detail on your monitor. (Photograph by Peter Burian.)

Now that all of the various pieces of the puzzle have been presented in previous chapters, it is time to put those pieces together into a cohesive workflow that helps you produce the most accurate results possible (see Figure 8.2).

Figure 8.2
Photographer Art Morris prepares images for a wide variety of output, including prints, books, magazine articles, calendars, and digital slideshow presentations. Following a proper color-managed workflow ensures accurate results for diverse processes. (Photograph by Art Morris, www.birdsasart.com.)

The Pre-Workflow Checklist

Certain aspects of a color-managed workflow should go without saying. Of course, in this book I'm not going to leave those items unstated. For all of the sample workflow procedures presented in this chapter, the following tasks, as applicable, should have been performed already:

> **Note:** I recommend confirming all of the items on this list anytime you begin a new project, especially when you are preparing images for a different type of output than you typically use.

- Confirm the Color Settings in Photoshop as appropriate to the type of output for which you are preparing images. This is a specific step in some workflow procedures, but it is always a good idea to confirm you are using the correct settings before starting on a big project.

- Calibrate and profile your monitor if you haven't done so within the past two weeks. While you can achieve very good results when calibrating less frequently, confirming the accuracy of your monitor display is a good idea whenever you embark on a new project.

- If you will be scanning film and prefer to use the "accuracy" method of scanning discussed in Chapter 4, "Scanning," create a profile for your scanner. Although the behavior of scanners doesn't change much over their useful life, updating your scanner profiles periodically (perhaps every six months, or anytime you feel you aren't getting the most accurate results) is a good idea.

- If you will be capturing images with a digital camera, consider what method you will use to ensure the most accurate color possible. Plan to use the in-camera settings, such as White Balance, and consider whether you will be using RAW capture or a custom digital camera profile. Refer to Chapter 5, "Digital Capture," for details on these issues.

Continue learning new methods for correcting the color in your images. Chapter 6, "Optimization," presents some of my favorite methods for dealing with color problems in photographic images, but there are countless other methods and tricks that can be employed. Read books, magazine articles, and other sources for a variety of tips and tricks from various authors. The more tricks you have at your disposal, the more likely you'll be able to solve any color problems that occur in your images.

- If you have the tools to generate custom profiles, create new profiles for any printer, ink, and paper combinations you'll be using. Whenever you find a new paper you'd like to print on, start by creating a custom profile to ensure the most accurate output possible.

- If you won't be creating custom profiles, test the output from your printer and determine the settings necessary to produce the most accurate prints. It may be necessary to use the color adjustment options in the printer properties to achieve accurate output. Remember, you never want to adjust the image to produce an accurate print. Rather, you want to adjust the printer settings so that the output matches the display on your calibrated and profiled monitor.

- Focus on your images. It is easy to get caught up in the numbers behind the pixels or the process of working in a color-managed workflow. In fact, that's what this book is all about. But don't forget that photography is about the final image. Color management is a way to help you get the best results possible, but the final analysis needs to be about the photo in its entirety.

Process-Specific Workflows

With your digital darkroom all set up and configured properly for your color-managed workflow, you're ready to start working with your images to produce output that matches the vision you had when you first took the picture (see Figure 8.3). While the information in this section is largely a review of the overall concepts presented in earlier chapters, it puts the full workflow in one place to help you understand the process of working with your images in a color-managed workflow. Think of these workflow guidelines as a checklist to use as you learn how to take advantage of color management for your images.

High-Bit Workflow

Working with high-bit files used to involve considerable compromise. While offering advantages in terms of image quality, many applications offered little or no support for high-bit files. That has all changed with Photoshop CS, which adds broad support for high-bit files. I highly recommend an upgrade to Photoshop CS if you work with high-bit files, such as high-bit film scans or digital captures in RAW mode. By upgrading, the workflow for your images will be exactly the same as it would be for 8-bit per channel images, eliminating all the tricks that might otherwise be required to get the results you are seeking.

Keep in mind that most output methods aren't able to take advantage of a 16-bit file, so you may need to convert the image to 8-bit per channel mode as part of the process of preparing your images.

Figure 8.3
Following a color-managed workflow will help ensure the most accurate results possible. For example, black-and-white images such as this one can be printed with no color cast. (Photograph by Jon Canfield, www.joncanfield.com.)

Scan-to-Print Workflow

Every day more photographers are making the switch to digital capture. However, just because you've left your film cameras to gather dust doesn't mean you won't need to scan film. You probably have a huge library of images captured on film, and you don't want to abandon them just because you have a great new digital camera (see Figure 8.4).

Figure 8.4 Images captured on film can easily be integrated into a digital color-managed workflow to create stunning results. (Photograph by Alice Cahill, www.alicecahill.com.)

Use the following steps to process your images from scan to print:

1. If you are using the "information" method of scanning presented in Chapter 4, use the following steps to scan the image:

   a. Perform a preview scan and adjust the image controls to produce the most accurate scan possible without clipping any highlight or shadow detail. The best scan is one that has relatively low contrast with maximum detail.

   b. Perform the scan.

   c. If you are importing directly into Photoshop, the image data will automatically be interpreted based on the current working space and no conversion is necessary.

   d. If you save the image file directly from the scanner software, a profile probably will not be embedded in the image file unless you are using software that specifically allows this. If there is no embedded profile, you'll need to assign a profile when the image is opened. Without a custom profile for your scanner, you can assign your working space profile. This won't necessarily produce the most accurate colors, but it provides a way for the colors to be interpreted and converts the image to your working space in the process.

2. If you are using the "accuracy" method of scanning presented in Chapter 4, use the following steps to scan the image:

   a. If you haven't created a profile for your scanner, create it so it can be assigned to your image after scanning.

   b. Scan the image with the same settings used when the profile was created.

   c. If you are not importing the image directly into Photoshop, open it.

   d. If a profile has not been assigned by the scanner software, the Missing Profile dialog box may be presented when you open the image. Assign your custom profile to the image at this point by selecting the Assign Profile option and choosing the custom scanner profile from the dropdown list, and click OK.

   e. If the Missing Profile dialog box is not displayed, select Image > Mode > Assign Profile. Select the Profile option and choose your custom profile from the dropdown list, and click OK.

Note: The steps below apply as the next step to 1 or 2, depending on the method used above.

3. Save the image file in TIFF or Photoshop PSD format by selecting File > Save As from the menu. Be sure the ICC Profile checkbox is checked and that the working space is set as the profile for the image.

4. Optimize the image to produce the intended result. This will represent the master image file, which can be fine-tuned for virtually any output method.

5. If you have a custom profile for the intended printer, ink, and paper combination, use the following steps:

   a. Configure the Proof Colors display by selecting View > Proof Setup > Custom from the menu. Select the profile and other settings recommended for the specific output conditions under which the image will be printed. When you click OK in the Proof Setup dialog box the Proof Colors option (View > Proof Setup) will automatically be enabled.

   b. Based on the colors that appear in the image you are working on, consider changing the Gamut Warning settings (Edit > Preferences > Transparency & Gamut) so that the color overlay will be easy to see in the image.

   c. Activate the Gamut Warning display by selecting View > Gamut Warning from the menu.

   d. Create a new layer set, and then create adjustment layers within that set to fine-tune the image to ensure the most accurate color possible with no colors that are out of gamut for the output profile.

6. When you are happy with the results, save this new "master" image that contains both the original image and the adjustments necessary to produce the best results for the planned output conditions.

7. Create a working copy for printing by selecting Image > Duplicate from the menu. You can then close the original master image file.

8. Flatten the working copy, resize it for your output, and sharpen it using Unsharp Mask (Filter > Sharpen > Unsharp Mask).

9. Select File > Print with Preview. Set the Print Space Profile based on the type of profile you will be using. If you are using a custom or generic profile, select it from the dropdown list. If you aren't using a profile, set the option to either Same As Source or Printer Color Management. Set the Intent as desired, preferably Relative Colorimetric or Perceptual. Be sure the Use Black Point Compensation checkbox is checked. Click Print to continue.

10. Select the printer to which you will be printing, and click the Properties button to access the printer properties.

11. If you are using a custom profile, select the option (such as No Color Adjustment) that will not cause any adjustment to the color data in the image. If you are using a generic printer profile, or no profile at all, use the controls available to produce the most accurate prints through trial-and-error.

12. Print the image and evaluate the results under a 5000 K illumination source, or under the type of lighting the print will be displayed under.

Digital Capture to Print Workflow

Digital capture provides a tremendous amount of flexibility for the photographer, especially when capturing in RAW mode. An appropriate workflow can help ensure that you produce images with exceptional quality with accurate color (see Figure 8.5).

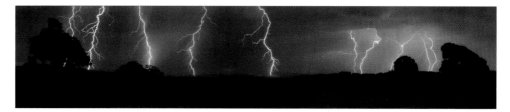

Figure 8.5 In many cases, the viewer would have no idea what the exact color in an image "should" be. However, as the photographer you still want the colors to appear exactly as intended. (Photograph by Jeff Greene, www.imagewestphoto.com.)

Use the following steps to process your images from digital capture to print:

1. Configure the camera settings for the desired workflow. The following basic options are available:

   - Use RAW capture, in which case the camera settings related to color aren't critical because they can be adjusted in the RAW conversion.

   - Capture a target image so you can generate a custom camera profile for the specific lighting conditions under which you are photographing.

   - Use a custom white balance setting to automatically compensate for the color cast produced by the particular lighting under which you are photographing. For RAW captures, the results can be fine-tuned in the RAW conversion.

   - Use a white balance preset based on the lighting under which you are photographing. For RAW captures, the results can be fine-tuned in the RAW conversion.

   - Use the Auto White Balance setting to let the camera decide on the best setting. For RAW captures, the results can be fine-tuned in the RAW conversion.

2. Capture your images. If you are using a custom camera profile or custom white balance setting, be sure to capture a new target image or adjust the white balance whenever the lighting conditions change.

3. For RAW captures, convert using your preferred software. If you are using a custom profile, use the same settings to convert the profile target image that you will use for all of the other settings.

4. If you are using a custom camera profile, generate the profile from the target image captured at the beginning of your photo shoot. Then do *one* of the following:

   - When you open the image, the Missing Profile dialog box may be presented if the camera has not assigned a profile. Assign your custom profile to the image at this point by selecting the Assign Profile option and choosing the custom camera profile from the dropdown list, and then click OK.

   - If the Missing Profile dialog box is not displayed, select Image > Mode > Assign Profile. Select the Profile option, and choose your custom profile from the dropdown list and click OK.

5. Upon opening, convert the image to your working space through the Profile Mismatch dialog box, or by selecting Image > Mode > Convert to Profile, and select your working space from the Destination Space Profile dropdown.

6. Save the image file in TIFF or Photoshop PSD format by selecting File > Save As from the menu. Make sure the ICC Profile checkbox is checked, and verify that the working space is set as the profile for the image.

7. Optimize the image to produce the intended result. This will represent the master image file, which can be fine-tuned for virtually any output method.

8. If you have a custom profile for the intended printer, ink, and paper combination, use the following steps:

    a. Configure the Proof Colors display by selecting View > Proof Setup > Custom from the menu. Select the profile and other settings recommended for the specific output conditions under which the image will be printed. When you click OK in the Proof Setup dialog box, the Proof Colors option (View > Proof Setup) will automatically be enabled.

    b. Based on the colors that appear in the image you are working on, consider changing the Gamut Warning settings (Edit > Preferences > Transparency & Gamut) so that the color overlay will be easy to see in the image.

    c. Activate the Gamut Warning display by selecting View > Gamut Warning from the menu.

    d. Create a new layer set, and then create adjustment layers within that set to fine-tune the image to ensure the most accurate color possible with no colors that are out of gamut for the output profile.

9. When you are happy with the results, save this new "master" image that contains both the original image and the adjustments necessary to produce the best results for the planned output conditions.

10. Create a working copy for printing by selecting Image > Duplicate from the menu. You can then close the original master image file.

11. Flatten the working copy, resize it for your output, and sharpen it using Unsharp Mask (Filter > Sharpen > Unsharp Mask).

12. Select File > Print with Preview. Set the Print Space Profile based on the type of profile you will be using. If you are using a custom or generic profile, select it from the dropdown. If you aren't using a profile, set the option to Same As Source or Printer Color Management. Set the Intent as desired, preferably Relative Colorimetric or Perceptual. Be sure the Use Black Point Compensation checkbox is checked. Click Print to continue.

13. Select the printer you will be printing to, and click the Properties button to access the printer properties.

14. If you are using a custom profile, select the option (such as No Color Adjustment) that will not cause any adjustment to the color data in the image. If you are using a generic printer profile, or no profile at all, use the controls available to produce the most accurate prints through trial-and-error.

15. Print the image and evaluate the results under a 5000 K illumination source, or under the type of lighting that will be used to display the print.

Web, E-mail, and Digital Projection Workflow

Prints are the most common output method for photographers, and they depend upon reflected light to be seen. Images shared via the Web, e-mail, or digital projection, on the other hand, are produced by emitted light (see Figure 8.6). As all of these images are produced with emitted light, they can be prepared with the same methods.

Figure 8.6 Luminous images such as this are ideally suited for display on a monitor or digital projector. The emitted light of these output methods adds tremendous depth to the image. (Photograph by Jon Canfield, www.joncanfield.com.)

Use the following steps to process your images for Web, e-mail, or digital projector display:

1. Open your master image file.

2. Select Image > Duplicate to create a working copy of the image.

3. Turn off the visibility of any adjustment layers designed to fine-tune the image for a specific print output method. If these adjustment layers are contained in a layer set, you can simply turn off the visibility of the layer set to disable the adjustment of all adjustment layers within the set.

4. Flatten the image (Layer > Flatten Image).

5. Resize the image for the desired output size. Keep in mind that for this type of output, the only critical factor is the pixel dimensions, not the output resolution and dimensions. The pixel dimensions should be set based on the expected output resolution of the monitor or digital projector that will be used to view the image.

6. Sharpen the image with Unsharp Mask (Filter > Sharpen > Unsharp Mask). The preview will accurately reflect the final appearance of the image, because the image will be displayed with pixels rather than ink that will spread on paper.

7. Convert the image to the sRGB color space by selecting Image > Mode > Convert to Profile from the menu, and select sRGB from the Destination Space Profile dropdown. Set the Engine to Adobe (ACE), the Intent to Relative Colorimetric, and be sure the Black Point Compensation checkbox is checked.

8. Select File > Save As from the menu. Select the desired location to save the file, enter a filename, set the Format to JPEG, and click Save.

9. In the JPEG Options dialog box that will be presented, set the desired Quality setting. For web or e-mail output, I recommend using a setting of 8. For digital projection, I recommend using a setting of 10. In all cases, I recommend using the Baseline Optimized option in the Format Options section. Click OK to save the image.

CMYK Output Workflow

Many photographers never have to deal with CMYK for their images. They either don't have any images printed with CMYK press output, or they aren't required to actually convert their RGB images to CMYK. For example, I only had to provide RGB images for use in this book. The publisher and the printer dealt with the issues of CMYK conversion. In situations where you actually have to convert your images to CMYK (for example, the book covers shown in Figure 8.7), you'll want to be sure you are following a workflow that will ensure the best results possible.

Figure 8.7
Book printing utilizes the CMYK printing process.

Note: The workflow presented here is a basic guideline for preparing CMYK images. More important than this workflow is the knowledge and experience of those who will actually be working the presses to produce output from your CMYK files. Although the workflow presented here is a good guide for the process, input from the print lab can be invaluable.

Use the following steps to process your images for CMYK output:

1. Contact the print lab or whoever is handling the files for the job for which you are preparing images. Discuss their requirements, how they want the file delivered, whether they have a profile for the specific output conditions, and what settings should be used when preparing the images. This is the most critical step, because the wrong settings and procedures cause unpredictable results. Make sure your questions are answered so that you understand exactly what you should be doing to optimize the files for the specific output conditions.

> **Note:** Keep in mind that you can make your work a lot easier if the print lab accepts an RGB image with a proof print they can attempt to match in the final output. Providing one will save you from the complexity of a CMYK conversion, leaving that work to those who have experience in producing accurate results.

2. In Photoshop, open the Color Settings dialog box (Edit > Color Settings), and configure the settings as recommended by the print lab or whoever will be producing the output from your CMYK files.

3. Check and recheck the Color Settings to ensure they are accurate for the specific print job for which you are preparing the files. If you will be preparing files for this specific output process frequently, save the settings so they can be easily accessed in the future.

4. Open the image that has already been optimized in the RGB color mode. Confirm that the image is indeed exactly as you want it based on the monitor display. Fine-tune the image if needed, and resave the master image file in RGB.

5. Configure the Proof Colors display by selecting View > Proof Setup > Custom from the menu. Select the profile and other settings recommended for the specific output conditions under which the image will be printed. When you click OK in the Proof Setup dialog box, the Proof Colors option (View > Proof Setup) will be enabled automatically.

> **Note:** Once you have saved your Proof Colors setup, you can simply select it from the menu under View > Proof Setup.

6. Examine the colors that appear in the image you are working on, and consider changing the Gamut Warning settings (Edit > Preferences > Transparency & Gamut) so that the color overlay will be easy to see in the image.

7. Activate the Gamut Warning display by selecting View > Gamut Warning from the menu.

8. Create a new layer set, and then create adjustment layers within that set to fine-tune the image to ensure the most accurate color possible with no colors that are out of gamut for the output profile. When you are happy with the results, save this new "master" image that contains both the original image and the adjustments necessary to produce the best results for the planned output conditions.

9. Duplicate this image (Image > Duplicate) to create a working copy. You can now close the original image if you like.

10. Flatten the image (Layer > Flatten Image).

11. Resize the image (Image > Image Size) to the final output dimensions and resolution, as requested by the print lab.

12. Sharpen the image (Filter > Sharpen > Unsharp Mask) using the settings recommended by the print lab. Note that this sharpening is designed to compensate for specific output conditions, and it may result in an image that looks over-sharpened on the monitor.

13. Convert the image to CMYK by selecting Image > Mode > CMYK. This will cause the image to be converted based on your current Color Settings, which should already represent the best settings for the specific output method being used.

14. Save this file as a TIFF with no compression applied, or save it in whatever format was requested by the print lab. Deliver this file to the printer. It is still a good idea to include a proof print you have created from your RGB master image file, so that the printer will know what the output should look like.

15. Maintain good communication with the printer. Confirm that the files were indeed prepared properly, and discuss any issues that arise related to the final output. With a good relationship, you should be able to resolve any issues related to the accuracy of colors, and you'll learn more about color management in the process.

CMYK output involves a huge number of variables, making it a real challenge to get the best results possible. I don't intend to make you a prepress expert, but being able to perform basic CMYK conversions with your images will help you achieve the best results. Although a print lab may have tremendous experience in getting good results, you're the one invested in your images. If you need to prepare images for CMYK output on a regular basis, learn as much as you can about the printing industry and the various processes used to create the final output. Nothing can replace experience, but reading as much as you can on the subject, visiting print labs to see how the results are created, and talking to those with experience can help you gain a better understanding of CMYK output.

Glossary

Absolute Colorimetric One of the four ICC rendering intents for handling out-of-gamut colors when converting colors from a source to destination profile. Colors that are within the gamut of the destination profile are reproduced accurately. Colors that are outside the color gamut of the destination profile are clipped to the nearest reproducible hue, with a possible change in brightness and saturation. The white point of the source is maintained, making this rendering intent useful primarily when simulating the output of one device using a different device.

additive primary colors The primary colors (red, green, and blue) for emitted light. All colors can be reproduced using these primaries. Combining all three primaries at maximum intensity would produce white light.

Adobe RGB (1998) A working space profile with a color gamut appropriate for a wide variety of output devices. Many experts consider this working space to be the best choice for images that will be printed.

assigning profiles The process of providing a profile that will be used to translate the color numbers in an image file so they relate to specific colors. When you assign a profile to an image, the color numbers will not be changed, and therefore the color appearance may change based on the translation provided by the profile.

black point compensation An option in profile conversions where the black in the source space is mapped to the black in the destination space, so that the full tonal range of the destination space is used and the darkest black possible is maintained.

brightness A measure of the amount of light reflected or emitted (see also lightness and luminance).

bronzing A phenomenon where certain inks (often black) have reflective properties that cause them to have a slightly "bronze" appearance under certain lighting conditions. This is often confused with metamerism (see metamerism).

calibration The process of actually changing the behavior of a device to match established standards. The behavior is typically changed by controls provided by the device itself, such as brightness and contrast controls on a monitor. Calibration is performed before profiling a device, reducing the amount of compensation the profile must include for the device.

camera profile A profile that describes the color behavior of a digital camera so that the colors can be corrected by assigning that profile to the captured image. A profile is specific to the specific camera, exposure settings, and lighting conditions, so camera profiling is not practical for photographers who photograph under a wide variety of lighting conditions, such as outdoor photographers. It can be beneficial when many photographs are captured under the same lighting conditions, such as for studio photographers.

candela A unit of measure for luminosity. One candela is equal to 1/60 of the luminosity per square centimeter of a blackbody radiating at 2046 Kelvin. See also color temperature and Kelvin.

characterization Typically referred to as "profiling." It is the process of gathering information about the color behavior of a device and assembling that information into a data file (the profile) that allows compensation for the device behavior to produce more accurate color.

chroma Typically referred to as "saturation" by most photographers, the property of a color that describes its purity. With higher purity, a color will appear more vibrant, while with lower purity it will appear duller. Chroma is one of the attributes in the LCH (Lightness, Chroma, Hue) color model. See also saturation.

CMYK A color model based on the subtractive primary colors of cyan, magenta, and yellow, with black added so that the final output can contain pure blacks. This model is used to represent how much of each ink color would be required to produce a given final color.

color A response in the human visual system based on an interpretation of light at different wavelengths. The range of colors that humans can perceive is the visible spectrum.

color gamut For a device, the range of colors that can be captured or produced. For a color model, the range of colors that can be defined.

color management A system that provides solutions to match color across a variety of devices. This system revolves around profiles that describe the color behavior of the devices in a workflow, so that color values can be interpreted accurately and consistently. A good color management system allows you to produce predictable output.

color model A method of describing color using numeric values for specific attributes. Examples include RGB, CMYK, HSB, and Lab. In the RGB color model, each color is described based on how much red, green, and blue light is required to produce it. In the CMYK color model, each color is described based on how much cyan, magenta, yellow, and black ink is required to produce it. In the HSB color model, each color is described based on its hue, saturation, and brightness. In the Lab color model, each color is described based on its lightness, balance between red and green (a), and balance between blue and yellow (b).

color space The range of colors available for a particular color model or profile. The color space represents the range of colors available for a particular image.

color temperature The color of white light, measured in degrees Kelvin. This measurement is based on the color of light emitted from a theoretical "black body radiator," with lower temperatures corresponding to the hues we think of as being "warm" colors (reds to yellows) and higher temperatures corresponding to the hues we think of as "cool" (greens to blues).

colorimeter An instrument that measures the relative intensities of red, green, and blue light; often used to measure colors from a monitor during the process of calibrating and profiling.

ColorSync The color management system included in the Macintosh operating system.

complementary colors Colors on opposite sides of the color wheel from each other. These colors represent the axes for color balance adjustments in the RGB and CMYK color models. Colors that are complementary to each other are generally pleasing to the eye when used together.

converting profiles The process of changing the profile that will be used to translate the color numbers in an image file so they relate to specific colors. When you convert an image from one profile to another, the color numbers are changed in an effort to produce the same result when interpreted based on the new profile. The rendering intent used determines how colors outside the destination gamut are dealt with.

D50 A standard illumination source with a color temperature of 5000 Kelvin. This is the standard used for evaluating prints in a color-managed workflow.

D65 A standard illumination source with a color temperature of 6500 Kelvin. This is the standard used for calibrating monitors in a color-managed workflow.

densitometer An instrument that measures the density of a sample, often used to measure the density of dye in photographic film or of ink on paper.

destination profile The profile that will be used to interpret colors after a profile conversion. See converting profiles.

device-dependent color space A color space where the actual colors produced depend on the device being used for output. Colors are described based on how a particular device produces color.

device-independent color space A color space where the colors are described based on how the human visual system perceives colors, so that the actual color is described accurately, without the need to know what type of device will be used to produce the color. Device-independent color spaces (such as Lab) are used as the translation space when converting colors between profiles.

dithering The process of arranging pixels or dots of colors to simulate colors that are outside the color gamut of a given device or color space.

dot gain The spreading of ink on paper, which can cause a loss of detail and color fidelity in the print.

DPI (dots per inch) The number of dots per linear inch on paper produced by a particular printer. This measurement is one of the attributes that determines overall print quality. See also PPI.

embedded profile A profile included within an image file, providing information on how to translate the color numbers stored in the image and making it possible to always render accurate color.

gamut See color gamut.

gamma The relationship between tonal values and perceived brightness. A gamma value of 2.2 is considered to be perceptually uniform (see perceptually uniform) and is the recommended target for monitor calibration.

gray balanced The property of a color model or profile where equal values of red, green, and blue correspond to a neutral gray value.

HSB (Hue/Saturation/Brightness) A color model where color is described based on relative values of hue, saturation, and brightness. See also hue, saturation, and brightness.

hue A color-related term that seems impossible to define without a circular definition. Hue is the property of color that we identify with the

name of the color, such as "red", "green", or "blue", or any other possible color. Hue is described as the number of degrees around a color wheel, starting at zero degrees for red. Hue is one of the attributes in the HSB (Hue, Saturation, Brightness) and LCH (Lightness, Chroma, Hue) color models.

ICC (International Color Consortium) A group of companies that develop industry-wide standards for color management. For more information, see the ICC website at www.color.org.

ICC profile A data file in a standard format defined by the ICC that describes the color behavior of a specific device. This allows color management systems to maintain consistent color throughout the complete color-managed workflow and across computer platforms.

ICM (Image Color Matching) The color management system included in the Windows operating system.

IT8 One of the standard targets used for calibrating and profiling scanners and printers.

Kelvin The unit of measure used to describe color temperature. One degree Kelvin equals one degree Celsius, but the Kelvin scale begins at absolute zero; as a result, 0 Kelvin equals −273 Celsius. For purposes of color management, the Kelvin scale is used to describe the color appearance of white. The scale used is based on the wavelengths of light given off by a theoretical black body radiator when it is heated.

Lab A color model where color is described based on lightness, color on a red/green axis (a), and color on a blue/yellow axis (b).

LCH (Lightness/Chroma/Hue) A color model where color is described based on lightness, chroma, and hue.

lightness A measure of the amount of light reflected or emitted. See also brightness and luminance.

linear A relationship where doubling the intensity (of light, for example) produces double the response. The human visual system is decidedly nonlinear.

linearization The process of calibrating a device to behave in a linear fashion.

luminance A measure of the amount of light emitted. See also brightness.

memory color A color that the observer is familiar with through personal experience. It is particularly important that such colors in an image be rendered accurately.

metamerism The phenomenon of two color samples appearing to match each other under one lighting condition but not matching under another condition. This behavior allows a wide variety of colors to be created with a small number of primary colorants. This behavior can cause inconsistent results in prints when the individual inks have different metameric properties.

monitor profile A profile that describes the color behavior of a monitor so the display can be compensated for based on that behavior.

nanometer One-millionth of a millimeter; used as a measure of wavelengths of visible light.

nonlinear A relationship where a change in stimulus does not necessarily produce a corresponding change in response. For example, if increasing the brightness value by 10 percent does not produce a 10 percent increase in perceived brightness, brightness will be nonlinear.

Perceptual One of the four ICC rendering intents for handling out-of-gamut colors when converting colors from a source to destination profile. With the Perceptual rendering intent, the full color gamut of the source space is compressed to fit into the destination space, maintaining the relationships between colors in the process.

perceptually uniform A property where the distances between two colors in a color space relate to the perceived differences between those colors.

PPI The number of pixels per linear inch on a monitor display or image file. This measurement is one of the attributes that determines overall display quality. See also DPI.

primary colors A minimal set of colors that can be used to produce all other colors. See also additive primary colors and subtractive primary colors.

printer profile A profile that describes the color behavior of a specific combination of printer, ink, and paper, used so the output can be compensated for based on that behavior.

profile See ICC profile.

profile mismatch A situation where the profile embedded in an image does not match the current working space profile.

profiling See characterization.

raster image processor (RIP) A hardware or software component that handles the job of converting computer data to printer data, often including color-management features.

Relative Colorimetric One of the four ICC rendering intents for handling out-of-gamut colors when converting colors from a source to destination profile. Colors that are within the gamut of the destination profile are reproduced accurately. Colors that are outside the color gamut of the destination profile are clipped to the nearest reproducible hue, with a possible change in brightness and saturation. White is mapped to the white of the destination space, with all colors adjusted based on that white point.

rendering intent A method for dealing with out-of-gamut colors when translating colors between two color space profiles. The four ICC rendering intents are Absolute Colorimetric, Relative Colorimetric, Perceptual, and Saturation.

RGB A color model based on the additive primary colors of red, green, and blue. This color model is used to represent colors based on how much light of each color would be required to produce a given color.

saturation (1) The property of a color that describes its purity. With higher purity, a color will appear more vibrant, while with lower purity it will appear duller. Saturation is one of the attributes in the HSB (Hue, Saturation, Brightness) color model. See also chroma.

(2) One of the four ICC rendering intents for handling out-of-gamut colors when converting colors from a source to destination profile. With the Saturation rendering intent, highly saturated colors in the source space are mapped to highly saturated colors in the destination space, with possible changes in hue and lightness.

scanner profile A profile that describes the color behavior of a scanner so the scanned images can be compensated for based on that behavior.

soft proofing A feature of Photoshop that allows you to get a preview of what the image will look like when printed using a specific profile.

source profile The profile that is used to interpret colors before a profile conversion.

spectrophotometer An instrument that measures the amount of light at each wavelength reflected or emitted by a color sample. This provides the most accurate data for building an ICC profile.

sRGB A working space profile with a color gamut designed to encompass a typical monitor. This makes it an appropriate choice for images that will be displayed only on a monitor rather than printed.

standard illuminant An established standard that defines a specific illumination source used in a color-managed workflow. See also D50 and D65.

standard observer An established standard that defines a hypothetical observer representing typical human color vision.

subtractive primary colors The primary colors (cyan, magenta, and yellow) for reflected light. All colors can be reproduced using these primaries, with black added so that true blacks can be produced in the final output.

video LUT The lookup table on a video card (display adapter) that contains the color signal values used to produce specific colors. This data is updated by monitor calibration tools to produce a more accurate display.

visible spectrum The portion of the electromagnetic spectrum that produces a response in the human visual system, encompassing wavelengths from about 380 to about 780 nanometers.

white balance An adjustment that compensates for the illumination color temperature, which ensures that white objects will appear neutral.

white point adaptation A method of adjusting the appearance of colors based on the color of white affected by specific print media or illumination influences. The human visual system is capable of white point adaptation.

working space A profile that determines the range of colors available for a given image, as a portion of the visible spectrum, used to define a color gamut available for images as they are optimized with photo-editing software. The working space profile is typically the profile that would serve as the embedded profile. See also Adobe RGB (1998), sRGB, and embedded profile.

Index

Note to the Reader: Page numbers in **bold** indicate the principle discussion of a topic or the definition of a term. Page numbers in *italic* indicate illustrations.

I

ICC (International Color Consortium), **243**
ICM (Image Color Matching), **243**
image controls in digital cameras, 115, *115*
Image Size dialog box, *196*, **196–197**, 220–221
Info palette, 148–149, 150, *150*, 191
inks, printer, 14, 171, 205, 213
Intent options, 27, **35**, *See also* rendering
interpolating images, 111
IT8 targets for profiling, 97, *97*, 101, 105, 243

J

Jones, Dewitt, 2, *2*, 90, *90*, 158, *158*
JPEG camera captures, **113–114**, *114*
JPEG compression, **162**
JPEG format, saving images in, *165*, **165**, 223, **223–224**

K

K (Kelvin) scale, 60, *60*, 242, **243**

L

LAB color model, **10**, 15, 16, **243**
Lasersoft Imaging company, 89, 101
layers. *See* adjustment layers
LCD monitor displays, *See also* monitor
    brightness, 47, 54–55
    choosing, 54, *54*
    contrast ratio, 47–48, 51, 55
    geometry, 49–50, 55
    on laptops, 57
    pixel pitch, 55
    pixel response time, 56
    resolution, 48–49, 55
    special concerns, 57
    viewable area, 50, 56
    viewing angle, 48, 51, 56, *56*
LCH color model, **243**
Lens settings in Camera Raw, **130**
Lepp, George D., 46
Levels control, *144–145*, **144–145**, 200, *200*
light
    color and, 3–5, *3–5*
    defined, **3**, 6
    human eyes and, 4, *4*
    overview, 2, *2*
    in photography, 5–6, *5*
    spectral curves, 4–5, *5*
    visible spectrum of, 3–4, *3*
light sources
    color perception and, 7, *7*, 13–14
    D50 and D65, 242
    Ott-Lite 5000K lamp, 208, *208–209*
    output evaluation and, 208–209, *208–209*, 212–213
lightness. *See* brightness
linear, **244**
loading color settings, 26
luminance. *See* brightness
Lynch, Richard, 142
LZW (Lempel Ziv Welch) compression, **162**

M

Macbeth. *See* Gretag Macbeth
magenta problem, 141, 153, *153*
maximum luminance of monitors, **61**
maximum output size of digital cameras, 111
memory colors, **138–139**, *139*, **244**
metamerism
    bronzing and, 14
    defined, **12–13**, *13*, **244**
    light sources and, 13–14, 212
    pitfall, 13
Meyer, Ira, 3, *3*
Minolta DiMAGE Scan Elite 5400 scanners, 84, *84*
Mismatch alerts, Embedded Profile, **41–42**, *42*
Mismatch dialog box, Embedded Profile, **38–39**, *39*, 134, *134*
Mismatch options, Paste Profile, **39–40**, *40*
mismatch problems, **210–213**, *211*
Mismatches checkboxes, Profile, **33–34**
Missing Profile dialog box, *See also* Photoshop setup
    Assign Profile option, *40*, 41, 103, *103*, 123, *123*
    Assign Working RGB option, *40*, 41
    defined, *40*, **40–41**
    Leave As Is option, *40*, 41, 135, *135*
Missing Profiles, Ask When Opening checkbox, 27, **34**, 40
MonacoEZcolor tool, **177–180**, *178–180*
MonacoOPTIX tool, **70–72**, *71–72*
monitor displays, **45–79**, *See also* CRT; LCD
    adding hoods, 79, *79*
    age, 61
    brightness, 47
    brightness, maximum, 61
    brightness uniformity, 49
    cleaning, 60
    color fidelity, 48, 51
    color management issues, 50–51
    contrast ratio, 47–48, 51
    CRT monitors, 47–54, *52–54*
    Desaturate Colors option, 36, *36*
    display adapters, 57–58
    environmental conditions, 77–79, *79*
    focus, 49
    geometry, 49–50
    glare, 49
    importance of, 45, 46, *46*
    LCD monitors, 47–51, 54–57, *54*, *56*
    using multiple monitors, 58
    power consumption, 49
    price, 50
    refresh rate, 48
    resolution, 48–49
    size and weight, 49
    target gamma values, 59
    target white point values, 59–60, *60*
    viewable area, 50
    viewing angle, 48, 51
monitor displays, calibrating/profiling, *See also* profiles
    using Adobe Gamma, 61, 72–74, *73–74*
    calibration, defined, **59**, **241**
    calibration frequency, 77
    calibration tools included with, 62
    using Color Vision Spyder, 61, 62–65, *63–64*

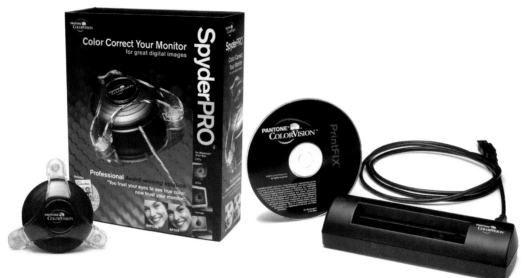

Get the Official Guide!

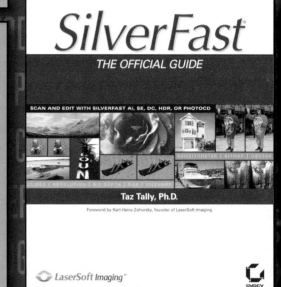